tasteofhome

EVERYDAY slow cooker 2011

& ONE DISH RECIPES

COOKING A DELICIOUS MEAL JUST GOT EASIER!

Putting a convenient and affordable dinner on the table is always a challenge, but *Taste of Home Everyday Slow Cooker & One Dish Recipes* will help ease this load for busy cooks! You'll love the home-style dishes that offer hundreds of ideas for fast, wholesome meals.

This beautiful book is divided into three main sections: Slow Cooker, Stovetop Suppers and Oven Entrees. At the end of the book, we have a new bonus chapter, Breads & Salads, that is full of hearty salads and baked breads—everything you need to complete a family-friendly feast. IT'S LIKE GETTING THREE BOOKS IN ONE!

SLOW COOKER. There's a good reason this simple cooking appliance is so popular—it does all the work for you! Knowing that dinner is simmering at home while you are away gives peace of mind, especially to those with busy lifestyles. This book features 50 NEVER-BEFORE PUBLISHED SLOW COOKER RECIPES, including yummy appetizers, hearty main courses and homespun desserts.

STOVETOP SUPPERS. This section has dozens of easy skillet and one-pot meals that come together fast. Hassle-free and family-friendly, these satisfying recipes require less cleanup because they usually utilize a single skillet or Dutch oven.

OVEN ENTREES. Hearty oven dinners, such as casseroles, baked pastas, beef and pork roasts, potpies, pizzas and more, are wonderful for potlucks, church suppers and banquets. You'll enjoy these meal-in-one specialties that make for heartwarming and nourishing family fare.

BONUS CHAPTER. To make it easier for you to create an entire meal, we've added 28 delicious main course accompaniments toward the end of the book in a chapter titled Breads & Salads. Whether you need an easy coleslaw, biscuit or pasta salad recipe, there are plenty of pairings to choose from!

You can prepare every recipe in this book with confidence because the Taste of Home Test Kitchen has tested each one for accuracy and flavor. Recipes on the light side include Nutrition Facts and Diabetic Exchanges when available and are marked with an asterisk next to the recipe title so you can find them easily.

So, set your slow cooker, grab your favorite pot or pan and preheat your oven! After one bite of any one of these tasty dishes, you'll see how easy it is to create memorable meals every day of the week.

VICE PRESIDENT, EDITOR-IN-CHIEF: Catherine Cassidy
VICE PRESIDENT, EXECUTIVE EDITOR/BOOKS: Heidi Reuter Lloyd
CREATIVE DIRECTOR: Howard Greenberg
FOOD DIRECTOR: Diane Werner, RD
SENIOR EDITOR/BOOKS: Mark Hagen
EDITOR: Krista Lanphier
ASSOCIATE CREATIVE DIRECTOR: Edwin Robles Jr.
ART DIRECTOR: Gretchen Trautman
CONTENT PRODUCTION MANAGER: Julie Wagner
DESIGN LAYOUT ARTIST: Kathy Crawford
PROOFREADER: Victoria Soukup Jensen
RECIPE ASSET SYSTEM MANAGER: Coleen Martin
RECIPE TESTING AND EDITING: Taste of Home Test Kitchen
ADMINISTRATIVE ASSISTANT: Barb Czysz
FOOD PHOTOGRAPHY: Taste of Home Photo Studio
COVER PHOTOGRAPHER: Jim Wieland
COVER FOOD STYLIST: Kathryn Conrad
COVER SET STYLIST: Dee Dee Jacq

NORTH AMERICAN CHIEF MARKETING OFFICER: Lisa Karpinski
VICE PRESIDENT/BOOK MARKETING: Dan Fink
CREATIVE DIRECTOR/CREATIVE MARKETING: Jim Palmen

THE READER'S DIGEST ASSOCIATION, INC.
PRESIDENT AND CHIEF EXECUTIVE OFFICER: Tom Williams
EXECUTIVE VICE PRESIDENT, RDA, AND PRESIDENT, NORTH AMERICA: Dan Lagani

FRONT COVER: No-Bean Chili (p. 62)
BACK COVER, LEFT TO RIGHT:
Lemon Cilantro Chicken (p. 29)
Savory Beef Stew (p. 103)
Cherry-Stuffed Pork Loin (p. 210)

International Standard Book Number (10): 0-89821-902-7
International Standard Book Number (13): 978-0-89821-902-9
International Standard Serial Number: 1944-6382

Printed in U.S.A.

For other Taste of Home books and products, visit **ShopTasteofHome.com**

table of contents

Slow Cooking 101

The original slow cooker, called a Crock-Pot®, was introduced in 1971 by Rival®. Today, the term "slow cooker" and the name Crock-Pot® are often used interchangeably, but technically, the term Crock-Pot® is a brand, and a slow cooker is the appliance.

Most slow cookers have two or more settings. Food cooks faster on the "high" setting, but the "low" setting is ideal for all-day cooking or for less tender cuts of meat. Use the "warm" setting to keep food hot until it's ready to serve. The slow cooker recipes in this book refer to cooking on either "high" or "low" settings.

Some newer slow cookers seem to heat up faster than older ones. If you have an older model and a recipe directs to cook on low, you may want to set the slow cooker on the highest setting for the first hour of cooking to be sure the food is thoroughly cooked.

ADVANTAGES of Slow Cooking

CONVENIENCE. Slow cookers provide people with the convenience of safely preparing meals while being away from home. The appliances are readily available and budget-friendly.

HEALTH BENEFITS. As more people make better food choices to improve their overall health, slow cooking has gained popularity. Low-temperature cooking retains more vitamins in the foods and healthier cuts of lean meat will become tender in the slow cooker without using extra fats. Many slow cooker recipes call for condensed soups, but lower sodium and lower fat versions can be used. And, for many busy folks, knowing that a healthy meal is waiting at home helps cooks to avoid less-healthy, "fast-food" meals after work.

Cabbage Patch Stew

Nutrition Facts:
1-1/2 cups (calculated without optional ingredients) equals 214 calories, 5 g fat (2 g saturated fat), 28 mg cholesterol, 642 mg sodium, 29 g carbohydrated, 6 g fiber, 16 g protein

Coconut Curry Chicken

Nutrition Facts:
1 serving (calculated without optional ingredients) equals 396 calories, 11 g fat (7 g saturated fat), 63 mg cholesterol, 309 mg sodium, 43 g carbohydrate, 3 g fiber, 27 g protein

The recipes above are just a sample of 50+ recipes in this cookbook that include Nutritional Facts and Diabetic Exchanges. It's easy to see how much fat, sodium, fiber, protein and more is in each serving of these dishes, helping you and your family maintain a healthier diet.

FINANCIAL SAVINGS. A slow cooker uses very little electricity because of its low wattage. For instance, it would cost roughly 21 cents to operate a slow cooker for a total of 10 hours. If you roast a pork roast for 2 hours in the oven instead of using the slow cooker for 10 hours, you would spend $2.51 to operate an electric oven or $1.49 to operate a gas oven. Plus, slow cookers do not heat the home as ovens do, providing summertime savings in home-cooling costs.

TIPS FOR TASTY OUTCOMES

- No peeking! Refrain from lifting the lid while food cooks in the slow cooker, unless you're instructed in a recipe to stir or add ingredients. The loss of steam can mean an extra 20 to 30 minutes of cooking time each time you lift the lid.
- Be sure the lid is well-placed over the ceramic insert, not tilted or askew. The steam during cooking creates a seal.
- When food is finished cooking, remove it from the slow cooker within 1 hour and promptly refrigerate any leftovers.
- Slow cooking may take longer at higher altitudes.
- Don't forget your slow cooker when you go camping, if electricity is available. When space is limited and you want "set-it-and-forget-it" meals, it's a handy appliance.
- Reheating food in a slow cooker isn't recommended. Cooked food can be heated on the stovetop or in the microwave and then put into a slow cooker to keep hot for serving.
- Use a slow cooker on a buffet table to keep soup, stew, savory dips or mashed potatoes hot.

WHEN USING YOUR SLOW COOKER...

- Slow cookers come in a range of sizes, from 1-1/2 to 7 quarts. It's important to use the right size for the amount of food you're making. To serve a dip from a buffet, the smallest slow cookers are ideal. For entertaining or potluck dinners, the larger sizes work best. Check the chart below to find a useful size for your household.
- To cook properly and safely, manufacturers and the USDA recommend slow cookers be filled at least half full but no more than two-thirds full.
- With many slow cooker recipes, the ingredients are added at once and are cooked all day. For make-ahead convenience, place the food items in the crock the night before, cover and refrigerate overnight (the removable stoneware insert makes this an easy task). In the morning, place the crock in the slow cooker and select the temperature.
- Do not preheat your slow cooker. An insert that has been in the refrigerator overnight should always be put into a cold base unit. Stoneware is sensitive to dramatic temperature changes, and cracking or breakage could occur if the base is preheated.
- After the recipe is finished cooking, if there are any leftovers, allow them to cool, then refrigerate. Slow cookers should not be used to reheat leftovers. Instead, use a microwave, stovetop burner or oven to reheat foods to 165°. This ensures that the food has been thoroughly heated and is safe to eat.
- Following a power outage of less than two hours, you can finish cooking food from your slow cooker on the stovetop or microwave. If it's been more than two hours or you are unsure how long the power has been out, discard the food for your safety.

SLOW COOKER SIZE

HOUSEHOLD SIZE	SLOW COOKER CAPACITY
1 person	1-1/2 quarts
2 people	2 to 3-1/2 quarts
3 or 4 people	3-1/2 to 4-1/2 quarts
4 or 5 people	4-1/2 to 5 quarts
6 or more people	5 to 7 quarts

A MELTING POT OF INGREDIENTS

BEANS. Minerals in water and variations in voltage affect different types of dried beans in different ways; therefore, dried beans can be tricky to work with in the slow cooker. As a result, dried beans should always be soaked before adding to a slow cooker recipe. To soak beans, place them in a Dutch oven or stockpot and add water to cover by 2 inches. Bring to a boil, and boil for 2 minutes. Remove from the heat, cover and let stand for 1 hour. Drain and rinse the beans, discarding the liquid. Sugar, salt and acidic ingredients, such as vinegar, have a hardening effect on beans and prevent them from becoming soft and tender. It's best not to cook beans with these flavorings, but to add them only after the beans are fully cooked. Lentils and split peas do not need to be soaked.

COUSCOUS. For the best results when preparing couscous, cook on a stovetop instead of in a slow cooker.

DAIRY. Milk-based products tend to break down during slow cooking. Add items like milk, sour cream, cream cheese or cream during the last hour of cooking unless the recipe instructs otherwise. Cheeses don't generally hold up over extended periods of cooking, so they should be added near the end of cooking. Condensed cream soups can be cooked in slow cookers for extended periods of time with minimal curdling concerns.

FISH & SEAFOOD. Since fish and seafood cook quickly in a slow cooker and can break down if cooked too long, they are often added toward the end of the cooking time.

MEATS. For enhanced flavor and appearance, meat may be browned before going into the slow cooker. Browning, although not vital, may improve the color and flavor of meat. When cooking a roast over 3 pounds, be sure to cut it in half before placing it in the slow cooker to ensure that it thoroughly cooks. Frozen meats should be completely thawed before being placed in a slow cooker. Trim excess fat from meat or poultry before placing in a slow cooker. A slow cooker retains heat, and large amounts of fat could raise the temperature of the cooking liquid, causing the meat to overcook and become tough.

OATS. Quick-cooking and old-fashioned oats are often interchangeable in recipes. However, old-fashioned oats hold up better in a slow cooker.

PASTA. If added to a slow cooker when dry, pasta tends to become very sticky. It's best to cook it according to the package directions and stir it into the slow cooker just before serving. Small types of pasta, like orzo and ditalini, may be cooked in the slow cooker. To keep them from becoming mushy, add during the last hour of cooking.

RICE. Converted rice is ideal for all-day cooking. If using instant rice, add it during the last 30 minutes of cooking.

VEGETABLES. Vegetables, especially potatoes and root vegetables (such as carrots), tend to cook slower than meat. Place these vegetables on the bottom and around the sides of the slow cooker and put meat on top of the vegetables. Add tender vegetables, like peas and zucchini, or those you'd prefer to be crisp-tender, during the last 50 to 60 minutes.

COOK TIMES
CONVENTIONAL OVEN 15 to 30 minutes **Slow Cooker** Low: 4 to 6 hours High: 1-1/2 to 2 hours
CONVENTIONAL OVEN 35 to 45 minutes **Slow Cooker** Low: 6 to 8 hours High: 3 to 4 hours
CONVENTIONAL OVEN 50 minutes or more **Slow Cooker** Low: 8 to 10 hours High: 4 to 6 hours

When a range in cooking time is provided, this accounts for variables such as thickness of meat, how full the slow cooker is and the temperature of the food going into the cooker. As you become used to how your slow cooker works, you'll be better able to judge which end of the range to use.

CONVERTING RECIPES FOR THE SLOW COOKER

Almost any recipe that bakes in the oven or simmers on the stovetop can be easily converted for the slow cooker. Here are some guidelines.

- Before converting recipes, check the manufacturer's guidelines for your particular slow cooker. Find a recipe that is similar to the one you want to convert and use it as a guide. Note the amount and size of meat and vegetables, heat setting, cooking time and liquid.
- Since there is no evaporation, adjusting the amount of liquid in your recipe may be necessary. If a recipe calls for 6 to 8 cups of water, try starting with 5 cups. Conversely, recipes should include some liquid. If a recipe does not include liquid, add 1/2 cup of water or broth.
- In general, 1 hour of simmering on the range or baking at 350°F in the oven is equal to 8-10 hours on low or 4-6 hours on high in a slow cooker. Check the chart, top left.
- Flour and cornstarch are often used to thicken soup, stew and sauce that are cooked in a slow cooker.

Useful Handles for Lifting Food

Layered dishes or meat loaves are easier to get out of the slow cooker using foil handles. Here's how to make and utilize them:

1. For a 3-qt. slow cooker, cut three 20- x 3-inch strips of heavy-duty foil (or 25- x 3-inch strips for large slow cookers). Or, cut 6-inch wide strips from regular foil and fold in half lengthwise. Criss-cross the strips to resemble spokes of a wheel.

2. Place the foil strips on the bottom and up the sides of the ceramic insert. Let the strips hang over the edge. To prevent food from sticking to the foil, coat the foil strips with cooking spray.

3. Place the food in the order suggested by the recipe in the center of the foil strips and lower until the food rests on the bottom of the slow cooker.

4. After the food cooks, grasp the foil strips and carefully lift the food from the ceramic insert. Remove the foil strips from the food before serving.

HINTS FOR CLEANING SLOW COOKERS

- Removable stoneware inserts make cleanup a breeze. Be sure to cool the insert before rinsing or cleaning with water to avoid cracking. Do not immerse the metal base unit in water. Clean it with a damp sponge.
- Wash the insert in the dishwasher or in warm, soapy water. Avoid using abrasive cleansers since they may scratch the stoneware.
- To remove mineral stains on a ceramic insert, fill the cooker with hot water and 1 cup white vinegar; cover. Set the control to high and allow to "cook" for 2 hours. Discard liquid, and when cool, wash with hot, sudsy water. Rinse well and dry.
- To remove water marks from a highly glazed crockery insert, rub the surface with vegetable oil and allow to stand for 2 hours before washing with hot, sudsy water.

page 29

SLOW
COOKER

Beef & Ground Beef

There's no better way to bring out the full flavor of beef than with a slow cooker. This chapter is full of robust, family-friendly main courses that make dinner preparation effortless. Putting smiles on the faces of those you love has never been easier!

Creamy Swiss Steak

Gloria Carpenter
BANCROFT, MICHIGAN

When I was working, I'd put this Swiss steak in the slow cooker before I left for the day. A creamy mushroom sauce made with canned soup nicely flavors the tender round steak.

Creamy Swiss Steak

PREP: 15 min. ■ COOK: 8 hours

- 3/4 cup all-purpose flour
- 1 teaspoon salt
- 1/2 teaspoon pepper
- 2 pounds boneless beef round steak, cut into serving-size portions
- 2 tablespoons butter
- 1/2 cup chopped onion
- 2 cans (10-3/4 ounces *each*) condensed cream of mushroom soup, undiluted
- 1 cup water
- Hot cooked noodles

■ In a large resealable plastic bag, combine the flour, salt and pepper. Add beef, a few pieces at a time, and shake to coat.

■ In a large skillet, brown beef in butter on both sides. Transfer to a 3-qt. slow cooker; top with onion. Combine soup and water; pour over onion. Cover and cook on low for 8-10 hours or until meat is tender. Serve with noodles.

Yield: 8 servings.

Saucy Italian Roast

Jan Roat
RED LODGE, MONTANA

This tender roast is one of my favorite fix-and-forget meals. I thicken the juices with a little flour and add ketchup, then serve the sauce and beef over pasta.

PREP: 10 min.
COOK: 8 hours

- 1 beef rump roast *or* bottom round roast (3 to 3-1/2 pounds)
- 1/2 to 1 teaspoon salt
- 1/2 teaspoon garlic powder
- 1/4 teaspoon pepper
- 1 jar (4-1/2 ounces) sliced mushrooms, drained
- 1 medium onion, diced
- 1 jar (14 ounces) spaghetti sauce
- 1/4 to 1/2 cup red wine *or* beef broth
- Hot cooked pasta

■ Cut roast in half. Combine the salt, garlic powder and pepper; rub over roast. Place in a 5-qt. slow cooker. Top with mushrooms and onion. Combine the spaghetti sauce and wine; pour over meat and vegetables.

■ Cover and cook on low for 8-10 hours or until meat is tender. Slice roast; serve with pasta and pan juices.

Yield: 10 servings.

Marie Rizzio
INTERLOCHEN, MICHIGAN

Here's a tasty dish made with meaty short ribs, cabbage, carrots and scallions. It makes a complete meal that is robust and rich. The Asian-inspired flavor, made with soy sauce, brown sugar, vinegar, gingerroot and garlic, is delicious.

Gingered Short Ribs

PREP: 25 min. ■ COOK: 7 hours

- 4 pounds bone-in beef short ribs
- 2 medium parsnips, peeled and halved widthwise
- 2 large carrots, halved widthwise
- 1/2 cup reduced-sodium soy sauce
- 1/3 cup packed brown sugar
- 1/4 cup rice vinegar
- 1 tablespoon minced fresh gingerroot
- 2 garlic cloves, minced
- 1/2 teaspoon crushed red pepper flakes
- 1 small head cabbage, cored and quartered
- 2 tablespoons cornstarch
- 2 tablespoons cold water
- 2 teaspoons sesame oil
- 4 green onions, thinly sliced
- Hot cooked couscous, optional

■ Place the ribs, parsnips and carrots in a 5- or 6-qt. slow cooker. In a small bowl, combine the soy sauce, brown sugar, vinegar, ginger, garlic and pepper flakes; pour over ribs. Top with cabbage. Cover and cook on low for 7-8 hours or until meat is tender.

■ Remove meat and vegetables to a serving platter; keep warm. Skim fat from cooking juices; transfer to a small saucepan. Bring liquid to a boil. Combine cornstarch and water until smooth. Gradually stir into the pan. Bring to a boil; cook and stir for 2 minutes or until thickened.

■ Stir in sesame oil. Serve with meat and vegetables. Sprinkle with green onions. Serve over couscous if desired.

Yield: 4 servings.

Roast Beef and Gravy

Abby Metzger
LARCHWOOD, IOWA

This is by far the simplest way to make roast beef and gravy. On busy days, I can put this main dish in the slow cooker and forget about it. My family likes it with mashed potatoes and fruit salad.

PREP: 15 min. ■ COOK: 8 hours

- 1 boneless beef chuck roast (3 pounds)
- 2 cans (10-3/4 ounces *each*) condensed cream of mushroom soup, undiluted
- 1/3 cup sherry *or* beef broth
- 1 envelope onion soup mix

■ Cut the roast in half; place in a 3-qt. slow cooker. In a large bowl, combine the remaining ingredients; pour over roast.

■ Cover and cook on low for 8-10 hours or until meat is tender.

Yield: 8-10 servings.

Easy Chow Mein

Kay Bade
MITCHELL, SOUTH DAKOTA

My daughter gave me this simple recipe, and it's one I turn to often. The exotic flavors make it a standout. I often make it for myself because the leftovers freeze so well.

PREP: 15 min.
COOK: 4 hours

- 1 pound ground beef
- 1 medium onion, chopped
- 1 bunch celery, sliced
- 2 cans (14 ounces *each*) Chinese vegetables, drained
- 2 envelopes brown gravy mix
- 2 tablespoons soy sauce
- Hot cooked rice

■ In a large skillet, cook beef and onion over medium heat until meat is no longer pink; drain. Transfer to a 3-qt. slow cooker. Stir in the celery, Chinese vegetables, gravy mixes and soy sauce. Cover and cook on low for about 4-6 hours or until celery is tender, stirring occasionally. Serve over rice.

Yield: 8 servings.

Party-Pleasing Beef Dish

Glee Witzke
CRETE, NEBRASKA

Mild and saucy, this mixture is served over tortilla chips and topped with popular taco ingredients. My guests can't get enough of it!

Party-Pleasing Beef Dish

PREP: 15 min. ■ COOK: 4 hours 10 min.

- 1 pound ground beef
- 1 medium onion, chopped
- 3/4 cup water
- 1 can (8 ounces) tomato sauce
- 1 can (6 ounces) tomato paste
- 2 teaspoons sugar
- 1 garlic clove, minced
- 1 teaspoon chili powder
- 1 teaspoon ground cumin
- 1 teaspoon dried oregano
- 1 cup cooked rice

Tortilla chips

Optional toppings: shredded cheddar cheese, chopped green onions, sliced ripe olives, sour cream, chopped tomatoes and taco sauce

■ In a large skillet, cook beef and onion over medium heat until meat is no longer pink; drain. Transfer to a 3-qt. slow cooker. Stir in the water, tomato sauce, tomato paste, sugar, garlic and seasonings.

■ Cover and cook on low for 4-5 hours or until heated through. Add rice; cover and cook about 10 minutes longer. Serve over tortilla chips with toppings of your choice.

Yield: 6-8 servings.

As a general rule, do not use the utensil that was used to prepare uncooked meats to later stir or serve cooked foods. To avoid cross-contamination, wash the utensils in hot soapy water before reusing or simply grab and use a different spoon.

Dana Cebolski
BESSEMER, MICHIGAN

My slow-cooked beef brisket has a sensational smoky flavor. It's a family favorite throughout the year, especially during the winter months. The tender beef slices taste great with hearty mashed potatoes.

Smoked Beef Brisket

Smoked Beef Brisket*

PREP: 10 min. ■ COOK: 8 hours

- 1 fresh beef brisket (2-1/2 pounds)
- 1 tablespoon Liquid Smoke, optional
- 1 teaspoon salt
- 1/2 teaspoon pepper
- 1/2 cup chopped onion
- 1/2 cup ketchup
- 2 teaspoons Dijon mustard
- 1/2 teaspoon celery seed

■ Place beef in a 3-qt. slow cooker; rub with Liquid Smoke if desired. Sprinkle with salt and pepper. Top with onion. Combine the ketchup, mustard and celery seed; spread over meat.

■ Cover and cook on low for 8-10 hours. Remove brisket and keep warm.

■ Transfer cooking juices to a blender; cover and process until smooth. Serve with brisket. To serve brisket, thinly slice across the grain.

Yield: 6 servings.

Editor's Note: This is a fresh beef brisket, not corned beef.

***Nutrition Facts:** 5 ounces equals 266 calories, 8 g fat (3 g saturated fat), 80 mg cholesterol, 750 mg sodium, 7 g carbohydrate, trace fiber, 39 g protein. **Diabetic Exchanges:** 5 lean meat, 1/2 starch.

Sweet-and-Sour Pot Roast

Erica Warkentin
DUNDAS, ONTARIO

I was so pleased to receive this recipe since it gives pot roast a new mouthwatering flavor.

PREP: 30 min.
COOK: 4 hours

- 12 small white potatoes, peeled
- 1 boneless beef chuck roast (about 3 pounds)
- 1 tablespoon canola oil
- 1 cup chopped onion
- 1 can (15 ounces) tomato sauce
- 1/4 cup packed brown sugar
- 2 to 3 tablespoons Worcestershire sauce
- 2 tablespoons cider vinegar
- 1 teaspoon salt

■ Place potatoes in a 5-qt. slow cooker. Trim fat from roast; cut in half. In a large skillet, brown roast in oil on all sides. Transfer to slow cooker.

■ Reserve 1 tablespoon drippings; saute onion in reserved drippings until tender. Stir in the tomato sauce, brown sugar, Worcestershire sauce, vinegar and salt. Pour over the roast.

■ Cover and cook on high for 4-6 hours or until the meat is tender. Before serving, pour sauce into a skillet. Cook and stir over medium-high heat until reduced and thickened. Serve with potatoes and meat.

Yield: 6-8 servings.

Cabbage Patch Stew

Karen Ann Bland
GOVE, KANSAS

I like to serve steaming helpings of hearty stew with thick crusty slices of homemade bread. For a quicker prep, substitute coleslaw mix for the chopped cabbage.

Cabbage Patch Stew*

PREP: 20 min. ■ COOK: 6 hours

- 1 pound lean ground beef (90% lean)
- 1 cup chopped onion
- 2 celery ribs, chopped
- 11 cups coarsely chopped cabbage (about 2 pounds)
- 2 cans (14-1/2 ounces *each*) stewed tomatoes
- 1 can (15 ounces) pinto beans, rinsed and drained
- 1 can (10 ounces) diced tomatoes with green chilies, undrained
- 1/2 cup ketchup
- 1 to 1-1/2 teaspoons chili powder
- 1/2 teaspoon dried oregano
- 1/2 teaspoon pepper
- 1/4 teaspoon salt

Optional ingredients: shredded cheddar cheese and sour cream

■ In a large skillet, cook the beef, onion and celery over medium heat until meat is no longer pink; drain.

■ Transfer to a 5-qt. slow cooker. Stir in the cabbage, stewed tomatoes, beans, diced tomatoes, ketchup, chili powder, oregano, pepper and salt. Cover and cook on low for 6-8 hours or until cabbage is tender.

■ Serve with cheese and sour cream if desired.

Yield: 8 servings (2 quarts).

***Nutrition Facts:** 1-1/2 cups (calculated without optional ingredients) equals 214 calories, 5 g fat (2 g saturated fat), 28 mg cholesterol, 642 mg sodium, 29 g carbohydrate, 6 g fiber, 16 g protein.
Diabetic Exchanges:
2 lean meat, 2 vegetable, 1 starch.

To quickly chop an onion, peel and cut in half from the root to the top. Leaving the root attached, place flat side down on a work surface. Cut vertically through the onion, leaving the root end uncut. Cut across the onion, discarding the root end. The closer the cuts, the finer the onion will be chopped.

Slow-Cooked Meat Loaf*

Taste of Home Test Kitchen

Chopped onion and garlic plus spicy seasonings add outstanding flavor to my slow-cooked entree.

PREP: 25 min. ■ COOK: 4 hours

- 6 tablespoons ketchup, *divided*
- 2 tablespoons Worcestershire sauce
- 12 saltines, crushed
- 1 medium onion, finely chopped
- 6 garlic cloves, minced
- 1 teaspoon paprika
- 1/2 teaspoon salt
- 1/2 teaspoon pepper
- 1/8 teaspoon cayenne pepper
- 2 pounds lean ground beef (90% lean)

■ Cut three 20-in. x 3-in. strips of heavy-duty foil; crisscross so they resemble spokes of a wheel. Place strips on the bottom and up the sides of a 3-qt. slow cooker. Coat strips with cooking spray.

■ In a large bowl, combine 2 tablespoons ketchup, Worcestershire sauce, saltines, onion, garlic, paprika, salt, pepper and cayenne. Crumble beef over mixture and mix well.

■ Shape into a round loaf. Place in the center of the strips. Cover and cook on low for 4-5 hours or until no pink remains and a meat thermometer reads 160°.

■ Using foil strips as handles, remove the meat loaf to a platter. Carefully spread remaining ketchup over top.

Yield: 8 servings.

***Nutrition Facts:** 1 slice equals 222 calories, 10 g fat (4 g saturated fat), 71 mg cholesterol, 447 mg sodium, 10 g carbohydrate, 1 g fiber, 23 g protein. **Diabetic Exchanges:** 3 lean meat, 1/2 starch.

Chunky Pasta Sauce

Christy Hinrichs

PARKVILLE, MISSOURI

Your kitchen will smell heavenly when it's time to dish up Chunky Pasta Sauce. Add the extra 1/2 cup water if you want your sauce a bit thinner.

PREP: 15 min.
COOK: 6 hours

- 1 pound ground beef
- 1/2 pound ground pork
- 2 cans (28 ounces *each*) diced tomatoes, undrained
- 1/2 to 1 cup water
- 1 can (6 ounces) tomato paste
- 1 medium onion, cut into wedges
- 1 medium sweet red pepper, cut into 1-inch pieces
- 1 cup chopped carrots
- 2 tablespoons sugar
- 2 teaspoons minced garlic
- 1 teaspoon salt
- 1 teaspoon dried basil
- 1 teaspoon dried oregano
- 1 teaspoon pepper
- 6 cups cooked bow tie pasta

■ In a large skillet, cook beef and pork over medium heat until no longer pink; drain.

■ Transfer to a 3-qt. slow cooker. Stir in the tomatoes, water, tomato paste, vegetables, sugar, garlic and seasonings. Cover and cook on low for 6-8 hours or until vegetables are tender. Serve with pasta.

Yield: 8 servings.

Hearty Beef Enchiladas

Marina Castle
NORTH HOLLYWOOD, CALIFORNIA

Created by my daughter, this spicy, meaty and cheesy casserole is great for get-togethers with family and friends. I make it frequently for potlucks.

PREP: 10 min. ■ **COOK:** 6 hours

- 1-1/2 pounds lean ground beef (90% lean)
- 1 small onion, chopped
- 1 garlic clove, minced
- 1 envelope taco seasoning
- 1/2 teaspoon salt
- 1/2 teaspoon pepper
- 9 corn tortillas (6 inches)
- 1/2 cup chicken broth
- 1/2 cup tomato sauce
- 1 can (10 ounces) enchilada sauce
- 1-1/2 cups (6 ounces) shredded cheddar cheese
- 2 cans (15 ounces *each*) pinto beans, rinsed and drained
- 1 can (11 ounces) Mexican-style corn, drained
- 1 can (4 ounces) chopped green chilies, drained
- 1 can (2-1/4 ounces) chopped ripe olives, drained
- Sour cream and avocado slices, optional

■ In a large skillet, cook the beef, onion and garlic over medium heat until meat is no longer pink; drain. Stir in the taco seasoning, salt and pepper.

■ In a greased 5-qt. slow cooker, layer 3 tortillas, beef mixture, broth, tomato sauce and enchilada sauce; sprinkle with 1/2 cup cheese. Add 3 tortillas, beans, corn, green chilies, half of the olives and 1/2 cup cheese. Top with remaining tortillas, cheese and olives.

■ Cover and cook on low heat for 6-7 hours. Serve with sour cream and avocado if desired.

Yield: 10 servings.

Ground meat is labeled and sold based on the percentage of fat by weight. If you want to purchase lean meat, check the label and look for less than 10% fat by weight.

Skier's Stew

Traci Gangwer
DENVER, COLORADO

Assemble a few ingredients in the morning, then put in the slow cooker and enjoy your day. It's wonderful to come home and have this hot meal waiting! Serve with a fresh, crusty loaf of bread.

PREP: 20 min.
COOK: 4-1/2 hours

- 2 pounds beef stew meat, cut into 1-inch cubes
- 2 tablespoons canola oil
- 8 medium carrots, cut into 1-inch slices
- 6 large potatoes, peeled and cut into 1-inch cubes
- 1 to 1-1/2 cups water
- 1 can (15 ounces) tomato sauce
- 1 envelope onion soup mix

■ In a large skillet, brown meat in oil on all sides; drain. Transfer to a 5-qt. slow cooker. Top with vegetables. Combine the water, tomato sauce and soup mix; pour over top. Cover and cook on low for 4-1/2 to 5 hours or until the meat and vegetables are tender.

Yield: 8 servings.

Slow-Cooked Pepper Steak

Sue Gronholz
BEAVER DAM, WISCONSIN

After a long day in our greenhouse raising bedding plants for sale, I appreciate coming home to this hearty beef dish for supper. Its delicious aroma fills the air!

Slow-Cooked Pepper Steak

PREP: 10 min. ■ COOK: 6 hours

- 1-1/2 to 2 pounds beef top round steak
- 2 tablespoons canola oil
- 1 cup chopped onion
- 1/4 cup reduced-sodium soy sauce
- 1 garlic clove, minced
- 1 teaspoon sugar
- 1/2 teaspoon salt
- 1/4 teaspoon pepper
- 1/4 teaspoon ground ginger
- 4 tomatoes, cut into eighths *or* 1 can (14-1/2 ounces) diced tomatoes, undrained
- 1 large green pepper, cut into strips
- 1 tablespoon cornstarch
- 1/2 cup cold water
- Cooked noodles *or* rice

■ Cut beef into 3-in. x 1-in. strips. In a large skillet, brown beef in oil. Transfer to a 3-qt. slow cooker. Combine the onion, soy sauce, garlic, sugar, salt, pepper and ginger; pour over beef. Cover and cook on low for 5-6 hours, or until meat is tender. Add tomatoes and green pepper; cook on low for 1 hour longer.

■ Combine the cornstarch and cold water until smooth; gradually stir into the slow cooker. Cover and cook on high for 20-30 minutes or until thickened. Serve with cooked noodles or rice.

Yield: 6-8 servings.

When a recipe calls for canola oil, vegetable oil can be substituted in equal amounts. There truly should be no difference in the flavor of the final product.

Two-Pot Dinner

Jean Roper
PALERMO, CALIFORNIA

My daughter received this recipe from a friend awhile ago. Bacon gives it a wonderfully rich flavor, making it a very popular option at covered-dish events.

Two-Pot Dinner

PREP: 20 min. ■ COOK: 10 min.

- 1 pound sliced bacon, cut into 2-inch pieces
- 1 large onion, chopped
- 1 pound ground beef
- 1 can (31 ounces) pork and beans
- 1 can (30 ounces) kidney beans, rinsed and drained
- 1 can (15 ounces) great northern beans, rinsed and drained
- 1 cup ketchup
- 1/3 cup packed brown sugar
- 3 tablespoons vinegar
- 1 tablespoon liquid smoke, optional

■ In a large skillet, cook bacon over medium heat until crisp. Remove to paper towels with a slotted spoon; drain, reserving 2 tablespoons drippings. Saute onion in drippings until tender; remove with a slotted spoon. Add bacon and onion to a 5-qt. slow cooker.

■ In the same skillet, cook beef until no longer pink; drain and transfer to slow cooker. Add the remaining ingredients and mix well. Cover and cook on low for 4-6 hours or until heated through.

Yield: 10 servings.

Mexican Pot Roast for Tacos

Connie Dicavoli
SHAWNEE, KANSAS

My son's friends used to request this recipe...10 years later they're still talking about it!

PREP: 25 min.
COOK: 8 hours

- 1-1/2 teaspoons chili powder
- 1 teaspoon ground cumin
- 1/2 teaspoon smoked paprika
- 1/2 teaspoon crushed red pepper flakes
- 1/4 teaspoon salt
- 1 boneless beef chuck roast (3 pounds)
- 1 can (4 ounces) chopped green chilies
- 1/2 cup chopped sweet onion
- 2 garlic cloves, minced
- 3/4 cup beef broth
- 8 taco shells *or* flour tortillas (8 inches)

Optional ingredients: chopped tomatoes, shredded lettuce, shredded Mexican cheese

■ Combine first five ingredients. Cut roast in half; rub spice mixture over meat. Transfer to a 3-qt. slow cooker. Top with chilies, onion and garlic. Pour broth over meat. Cover; cook on low for 8-10 hours or until meat is tender.

■ Remove meat from slow cooker; shred with two forks. Skim fat from cooking juices. Return meat to slow cooker; heat through. Use a slotted spoon to place 1/2 cup meat on each taco shell. Top with tomatoes, lettuce and cheese or toppings of your choice.

Yield: 9 servings.

Beef Burgundy

Sherri Melotik
OAK CREEK, WISCONSIN

Here is a new recipe I tried this year. The whole family loved it, and I plan to make it many times in the future.

PREP: 25 min. + marinating ■ **COOK:** 9 hours

- 2-1/4 cups Burgundy wine, *divided*
- 1/4 cup olive oil
- 1-1/2 teaspoons pepper, *divided*
- 1 teaspoon salt, *divided*
- 4 pounds beef stew meat, cut into 1-inch cubes
- 8 bacon strips, chopped
- 1 large onion, chopped
- 1 pound medium fresh mushrooms, halved
- 2 garlic cloves, minced
- 1/4 cup plus 1/3 cup all-purpose flour, *divided*
- 1 tablespoon tomato paste
- 1 teaspoon dried thyme
- 1 teaspoon dried parsley flakes
- 1/2 cup beef broth
- Hot cooked noodles, optional

■ In a large resealable plastic bag, combine 1 cup wine, oil, 1 teaspoon pepper and 1/2 teaspoon salt. Add the beef; seal bag and turn to coat. Refrigerate for 8 hours or overnight.

■ In a large skillet, cook bacon over medium heat until almost crisp. Remove to paper towels with a slotted spoon; drain, reserving 2 tablespoons drippings. Brown onion in drippings. Add mushrooms and garlic; cook 3 minutes longer. Transfer onion mixture and bacon to a 4-qt. slow cooker.

■ Drain and discard marinade. Add 1/4 cup flour to beef in bag; toss to coat. Transfer beef to slow cooker. In a small bowl, combine the tomato paste, thyme, parsley and remaining wine, pepper and salt. Pour over the beef. Cover and cook on low for 9-10 hours or until meat is tender.

■ Combine remaining flour and broth until smooth; gradually stir into beef mixture. Cover and cook on high for 30 minutes or until gravy is thickened; serve with noodles if desired.

Yield: 11 servings (2-3/4 quarts).

Hungarian Goulash

Jackie Kohn
DULUTH, MINNESOTA

This great family dish boasts a rich creamy sauce certain to satisfy goulash lovers. I enjoy sharing recipes with friends and family, and this one's ideal for potluck suppers, too.

PREP: 15 min.
COOK: 8 hours

- 2 pounds beef top round steak, cut into 1-inch cubes
- 1 cup chopped onion
- 2 tablespoons all-purpose flour
- 1-1/2 teaspoons paprika
- 1 teaspoon garlic salt
- 1/2 teaspoon pepper
- 1 can (14-1/2 ounces) diced tomatoes, undrained
- 1 bay leaf
- 1 cup (8 ounces) sour cream
- Hot cooked noodles
- Minced fresh parsley, optional

■ Place beef and onion in a 3-qt. slow cooker. Combine the flour, paprika, garlic salt and pepper; sprinkle over beef and stir to coat. Stir in tomatoes; add bay leaf. Cover and cook on low for 8-10 hours or until meat is tender.

■ Discard bay leaf. Just before serving, stir in sour cream; heat through. Serve with noodles. Sprinkle with parsley if desired.

Yield: 6-8 servings.

Lots-A-Veggies Stew*

Judy Page
EDENVILLE, MICHIGAN

When I needed a no-fuss meal, I went through my pantry and refrigerator to gather whatever ingredients I had on hand. The result was a nicely seasoned stew packed with colorful vegetables.

PREP: 10 min. ■ COOK: 5 hours

- 1 pound ground beef
- 1 medium onion, diced
- 2 garlic cloves, minced
- 1 can (16 ounces) baked beans, undrained
- 1 can (16 ounces) kidney beans, rinsed and drained
- 1 can (16 ounces) butter beans, rinsed and drained
- 1 can (14-1/2 ounces) beef broth
- 1 can (11 ounces) whole kernel corn, undrained
- 1 can (10-1/2 ounces) condensed vegetable soup, undiluted
- 1 can (6 ounces) tomato paste
- 1 medium green pepper, diced
- 1 cup sliced carrots
- 1 cup sliced celery
- 2 tablespoons chili powder
- 1 teaspoon dried oregano
- 1 teaspoon dried thyme
- 1 teaspoon salt, optional
- 1/2 teaspoon dried marjoram
- 1/2 teaspoon pepper

■ In a large skillet, cook beef and onion over medium heat until meat is no longer pink. Add garlic; cook 1 minute longer. Drain. Transfer to a 5-qt. slow cooker. Stir in the remaining ingredients. Cover and cook on low for 5-6 hours or until vegetables are tender.

Yield: 10 servings.

***Nutrition Facts:** 1 cup equals 272 calories, 6 g fat (2 g saturated fat), 21 mg cholesterol, 1,088 mg sodium, 40 g carbohydrate, 9 g fiber, 20 g protein. **Diabetic Exchanges:** 2 starch, 2 vegetable, 1 lean meat.

Pizza Casserole

Julie Sterchi
HARRISBURG, ILLINOIS

This is one of the first dishes finished at potlucks. It can be adapted to personal tastes.

PREP: 25 min.
COOK: 1 hour

- 3 pounds ground beef
- 1/2 cup chopped onion
- 1 jar (28 ounces) spaghetti sauce
- 2 jars (4-1/2 ounces *each*) sliced mushrooms, drained
- 1 teaspoon salt
- 1/2 teaspoon garlic powder
- 1/2 teaspoon dried oregano
- Dash pepper
- 1 package (16 ounces) wide egg noodles, cooked and drained
- 2 packages (3-1/2 ounces *each*) sliced pepperoni
- 2 cups (8 ounces) shredded cheddar cheese
- 2 cups (8 ounces) shredded part-skim mozzarella cheese

■ In a Dutch oven, brown beef and onion over medium heat until meat is no longer pink; drain. Add the spaghetti sauce, mushrooms, salt, garlic powder, oregano and pepper; heat through.

■ Spoon 4 cups into a 5-qt. slow cooker. Top with half of the noodles, pepperoni and cheeses. Repeat layers.

■ Cover; cook on high for 1-2 hours or until cheese is melted.

Yield: 12 servings.

Editor's Note: This recipe can be halved to use in a 3-qt. slow cooker.

Dilled Pot Roast

Amy Lingren
JACKSONVILLE, FLORIDA

It's hard to believe that this mouthwatering pot roast comes together so easily. Dill weed, cider vinegar and a simple sour cream sauce gives great flavor to the meat.

Dilled Pot Roast

PREP: 15 min. ■ COOK: 7 to 8 hours

- 2 teaspoons dill weed, *divided*
- 1 teaspoon salt
- 1/4 teaspoon pepper
- 1 boneless beef chuck roast (2-1/2 pounds)
- 1/4 cup water
- 1 tablespoon cider vinegar
- 3 tablespoons all-purpose flour
- 1/4 cup cold water
- 1 cup (8 ounces) sour cream
- 1/2 teaspoon browning sauce, optional
- Hot cooked rice

■ In a small bowl, combine 1 teaspoon dill, salt and pepper. Sprinkle over both sides of roast. Transfer to a 3-qt. slow cooker. Add water and vinegar. Cover and cook on low for 7-8 hours or until meat is tender.

■ Remove meat and keep warm. In a small bowl, combine flour and remaining dill; stir in cold water until smooth. Gradually stir into slow cooker.

■ Cover and cook on high for 30 minutes or until thickened. Stir in sour cream and browning sauce if desired; heat through. Slice the meat; serve with the sour cream sauce and rice.

Yield: 6-8 servings.

Pot roasts are done when a long-handled fork can be inserted into the thickest part of the roast easily. If the pot roast is cooked until it falls apart, the meat is actually overcooked and will be stringy, tough and dry.

Taste of Home Test Kitchen

If you need a main dish recipe from a slow cooker that offers an upscale feel, this one is a great choice! Elegant enough for company, the rolled flank steak looks very pretty on a plate. Served with a simple side dish of potatoes, it's a sure-fire winner!

Spinach & Feta Stuffed Flank Steak

PREP: 30 min. ■ COOK: 6 hours

- 1 beef flank steak (1-1/2 pounds)
- 2 cups (8 ounces) crumbled feta cheese
- 3 cups fresh baby spinach
- 1/2 cup oil-packed sun-dried tomatoes, drained and chopped
- 1/2 cup finely chopped onion
- 5 tablespoons all-purpose flour, *divided*
- 1/2 teaspoon salt
- 1/2 teaspoon pepper
- 2 tablespoons canola oil
- 1 cup beef broth
- 1 tablespoon Worcestershire sauce
- 2 teaspoons tomato paste
- 1/3 cup dry red wine *or* additional beef broth
- Hot cooked egg noodles, optional
- Potatoes *or* hot cooked egg noodles, optional

■ Cut steak horizontally from the long side to within 1/2 in. of opposite side. Open steak so it lies flat; cover with plastic wrap. Flatten to 1/2-inch thickness; remove plastic.

■ Sprinkle 1 cup cheese over steak to within 1 inch of edges. Layer with spinach, tomatoes, onion and remaining cheese. Roll up jelly-roll style, starting with a long side; tie with kitchen string. Sprinkle steak with 2 tablespoons flour, salt and pepper.

■ In a large skillet, brown steak in oil; drain. Transfer to an oval 6-qt. slow cooker. Combine the broth, Worcestershire sauce and tomato paste; pour over steak. Cover and cook on low for 6-8 hours or until beef is tender.

■ Remove meat to a serving platter; keep warm. Skim fat from cooking juices; transfer to a small saucepan. Bring liquid to a boil. Combine remaining flour and wine until smooth. Gradually stir into the pan. Bring to a boil; cook and stir for 2 minutes or until thickened.

■ To serve, thinly slice beef across the grain. Serve with gravy and potatoes or noodles if desired.

Yield: 6 servings.

Family-Friendly Pizza

Hollie Clark
AMES, IOWA

This slow cooker casserole has lots of cheese and pepperoni, so it's family- and kid-friendly. It makes a lot, is easy to prepare and has the great flavors of pizza!

PREP: 30 min.
COOK: 3 hours

- 6 cups uncooked egg noodles
- 1-1/2 pounds ground beef
- 1 medium onion, chopped
- 1 medium green pepper, chopped
- 2 cans (15 ounces *each*) pizza sauce
- 1 can (4 ounces) mushroom stems and pieces, drained
- 2 cups (8 ounces) shredded cheddar cheese
- 2 cups (8 ounces) shredded part-skim mozzarella cheese
- 1 package (3-1/2 ounces) sliced pepperoni

■ Cook noodles according to package directions; drain. In a large skillet, cook the beef, onion and green pepper over medium heat until meat is no longer pink; drain. Stir in pizza sauce and mushrooms.

■ In a greased 5-qt. slow cooker, layer half of the noodles, meat sauce, cheese and pepperoni. Repeat layers. Cover and cook on low for 3-4 hours or until heated through.

Yield: 8 servings.

Poultry

Delicious dinners are as easy as the touch of a button with the wonderful variety of slow-cooked chicken and turkey dishes offered here. After trying one of these super satisfying recipes, you just might find a new family favorite!

Lemon Cilantro Chicken

Taste of Home Test Kitchen

This fall-off-the-bone chicken with lemony gravy is very easy to prepare and is a wonderful way to cook a whole chicken in the slow cooker.

Lemon Cilantro Chicken

PREP: 25 min. ■ COOK: 4 hours

- 1/2 cup chopped fresh cilantro
- 3 tablespoons canola oil, *divided*
- 2 tablespoons lemon juice
- 2 garlic cloves, minced
- 2 teaspoons salt
- 1 teaspoon grated lemon peel
- 1 broiler/fryer chicken (3 to 4 pounds)
- 1/2 teaspoon paprika
- 1/2 teaspoon pepper
- 1/2 cup white wine *or* chicken broth

■ In a small bowl, combine the cilantro, 2 tablespoons oil, lemon juice, garlic, salt and lemon peel. Loosen skin around the chicken breast, leg and thigh. Rub the cilantro mixture under and over the skin. Rub any remaining mixture into the cavity. Drizzle with remaining oil. Sprinkle with paprika and pepper.

■ Place in a 6- or 7-qt. slow cooker. Add the wine to slow cooker. Cover and cook on low for 4-5 hours or until a meat thermometer reads 180°. Remove the chicken to a serving platter; cover and let stand 15 minutes before carving. Skim the fat and thicken juices if desired. Serve with chicken.

Yield: 6 servings.

Turkey with Cranberry Sauce

Marie Ramsden

FAIRGROVE, MICHIGAN

Here's a delicious, easy way to cook a turkey breast in the slow cooker. Ideal for holiday potlucks, the sweet cranberry sauce complements the poultry nicely.

PREP: 15 min.
COOK: 4 hours

- 2 boneless skinless turkey breast halves (4 pounds *each*)
- 1 can (14 ounces) jellied cranberry sauce
- 1/2 cup plus 2 tablespoons water, *divided*
- 1 envelope onion soup mix
- 2 tablespoons cornstarch

■ Cut each turkey breast in half; place in two 5-qt. slow cookers. In a large bowl, combine the cranberry sauce, 1/2 cup water and soup mix. Pour half over each turkey. Cover and cook on low for 4-6 hours or until a meat thermometer reads 170°. Remove turkey and keep warm.

■ Transfer both cranberry mixtures to a large saucepan. Combine the cornstarch and remaining water until smooth. Bring cranberry mixture to a boil; gradually stir in cornstarch mixture until smooth. Cook and stir for 2 minutes or until thickened. Slice turkey; serve with cranberry sauce.

Yield: 20-25 servings.

Teriyaki Chicken

Gigi Miller
STOUGHTON, WISCONSIN

Chicken, rice and sweet-salty sauce create an entree that's packed with Asian flavor. Your family will love this moist and tender meal.

Teriyaki Chicken

PREP: 15 min. ■ COOK: 4 hours

- 12 boneless skinless chicken thighs (about 3 pounds)
- 3/4 cup sugar
- 3/4 cup soy sauce
- 6 tablespoons cider vinegar
- 3/4 teaspoon ground ginger
- 3/4 teaspoon minced garlic
- 1/4 teaspoon pepper
- 4-1/2 teaspoons cornstarch
- 4-1/2 teaspoons cold water
- Hot cooked rice, optional

■ Place chicken in a 4-qt. slow cooker. In a large bowl, combine the sugar, soy sauce, vinegar, ginger, garlic and pepper. Pour over the chicken. Cover; cook on low for 4-5 hours or until chicken is tender.

■ Remove chicken to a serving platter; keep warm. Skim the fat from cooking juices; transfer to a small saucepan. Bring liquid to a boil. Combine cornstarch and water until smooth. Gradually stir into the pan. Bring to a boil; cook and stir for 2 minutes or until thickened. Serve with chicken and rice if desired.

Yield: 6 servings.

Tender Barbecued Chicken

Jacqueline Blanton
GAFFNEY, SOUTH CAROLINA

I'm a teacher and work most of the day, so slow-cooked meals are a great help. A family favorite is this moist slow-simmered chicken. For an appealing look, simply choose a dark brown barbecue sauce.

PREP: 15 min.
COOK: 8 hours

- 1 broiler/fryer chicken (3 to 4 pounds), cut up
- 1 tablespoon canola oil
- 1 medium onion, thinly sliced
- 1 medium lemon, thinly sliced
- 1 bottle (18 ounces) barbecue sauce
- 3/4 cup cola

■ In a large skillet, brown chicken in oil in batches. Transfer to a 3-qt. slow cooker. Top with onion and lemon slices. Combine barbecue sauce and cola; pour over chicken.

■ Cover and cook on low for 8-10 hours or until chicken is tender.

Yield: 4 servings.

Helen Toulantis
WANTAGH, NEW YORK

We adopted three children from Thailand and enjoy curry dishes. All of us love the spicy flavors found in this savory favorite.

Slow-Cooked Curry Chicken

Slow-Cooked Curry Chicken

PREP: 25 min. ■ COOK: 4 hours

- 6 boneless skinless chicken breast halves (6 ounces *each*)
- 1-1/4 teaspoons salt
- 1 can (14 ounces) light coconut milk
- 1 teaspoon curry powder
- 1/2 teaspoon ground turmeric
- 1/2 teaspoon cayenne pepper
- 3 green onions, sliced, *divided*
- 2 tablespoons cornstarch
- 2 tablespoons cold water
- 1 to 2 tablespoons lime juice
- 3 cups hot cooked rice

■ Sprinkle chicken with salt. In a large nonstick skillet coated with cooking spray, brown chicken on both sides. Place in a 5-qt. slow cooker.

■ Combine the coconut milk, curry, turmeric and cayenne; pour over chicken. Sprinkle with half of the onions. Cover and cook on low for 4-5 hours or until chicken is tender.

■ Combine cornstarch and water until smooth; stir into slow cooker. Cover and cook on high for 30 minutes or until sauce is thickened. Stir in lime juice. Serve chicken with rice and sauce; sprinkle with remaining onions.

Yield: 6 servings.

Thai Chicken Thighs

Taste of Home Test Kitchen

These tender and moist chicken thighs come with a tangy peanut butter sauce that is irresistible.

PREP: 25 min.
COOK: 5 hours

- 8 bone-in chicken thighs (about 3 pounds), skin removed
- 1/2 cup salsa
- 1/4 cup creamy peanut butter
- 2 tablespoons lemon juice
- 2 tablespoons reduced-sodium soy sauce
- 1 tablespoon chopped seeded jalapeno pepper
- 2 teaspoons Thai chili sauce
- 1 garlic clove, minced
- 1 teaspoon minced fresh gingerroot
- 2 green onions, sliced
- 2 tablespoons sesame seeds, toasted

Hot cooked basmati rice, optional

■ Place chicken in a 3-qt. slow cooker. In a small bowl, combine the salsa, peanut butter, lemon juice, soy sauce, jalapeno pepper, Thai chili sauce, garlic and ginger; pour over chicken.

■ Cover and cook on low for 5-6 hours or until chicken is tender. Sprinkle with green onions and sesame seeds. Serve with rice if desired.

Yield: 8 servings.

Editor's Note: We recommend wearing disposable gloves when cutting hot peppers. Avoid touching your face.

Michele Trantham
WAYNESVILLE, NORTH CAROLINA

Try this moist and tender chicken-and-potato dish! Just fix it in the morning, then forget about it until dinner time.

Chicken and Red Potatoes

Chicken and Red Potatoes

PREP: 20 min. ■ COOK: 3-1/2 hours

- 3 tablespoons all-purpose flour
- 4 boneless skinless chicken breast halves (6 ounces *each*)
- 2 tablespoons olive oil
- 4 medium red potatoes, cut into wedges
- 2 cups fresh baby carrots, halved lengthwise
- 1 can (4 ounces) mushroom stems and pieces, drained
- 4 canned whole green chilies, cut into 1/2-inch slices
- 1 can (10-3/4 ounces) condensed cream of onion soup, undiluted
- 1/4 cup 2% milk
- 1/2 teaspoon chicken seasoning
- 1/4 teaspoon salt
- 1/4 teaspoon dried rosemary, crushed
- 1/4 teaspoon pepper

■ Place flour in a large resealable plastic bag. Add chicken, one piece at a time, and shake to coat. In a large skillet, brown chicken in oil on both sides.

■ Meanwhile, place the potatoes, carrots, mushrooms and chilies in a greased 5-qt. slow cooker. In a small bowl, combine the remaining ingredients. Pour half of soup mixture over vegetables.

■ Transfer chicken to slow cooker; top with remaining soup mixture. Cover and cook on low for 3-1/2 to 4 hours or until a meat thermometer reads 170°.

Yield: 4 servings.

Editor's Note: This recipe was tested with McCormick's Montreal Chicken Seasoning. Look for it in the spice aisle.

Maple Mustard Chicken*

Jennifer Seidel
MIDLAND, MICHIGAN

This recipe is one of my husband's favorites. It only calls for five ingredients, and we try to have them on hand all the time for a delicious and cozy dinner any night of the week.

PREP: 5 min.
COOK: 3 hours

- 6 boneless skinless chicken breast halves (6 ounces *each*)
- 1/2 cup maple syrup
- 1/3 cup stone-ground mustard
- 2 tablespoons quick-cooking tapioca

Hot cooked brown rice

■ Place chicken in a 3-qt. slow cooker. Combine the syrup, mustard and tapioca; pour over chicken. Cover and cook on low for 3-4 hours or until a meat thermometer reads 170°. Serve with rice.

Yield: 6 servings.

***Nutrition Facts:** 1 chicken breast half with 3 tablespoons sauce (calculated without rice) equals 289 calories, 4 g fat (1 g saturated fat), 94 mg cholesterol, 296 mg sodium, 24 g carbohydrate, 2 g fiber, 35 g protein. **Diabetic Exchanges:** 5 lean meat, 1-1/2 starch.

Herbed Chicken with Wild Rice

Becky Gifford
CONWAY, ARKANSAS

My family is always very busy. With three kids involved in many different after-school and evening activities, it's nice to come home to a meal that's prepared and ready to eat!

Herbed Chicken with Wild Rice

PREP: 20 min. ■ COOK: 4 hours

- 1 package (6 ounces) long grain and wild rice mix
- 6 boneless skinless chicken breast halves (5 ounces *each*)
- 1 tablespoon canola oil
- 1 teaspoon butter
- 1/2 pound sliced fresh mushrooms
- 1 can (10-3/4 ounces) condensed cream of chicken soup, undiluted
- 1 cup water
- 3 bacon strips, cooked and crumbled
- 1 teaspoon dried parsley flakes
- 1/2 teaspoon dried thyme
- 1/4 teaspoon dried tarragon

■ Place rice in a 5-qt. slow cooker; set aside seasoning packet. In a large skillet, brown chicken in oil and butter. Add to slow cooker. In the same skillet, saute mushrooms until tender; place over chicken.

■ In a small bowl, combine the soup, water, bacon, herbs and contents of seasoning packet. Pour over top. Cover and cook on low for 4-5 hours or until meat is tender.

Yield: 6 servings.

Slow Cooker Chicken Dinner

Jenet Cattar
NEPTUNE BEACH, FLORIDA

This meal-in-one, which includes juicy chicken and tasty veggies in a creamy sauce, is ready to eat when I get home from the office.

PREP: 10 min.
COOK: 8-1/2 hours

- 6 medium red potatoes, cut into chunks
- 4 medium carrots, cut into 1/2-inch pieces
- 4 boneless skinless chicken breast halves
- 1 can (10-3/4 ounces) condensed cream of chicken soup, undiluted
- 1 can (10-3/4 ounces) condensed cream of mushroom soup, undiluted
- 1/8 teaspoon garlic salt
- 2 to 4 tablespoons mashed potato flakes, optional

■ Place potatoes and carrots in a 5-qt. slow cooker. Top with chicken. Combine soups and garlic salt; pour over chicken.

■ Cover and cook on low for 6-8 hours or until meat is tender. To thicken if desired, stir the potato flakes into the gravy and cook 30 minutes longer.

Yield: 4 servings.

Lorie Miner
KAMAS, UTAH

My husband grew up in an area with lots of turkey farms, so he learned early to love dishes that use turkey. This makes a tasty dinner that requires no last minute fuss, so I like to serve it when I have company over.

Mandarin Turkey Tenderloin

PREP: 15 min. ■ COOK: 4-1/2 hours

- 8 turkey breast tenderloins (4 ounces *each*)
- 1/2 teaspoon ground ginger
- 1/2 teaspoon crushed red pepper flakes
- 1 can (11 ounces) mandarin oranges, drained
- 1 cup sesame ginger marinade
- 1/2 cup chicken broth
- 1 package (16 ounces) frozen stir-fry vegetable blend, thawed
- 1 tablespoon sesame seeds, toasted
- 1 green onion, sliced
- Hot cooked rice, optional

■ Place turkey in a 3-qt. slow cooker. Sprinkle with ginger and pepper flakes. Top with oranges. In a small bowl, combine marinade and broth; pour over turkey. Cover and cook on low for 4-5 hours or until a meat thermometer reads 170°.

■ Stir vegetables into the slow cooker. Cover and cook 30 minutes longer or until vegetables are heated through.

■ Sprinkle with sesame seeds and sliced green onion. Serve with the rice if desired.

Yield: 8 servings.

Sweet Orange Chicken

Louise Gilbert
QUESNEL, BRITISH COLUMBIA

Orange marmalade and tangy barbecue sauce make my simple chicken entree a tasty sensation.

PREP: 15 min. ■ COOK: 6 hours

- 3 tablespoons all-purpose flour
- 1 broiler/fryer chicken (3 to 4 pounds), cut up and skin removed
- 2/3 cup orange marmalade
- 2/3 cup barbecue sauce
- 1/4 cup soy sauce
- 2 tablespoons minced fresh gingerroot
- Hot cooked rice *or* rice noodles, optional

■ Place flour in a large resealable plastic bag. Add chicken, a few pieces at a time, and shake to coat. Place in a 3-qt. slow cooker.

■ Combine the orange marmalade, barbecue sauce, soy sauce and ginger; pour over chicken. Cover and cook on low for 6-8 hours or until chicken juices run clear. Serve with rice or noodles if desired.

Yield: 6 servings.

Wild Rice Turkey Dinner

Tabitha Dodge
CONOVER, WISCONSIN

We live in the northwoods of Wisconsin, and the wild rice, squash and cranberries I use for this meal are locally grown. I combine these ingredients with turkey tenderloins for a complete and satisfying supper.

PREP: 10 min.
COOK: 7 hours

- 3/4 cup uncooked wild rice
- 1 medium butternut squash, peeled, seeded and cut into 1-inch pieces
- 1 medium onion, cut into 1-inch pieces
- 2 turkey breast tenderloins (8 ounces *each*)
- 3 cups chicken broth
- 1/2 teaspoon salt
- 1/2 teaspoon pepper
- 1/2 teaspoon dried thyme
- 1/2 cup dried cranberries

■ In a 4 qt. slow cooker, layer the rice, squash, onion and turkey. Add broth; sprinkle with salt, pepper and thyme. Cover and cook on low for 6-8 hours or until meat is tender.

■ Remove turkey; cut into slices. Stir cranberries into rice mixture. Using a slotted spoon, serve the squash mixture with the turkey.

Yield: 4 servings.

Chicken with Veggies 'n' Gravy

Susan Dalrymple
MARATHON, FLORIDA

I couldn't bear the thought of going to the supermarket one day and was determined to come up with something for dinner from what I had. I created this comforting chicken mix, and my husband loved it!

PREP: 10 min. ■ COOK: 4 hours

- 3 medium carrots, chopped
- 2 celery ribs, chopped
- 1 medium onion, chopped
- 2 boneless skinless chicken breast halves (5 ounces *each*)
- 1/8 teaspoon pepper
- 1 can (10-3/4 ounces) condensed cream of chicken soup, undiluted
- 2/3 cup water
- 1/4 cup white wine *or* chicken broth
- 2 individually frozen biscuits

■ Place the carrots, celery and onion in a 1-1/2-qt. slow cooker; top with chicken. Sprinkle with pepper.

■ In a small bowl, combine the soup, water and wine; pour over the chicken. Cover and cook on low for 4-5 hours or until the meat and vegetables are tender.

■ If desired, thicken cooking juices. Meanwhile, bake biscuits according to package directions. Serve with chicken and gravy.

Yield: 2 servings.

Saucy Apricot Chicken

Dee Gray
KOKOMO, INDIANA

Four ingredients are all you'll need for a tender chicken entree. The tangy glaze is just as wonderful with ham or turkey. Leftovers reheat nicely in the microwave.

PREP: 5 min. ■ COOK: 4 hours

- 6 boneless skinless chicken breast halves (4 ounces *each*)
- 2 jars (12 ounces *each*) apricot preserves
- 1 envelope onion soup mix
- Hot cooked rice

■ Place chicken in a 3-qt. slow cooker. Combine the preserves and soup mix; spoon over chicken. Cover and cook on low for 4-5 hours or until meat is tender. Serve with rice.

Yield: 6 servings.

Chili-Lime Chicken Tostadas

PREP: 10 min.
COOK: 5 hours

- 4 pounds bone-in chicken breast halves, skin removed
- 1 medium onion, chopped
- 1 can (4 ounces) chopped green chilies
- 3 tablespoons lime juice
- 4-1/2 teaspoons chili powder
- 4 garlic cloves, minced
- 10 tostada shells
- 1 can (16 ounces) fat-free refried beans

Optional ingredients: shredded red cabbage, shredded cheddar cheese, salsa, sour cream and sliced ripe olives

■ In a 4-qt. slow cooker, combine chicken and onion. In a small bowl, combine green chilies, lime juice, chili powder and garlic; pour over chicken. Cover and cook on low for 5-6 hours or until meat is tender.

■ Remove chicken; cool slightly. Set aside 2/3 cup cooking juices. Discard remaining juices. Shred chicken with two forks and return to slow cooker. Stir in reserved cooking juices.

■ Spread tostadas with refried beans; top with chicken. Layer with shredded cabbage, cheese, salsa, sour cream and olives if desired.

Yield: 5 servings.

Laura Powell
SOUTH JORDAN, UTAH

These are family-friendly, fun and super tasty. The flavor of the tender chicken is delicious with a hint of lime, and it has just the right amount of heat to spice it up but still keep it popular with kids. Top the tostadas with anything you like!

Taste of Home Test Kitchen

Take a trip to Morocco with an exotic and rich dish. A tagine is a North African slow-cooked stew that is named after the pot in which it is cooked. The tagine that follows is full of delicious ingredients and aromatic spices that cook together for a fabulously flavorful meal.

Moroccan Vegetable Chicken Tagine

PREP: 45 min. ■ COOK: 7-1/2 hours

- 1 medium butternut squash (about 3 pounds), peeled and cut into 1-inch cubes
- 2 medium red potatoes, cut into 1-inch cubes
- 1 medium sweet potato, peeled and cut into 1-inch cubes
- 1 large onion, halved and sliced
- 2 garlic cloves, minced
- 6 chicken leg quarters, skin removed
- 1/2 teaspoon salt
- 1/4 teaspoon pepper
- 1/2 cup dried apricots, chopped
- 1/2 cup dried cranberries, chopped
- 2 tablespoons all-purpose flour
- 1 can (14-3/4 ounces) reduced-sodium chicken broth
- 1/4 cup chili sauce
- 1 tablespoon minced fresh gingerroot
- 1 teaspoon curry powder
- 1/2 teaspoon ground cinnamon
- 1/2 teaspoon ground cumin
- 1 can (15 ounces) garbanzo beans *or* chickpeas, rinsed and drained

Hot cooked couscous, optional

■ In a 6-qt. slow cooker, combine the squash, potatoes, onion and garlic. Sprinkle chicken with salt and pepper; place over vegetables. Top with apricots and cranberries.

■ In a small bowl, combine flour and broth until smooth. Stir in the chili sauce, ginger, curry, cinnamon and cumin. Pour over chicken. Cover and cook on low for 7-8 hours or until chicken and vegetables are tender.

■ Stir in garbanzo beans; cover and cook for 30 minutes or until heated through. Serve with couscous if desired.

Yield: 6 servings.

Couscous is a commercially produced grain product usually made from semolina, shaped into tiny beads with origins in the Middle East and North Africa. Found in the rice or pasta section of the grocery store, it is available in regular or quick-cooking forms. Use as a side dish and in salads like rice or pasta.

Lemon Chicken

Elizabeth Hokanson

ARBORG, MANITOBA

This easy and attractive meal is bound to become a staple in your home. Made with everyday ingredients, there's nothing complicated or fancy about it.

PREP: 20 min.
COOK: 4-1/4 hours

- 1 teaspoon dried oregano
- 1/2 teaspoon seasoned salt
- 1/4 teaspoon pepper
- 6 boneless skinless chicken breast halves (6 ounces *each*)
- 2 teaspoons chicken bouillon granules
- 1/4 cup boiling water
- 3 tablespoons lemon juice
- 1-1/2 teaspoons minced garlic
- 1-1/2 cups (12 ounces) sour cream
- 2 teaspoons minced fresh parsley

Hot cooked brown rice, optional

■ Combine oregano, seasoned salt and pepper and rub over the chicken. Place in a 3-qt. slow cooker.

■ In a small bowl, dissolve bouillon in boiling water. Stir in lemon juice and garlic. Pour over chicken. Cover and cook on low for 4-5 hours or until meat is tender.

■ Remove chicken and keep warm. Stir in sour cream and parsley; cover and cook for 15 minutes or until heated through. Serve chicken with sauce and rice if desired.

Yield: 6 servings.

Andi Kauffman
BEAVERCREEK, OREGON

My husband and I love this yummy dish! It's a breeze to prepare in the slow cooker, and it tastes just like a meal you'd have at your favorite Indian or Thai restaurant.

Coconut Curry Chicken

Coconut Curry Chicken*

PREP: 20 min. ■ COOK: 5 hours

- 2 medium potatoes, peeled and cubed
- 1 small onion, chopped
- 4 boneless skinless chicken breast halves (4 ounces *each*)
- 1 cup light coconut milk
- 4 teaspoons curry powder
- 1 teaspoon reduced-sodium chicken bouillon granules
- 1 garlic clove, minced
- 1/4 teaspoon salt
- 1/4 teaspoon pepper
- 2 cups hot cooked rice
- 1/4 cup thinly sliced green onions

Optional ingredients: raisins, flaked coconut and chopped unsalted peanuts

■ Place potatoes and onion in a 3- or 4-qt. slow cooker. In a large nonstick skillet coated with cooking spray, brown chicken on both sides.

■ Transfer to slow cooker. In a small bowl, combine the coconut milk, curry, bouillon, garlic, salt and pepper; pour over chicken. Cover and cook on low for 5-6 hours or until meat is tender.

■ Serve the chicken and sauce with rice; sprinkle with green onions. Garnish with raisins, coconut and peanuts if desired.

Yield: 4 servings.

***Nutrition Facts:** 1 serving (calculated without optional ingredients) equals 396 calories, 11 g fat (7 g saturated fat), 63 mg cholesterol, 309 mg sodium, 43 g carbohydrate, 3 g fiber, 27 g protein. **Diabetic Exchanges:** 3 lean meat, 2-1/2 starch, 2 fat.

Herbed Slow Cooker Chicken

Sundra Hauck
BOGALUSA, LOUISIANA

I use my slow cooker to prepare these well-seasoned chicken breasts that cook up moist and tender. My daughter, who has two young sons to keep up with, shared the recipe with me several years ago, and I've made it repeatedly since then!

PREP: 5 min.
COOK: 4 hours

- 1 tablespoon olive oil
- 1 teaspoon paprika
- 1/2 teaspoon garlic powder
- 1/2 teaspoon seasoned salt
- 1/2 teaspoon dried thyme
- 1/2 teaspoon dried basil
- 1/2 teaspoon pepper
- 1/2 teaspoon browning sauce, optional
- 4 bone-in chicken breast halves (6 ounces *each*)
- 1/2 cup chicken broth

■ In a small bowl, combine the oil, paprika, garlic powder, seasoned salt, thyme, basil, pepper and browning sauce, if desired; rub over chicken. Place chicken in a 5-qt. slow cooker; add broth. Cover and cook on low for 4-5 hours or until meat is tender.

Yield: 4 servings.

Zesty Mexican Chicken

Michelle Sheldon
MIDDLETOWN, DELAWARE

A hint of lime juice helps tame the heat in zesty, tender chicken with crunchy vegetables. And because it's all prepared in the slow cooker, you and your kitchen will stay cool, too!

Zesty Mexican Chicken*

PREP: 15 min. ■ COOK: 3-1/2 hours

- 6 boneless skinless chicken breast halves (4 ounces *each*)
- 1 can (14-1/2 ounces) diced tomatoes, undrained
- 1 large onion, chopped
- 1 medium green pepper, chopped
- 3 garlic cloves, minced
- 2 tablespoons lime juice
- 1 tablespoon hot pepper sauce
- 1/4 teaspoon salt
- 1/4 teaspoon pepper
- 3 cups hot cooked rice

■ Place chicken in a 4-qt. slow cooker coated with cooking spray. In a large bowl, combine the tomatoes, onion, green pepper, garlic, lime juice, pepper sauce, salt and pepper. Pour over chicken.

■ Cover and cook on low for 3-4 hours or until meat is tender. Serve with rice.

Yield: 6 servings.

***Nutrition Facts:** 1 chicken breast half with 1/2 cup rice and 1/2 cup tomato mixture equals 256 calories, 3 g fat (1 g saturated fat), 63 mg cholesterol, 257 mg sodium, 30 g carbohydrate, 2 g fiber, 26 g protein. **Diabetic Exchanges:** 3 lean meat, 1-1/2 starch, 1 vegetable.

Saucy Chicken With Veggies And Rice

Teri Lindquist
GURNEE, ILLINOIS

I'm proud to share a recipe that I created many years ago for a slow-cooker contest where it won first place! The rich and flavorful dish is so easy to put together.

PREP: 15 min.
COOK: 4-1/2 hours

- 3 cups sliced celery
- 3 cups sliced fresh carrots
- 2 cups sliced onion
- 6 boneless skinless chicken breast halves (5 ounces *each*)
- 1 can (10-3/4 ounces) condensed cream of mushroom soup, undiluted
- 1 envelope onion soup mix
- 1 teaspoon dried thyme
- 1 teaspoon pepper
- 1/2 teaspoon dried tarragon
- 2 tablespoons cornstarch
- 1/3 cup white wine *or* chicken broth

Hot cooked rice

■ Place the celery, carrots, onion and chicken in a 5-qt. slow cooker. In a small bowl, combine the soup, soup mix, thyme, pepper and tarragon; pour over chicken.

■ Cover and cook on low for 4-5 hours or until meat is tender. Mix cornstarch and wine until smooth; stir into slow cooker. Cover and cook on high for 30 minutes or until gravy is thickened. Serve with rice.

Yield: 6 servings.

Nostalgic Chicken and Dumplings

Brenda Edwards
HERFORD, ARIZONA

Enjoy old-fashioned goodness without all the fuss when you fix this supper in your slow cooker. It features tender chicken, wonderfully light dumplings and a full-flavored sauce.

Nostalgic Chicken and Dumplings

PREP: 20 min. ■ COOK: 5 hours

- 6 bone-in chicken breast halves (10 ounces *each*), skin removed
- 2 whole cloves
- 1/2 cup frozen pearl onions, thawed
- 1 bay leaf
- 1 garlic clove, minced
- 1/2 teaspoon salt
- 1/2 teaspoon dried thyme
- 1/2 teaspoon dried marjoram
- 1/4 teaspoon pepper
- 1/2 cup reduced-sodium chicken broth
- 1/2 cup white wine *or* additional chicken broth
- 3 tablespoons cornstarch
- 1/4 cup cold water
- 1/2 teaspoon browning sauce, optional
- 1 cup reduced-fat biscuit/baking mix
- 6 tablespoons fat-free milk
- 1 tablespoon minced fresh parsley

■ Place the chicken in a 5-qt. slow cooker. Insert cloves into one onion; add to slow cooker. Add bay leaf and remaining onions. Sprinkle mixture with the garlic, salt, thyme, marjoram and pepper. Add broth and wine or additional broth to the slow cooker. Cover and cook on low for 4-1/2 to 5 hours or until meat is tender.

■ Remove chicken to a serving platter and keep warm. Discard cloves and bay leaf. In a small bowl, combine the cornstarch, water and browning sauce if desired until smooth. Stir into slow cooker. Cover and cook on high until mixture reaches a simmer.

■ Meanwhile, combine the biscuit mix, milk and parsley. Drop by tablespoonfuls onto simmering liquid. Reduce heat to low; cover and cook for 20-25 minutes or until a toothpick inserted into dumplings comes out clean (do not lift cover while simmering). Serve with chicken and sauce.

Yield: 6 servings.

Dried herbs don't spoil, but they do lose flavor and potency over time. For maximum flavor in your cooking, you may want to replace herbs that are over a year old. Store dried herbs in airtight containers and keep them away from heat and light.

Sandra Bonow
LEWISTON, MINNESOTA

When my mother was pregnant with me, one of the only things she could eat was home-canned peaches. To this day, I love recipes with peaches. This dish is so delicious and fills the house with such wonderful aromas, you'll hardly be able to wait to eat it.

Peachy Chicken with Sweet Potatoes

Peachy Chicken With Sweet Potatoes

PREP: 25 min. ■ COOK: 6 hours

- 2 medium sweet potatoes, peeled and cubed
- 1 medium onion, chopped
- 8 boneless skinless chicken thighs (about 2 pounds)
- 1 teaspoon paprika
- 1 teaspoon dried thyme
- 1/2 teaspoon salt
- 1/8 teaspoon cayenne pepper
- 1 cup peach preserves
- 2 tablespoons cornstarch
- 1/2 cup cold water

■ In a 4- or 5-qt. slow cooker, combine sweet potatoes and onion. Sprinkle chicken with paprika, thyme, salt and cayenne; arrange over sweet potatoes. Top with preserves. Cover and cook on low for 6-8 hours or until chicken and potatoes are tender.

■ Remove chicken and vegetables to a serving platter; keep warm. Skim fat from cooking juices; transfer to a small saucepan. Bring liquid to a boil. Combine cornstarch and water until smooth. Gradually stir into the pan. Bring to a boil; cook and stir for 2 minutes or until thickened. Serve with chicken and vegetables.

Yield: 4 servings.

Lemony Turkey Breast*

Lynn Laux
BALLWIN, MISSOURI

Here, lemon and garlic add a lovely touch to turkey breast.

PREP: 10 min.
COOK: 5 hours

- 1 bone-in turkey breast (5 pounds), halved
- 1 medium lemon, halved
- 1 teaspoon salt-free lemon-pepper seasoning
- 1 teaspoon garlic salt
- 4 teaspoons cornstarch
- 1/2 cup reduced-sodium chicken broth

■ Remove skin from turkey, pat dry with paper towels and spray with cooking spray. Place breast side up in 5-qt. slow cooker. Squeeze half of the lemon over turkey; sprinkle with lemon-pepper and garlic salt. Place lemon halves under turkey.

■ Cover and cook on low for 5-7 hours or until meat is tender. Remove turkey and keep warm. Discard lemon.

■ For gravy, pour cooking liquid into measuring cup; skim fat. In a pan, combine cornstarch and broth until smooth. Gradually stir in cooking liquid. Bring to a boil. Cook; stir for 2 minutes or until thickened. Serve with turkey.

Yield: 14 servings.

***Nutrition Facts:** 4 ounces cooked turkey with 2 tablespoons gravy equals 154 calories, 1 g fat (trace saturated fat), 92 mg cholesterol, 149 mg sodium, 1 g carbohydrate, trace fiber, 34 g protein. **Diabetic Exchange:** 4 lean meat.

Pork, Ham & More

48

52

56

So many items turn out succulent in a slow cooker, and pork is certainly one of them! Whether you prefer simmering stews or fall-off-the-bone ribs, this section is your ticket to a satisfying supper. You'll also discover meatless recipes and other dishes sure to have your gang racing to the table!

Tender Spareribs

Julie Czmer
WEST BLOOMFIELD, MICHIGAN

Even my three little ones love this easy-to-make and delicious-to-eat meal. The succulent meat simmers to perfection in the slow cooker!

Tender Spareribs

PREP: 10 min. ■ COOK: 5-1/2 hours

- 4 pounds pork spareribs, cut into serving-size pieces
- 1/4 cup soy sauce
- 1/4 cup prepared mustard
- 1/4 cup molasses
- 3 tablespoons cider vinegar
- 2 tablespoons Worcestershire sauce
- 1 to 2 teaspoons hot pepper sauce

■ Place ribs in a 5-qt. slow cooker. Combine the remaining ingredients; pour over ribs. Cover and cook on low for 5-6 hours or until meat is tender.

Yield: 8 servings.

Pork and Sauerkraut With Potatoes

Valerie Hay
LONGMONT, COLORADO

This is a wintertime favorite in our home. The aroma is irresistible as it simmers.

PREP: 15 min.
COOK: 5 hours

- 2 cans (14 ounces *each*) sauerkraut, undrained
- 1 cup thinly sliced onion
- 2 medium tart apples, peeled and sliced
- 1/2 cup dark corn syrup
- 2 bay leaves
- 1 teaspoon caraway seeds
- 1/2 teaspoon pepper
- 3 large potatoes, peeled and cut into 2-inch chunks
- 6 bone-in pork loin chops (3/4 inch thick and 7 ounces *each*)

■ In a large bowl, combine the sauerkraut, onion, apples, corn syrup, bay leaves, caraway and pepper. Spoon half into a 5-qt. slow cooker; top with potatoes.

■ Broil pork chops 6 in. from the heat for 3-4 minutes on each side or until browned; place over potatoes. Spoon remaining sauerkraut mixture over pork.

■ Cover and cook on high for 1 hour. Reduce heat to low; cook 4-5 hours longer or until meat is tender. Discard bay leaves.

Yield: 6 servings.

Veggie Lasagna

Laura Davister
LITTLE SUAMICO, WISCONSIN

Perfect for two, this "veggie-licious" alternative to traditional lasagna makes use of slow-cooker convenience. Use chunky spaghetti sauce for the best results.

Veggie Lasagna

PREP: 25 min. ■ COOK: 3-1/2 hours

- 3/4 cup meatless spaghetti sauce
- 1/2 cup sliced zucchini
- 1/2 cup shredded part-skim mozzarella cheese
- 3 tablespoons 1% cottage cheese
- 2 tablespoons grated Parmesan cheese
- 2 tablespoons egg substitute
- 1/2 teaspoon Italian seasoning
- 1/8 teaspoon garlic powder
- 2 no-cook lasagna noodles
- 4 cups fresh baby spinach
- 1/2 cup sliced fresh mushrooms

■ Spread 1 tablespoon spaghetti sauce in a 1-1/2-qt. slow cooker coated with cooking spray. Top with half of the zucchini. Combine the cheeses, egg substitute, Italian seasoning and garlic powder; spoon a third over zucchini.

■ Break noodles into 1-in. pieces; sprinkle half over cheese mixture. Spread 1 tablespoon sauce over noodles. Top with half of the spinach and mushrooms. Repeat layers. Top with remaining cheese mixture and spaghetti sauce.

■ Cover; cook on low for 3-1/2 to 4 hours or until noodles are tender.

Yield: 2 servings.

Butternut Coconut Curry

Jeff Apfe
TASTE OF HOME ONLINE COMMUNITY

I love my slow cooker because it makes dinner so easy to make! This meatless curry was first created for a potluck and since then, the recipe has been requested often.

PREP: 35 min.
COOK: 4 hours

- 1 cup chopped carrots
- 1 small onion, chopped
- 1 tablespoon olive oil
- 1-1/2 teaspoons brown sugar
- 1-1/2 teaspoons curry powder
- 1 garlic clove, minced
- 1/2 teaspoon ground cinnamon
- 1/4 teaspoon ground ginger
- 1/8 teaspoon salt
- 1 medium butternut squash (about 2-1/2 pounds), cut into 1-inch cubes
- 2-1/2 cups vegetable broth
- 3/4 cup coconut milk
- 1/2 cup uncooked basmati *or* jasmine rice

■ In a large skillet, saute carrots and onion in oil until onion is tender. Add the brown sugar, curry, garlic, cinnamon, ginger and salt. Cook and stir 2 minutes longer.

■ In a 3- or 4-qt. slow cooker, combine the butternut squash, broth, coconut milk, rice and carrot mixture. Cover and cook on low for 4-5 hours or until rice is tender.

Yield: 9 servings.

Corina Flansberg
CARSON CITY, NEVADA

This pork roast is so moist and tender, it melts in your mouth. My son puts it on his list of most-favorite foods. We like it with mashed potatoes.

Country-Style Pork Loin

Country-Style Pork Loin*

PREP: 20 min. ■ COOK: 5 hours

- 1 boneless whole pork loin roast (3 pounds)
- 1/2 cup all-purpose flour
- 1 teaspoon onion powder
- 1 teaspoon ground mustard
- 2 tablespoons canola oil
- 2 cups reduced-sodium chicken broth
- 1/4 cup cornstarch
- 1/4 cup cold water
- Hot mashed potatoes, optional

■ Cut roast in half. In a large resealable plastic bag, combine the flour, onion powder and mustard. Add pork, one portion at a time, and shake to coat. In a large skillet, brown pork in oil on all sides.

■ Transfer to a 5-qt. slow cooker. Pour broth over pork. Cover and cook on low for 5-6 hours or a meat thermometer reads 160°. Remove pork and keep warm.

■ Strain cooking juices, reserving 2 1/2 cups juices; skim fat from reserved juices. Transfer to a small saucepan. Bring liquid to a boil. Combine cornstarch and water until smooth; gradually stir into the pan. Bring to a boil; cook and stir for 2 minutes or until thickened. Slice pork; serve with gravy and mashed potatoes if desired.

Yield: 8 servings.

***Nutrition Facts:** 5 ounces cooked meat with 1/4 cup gravy (calculated without potatoes) equals 291 calories, 11 g fat (3 g saturated fat), 85 mg cholesterol, 204 mg sodium, 10 g carbohydrate, trace fiber, 34 g protein. **Diabetic Exchanges:** 5 lean meat, 1 fat, 1/2 starch.

Root Beer BBQ Ribs

mairyn s
TASTE OF HOME ONLINE COMMUNITY

The slow cooker does a great job of creating super tender and juicy ribs. The yummy sauce has a mildly sweet flavor.

PREP: 25 min.
COOK: 6 hours

- 1 cup root beer
- 1 cup ketchup
- 1/4 cup orange juice
- 3 tablespoons Worcestershire sauce
- 2 tablespoons molasses
- 1 teaspoon onion powder
- 1 teaspoon garlic powder
- 1/2 teaspoon ground ginger
- 1/2 teaspoon paprika
- 1/4 teaspoon crushed red pepper flakes
- 4-1/2 pounds pork baby back ribs
- 1 teaspoon salt
- 1/2 teaspoon pepper

■ In a small saucepan, combine the first 10 ingredients. Bring to a boil over medium heat. Reduce heat; simmer, uncovered, for 10 minutes or until sauce is reduced to 2 cups. Set aside.

■ Cut ribs into five serving-size pieces; sprinkle with salt and pepper. Place in a 5- or 6-qt. slow cooker. Pour sauce over ribs. Cover and cook on low for 6-8 hours or until meat is tender. Serve with sauce.

Yield: 5 servings.

Cabbage Kielbasa Supper

Margery Bryan
MOSES LAKE, WASHINGTON

If you're a fan of German food, you'll enjoy my traditional combination of sausage, cabbage and potatoes. The hearty main dish is so good, all you need is a bowl of fruit and dinner's ready.

PREP: 10 min. ■ COOK: 8 hours

- 8 cups coarsely shredded cabbage
- 3 medium potatoes, cut into 1/2-inch cubes
- 1 medium onion, chopped
- 1-3/4 teaspoons salt
- 1/4 teaspoon pepper
- 1 can (14-1/2 ounces) chicken broth
- 2 pounds fully cooked kielbasa *or* Polish sausage, cut into serving-size pieces

■ In a 5-qt. slow cooker, combine the cabbage, potatoes, onion, salt and pepper. Pour broth over vegetables. Place sausage on top (slow cooker will be full, but cabbage will cook down).

■ Cover and cook on low for 8-9 hours or until vegetables are tender and sausage is heated through.

Yield: 6-8 servings.

Overnight Irish Oatmeal

Susan Smith
OCEAN VIEW, NEW JERSEY

Fans of the healthy benefits of flaxseed will enjoy this slow-cooked oatmeal. It's full of yummy raisins and dried cranberries, too!

PREP: 10 min. ■ COOK: 7 hours

- 3 cups water
- 1 cup old-fashioned oats
- 1 cup raisins
- 1/2 cup dried cranberries
- 1/2 cup ground flaxseed
- 1/2 cup 2% milk
- 1 teaspoon vanilla extract
- 1 teaspoon molasses

■ In a 3-qt. slow cooker, combine all ingredients. Cover and cook on low for 7-8 hours or until liquid is absorbed and oatmeal is tender.

Yield: 4 servings.

Easy Citrus Ham

PREP: 15 min.
COOK: 4 hours + standing

- 1 boneless fully cooked ham (3 to 4 pounds)
- 1/2 cup packed dark brown sugar
- 1 can (12 ounces) lemon-lime soda, *divided*
- 1 medium navel orange, thinly sliced
- 1 medium lemon, thinly sliced
- 1 medium lime, thinly sliced
- 1 tablespoon chopped crystallized ginger

■ Cut ham in half; place in a 5-qt. slow cooker. In a small bowl, combine brown sugar and 1/4 cup soda; rub over ham. Top with orange, lemon and lime slices. Add candied ginger and remaining soda to the slow cooker.

■ Cover and cook on low for 4-5 hours or until a meat thermometer reads 140°, basting occasionally with cooking juices. Let stand for about 10 minutes before slicing.

Yield: 10-12 servings.

Sheila Christensen

SAN MARCOS, CALIFORNIA

I created this recipe many years ago with items I already had on hand. Since then, it has become a family favorite. The ham is succulent with a mild citrus flavor. I was asked to share the recipe with a church social, and there were so many raves that I knew the recipe was a winner!

Betty Kercheval
BELLEVUE, WASHINGTON

I have always enjoyed Asian food, and when I had pork chops, I put this recipe together. The sauce is sweet and tangy and the meat is oh-so moist and tender.

Asian Pork Chops

Asian Pork Chops

PREP: 20 min. ■ COOK: 3 hours

- 4 boneless pork loin chops (5 ounces *each*)
- 1/4 teaspoon salt
- 1/8 teaspoon pepper
- 1 medium onion, chopped
- 1 medium green pepper, chopped
- 4 green onions, chopped
- 1/4 cup packed brown sugar
- 1/4 cup white wine *or* chicken broth
- 1/4 cup soy sauce
- 1 tablespoon crystallized ginger, finely chopped
- 1-1/2 teaspoons sesame oil
- 1 garlic clove, minced
- 2 tablespoons cornstarch
- 2 tablespoons cold water
- Hot cooked rice, optional

■ Sprinkle pork chops with salt and pepper. Place in a 3-qt. slow cooker. Add the onion, green pepper and green onions. In a small bowl, combine the brown sugar, wine, soy sauce, ginger, sesame oil and garlic; pour over chops. Cover and cook on low for 3-4 hours or until meat is tender.

■ Remove meat to a serving platter; keep warm. Skim fat from cooking juices; transfer to a small saucepan. Bring liquid to a boil. Combine cornstarch and water until smooth. Gradually stir into the pan. Bring to a boil; cook and stir for 2 minutes or until thickened. Serve with meat and rice if desired.

Yield: 4 servings.

Three Beans And Sausage

Judy Sumner
RIVERTON, UTAH

For a stick-to-your ribs meal, try my hearty combination of beans and sausage. Because it calls for several canned items, it's easy to prepare and let simmer by itself for the afternoon. It's also inexpensive to serve.

PREP: 15 min.
COOK: 4 hours

- 1-1/2 pounds smoked sausage, cut into 1-inch pieces
- 1 can (16 ounces) kidney beans, rinsed and drained
- 1 can (15-1/2 ounces) great northern beans, rinsed and drained
- 1 can (15 ounces) black beans, rinsed and drained
- 1 cup chopped onion
- 1 cup water
- 1 can (8 ounces) tomato sauce
- 2/3 cup chopped celery
- 1 teaspoon chicken bouillon granules
- 1 teaspoon minced garlic
- 1 bay leaf
- 1/2 teaspoon pepper
- 1/4 teaspoon dried oregano, optional
- 1/4 teaspoon dried thyme, optional
- Hot cooked rice

■ In a 5-qt. slow cooker, combine the first 12 ingredients. Sprinkle with oregano and thyme if desired. Cover and cook on low for 4-5 hours or until heated through. Discard bay leaf. Serve with rice.

Yield: 8 servings.

Parmesan Pork Roast

Karen Warner
LOUISVILLE, OHIO

For a pork roast with sweet and savory flavors, all you need are a few pantry staples. With only a bit of effort, I can enjoy a lovely entree any night of the week!

Parmesan Pork Roast

PREP: 15 min. ■ COOK: 5-1/2 hours

- 1 boneless whole pork loin roast (4 pounds)
- 2/3 cup grated Parmesan cheese
- 1/2 cup honey
- 3 tablespoons soy sauce
- 2 tablespoons dried basil
- 2 tablespoons minced garlic
- 2 tablespoons olive oil
- 1/2 teaspoon salt
- 2 tablespoons cornstarch
- 1/4 cup cold water

■ Cut roast in half. Transfer to a 3-qt. slow cooker. In a small bowl, combine the cheese, honey, soy sauce, basil, garlic, oil and salt; pour over pork. Cover and cook on low for 5-1/2 to 6 hours or until a meat thermometer reads 160°.

■ Remove meat to a serving platter; keep warm. Skim fat from cooking juices; transfer to a small saucepan. Bring liquid to a boil. Combine cornstarch and water until smooth. Gradually stir into pan. Bring to a boil; cook and stir for 2 minutes or until thickened. Slice roast; serve with gravy.

Yield: 10 servings.

Maple Pork Ribs

Phyllis Eismann Schmalz
KANSAS CITY, KANSAS

These tender ribs are draped in a luscious maple-mustard sauce. This is one of our favorite recipes.

PREP: 10 min.
COOK: 5 hours

- 1 pound boneless country-style pork ribs, trimmed and cut into 3-inch pieces
- 2 teaspoons canola oil
- 1 medium onion, cut into 1/4-inch slices and separated into rings
- 3 tablespoons maple syrup
- 2 tablespoons spicy brown *or* Dijon mustard

■ In a large skillet, brown ribs in oil on all sides; drain. Place ribs and onion in a 1-1/2-qt. slow cooker. Combine syrup and mustard; pour over ribs. Cover and cook on low for 5-7 hours or until meat is tender.

Yield: 2 servings.

To help remove the odor of onions from your hands after chopping them, sprinkle your hands with table salt, rub them together a few times, then wash them.

Vegetarian Stew in Bread Bowls

Maria Keller
ANTIOCH, ILLINOIS

My husband had just gotten me a slow cooker after our third baby was born and I didn't have a lot of time to cook. This was our first meal out of it!

Vegetarian Stew in Bread Bowls

PREP: 30 min. ■ COOK: 8 -1/2 hrs.

- 1 can (28 ounces) Italian crushed tomatoes, undrained
- 4 medium red potatoes, cubed
- 2 cups chopped celery
- 1-1/2 cups chopped carrots
- 2 medium parsnips, cut unto 1/2-inch pieces
- 2 medium leeks (white portion only), cut into 1/2-inch pieces
- 1 can (14-1/2 ounces) vegetable broth
- 2 teaspoons sugar
- 1/2 teaspoon salt
- 1/2 teaspoon dried thyme
- 1/2 teaspoon dried rosemary, crushed
- 3 tablespoons cornstarch
- 3 tablespoons cold water
- 10 round loaves sourdough bread (8 to 9 ounces *each*)

■ In a 4- or 5-qt. slow cooker, combine the first 11 ingredients. Cover and cook on low for 8-9 hours or until vegetables are tender.

■ Combine cornstarch and water until smooth; stir into stew. Cover and cook on high for 30 minutes or until gravy is thickened.

■ Cut a thin slice off the top of bread. Hollow out bottom of loaf, leaving a 1/2-in. shell (discard removed bread or save for another use). Fill bread shell with stew.

Yield: 10 servings.

Pork Chop Dinner

Mike Avery
BATTLE CREEK, MICHIGAN

Canned soup creates a comforting gravy for tender pork and potatoes in this simple meal-in-one. Feel free to vary the amount of onion soup mix in the recipe to suit your family's tastes.

PREP: 10 min.
BAKE: 6 hours

- 6 to 8 medium carrots (1 pound), coarsely chopped
- 3 to 4 medium potatoes, cubed
- 4 boneless pork loin chops (3/4 inch thick)
- 1 large onion, sliced
- 1 envelope onion soup mix
- 2 cans (10-3/4 ounces *each*) condensed cream of mushroom soup, undiluted

■ Place the carrots and potatoes in a 3-qt. slow cooker. Top with the pork chops, onion, soup mix and soup. Cover and cook on low for 6-8 hours or until meat and vegetables are tender.

Yield: 4 servings.

Island Pork Roast

Heather Campbell
LAWRENCE, KANSAS

This fork tender roast is a nice mixture of sweet and tangy. I like to serve it over rice and the leftovers make wonderful sandwiches.

PREP: 25 min. ■ **COOK:** 5 hours

- 1 boneless pork loin roast (about 4 pounds)
- 1 large onion, sliced
- 2 cans (8 ounces *each*) unsweetened pineapple chunks, undrained
- 1/2 cup sugar
- 1/2 cup lime juice
- 1/2 cup soy sauce
- 1/4 cup packed brown sugar
- 2 tablespoons teriyaki sauce
- 2 garlic cloves, minced
- 1 teaspoon ground ginger
- 1 teaspoon curry powder
- 1/4 teaspoon salt
- 1/4 teaspoon pepper
- 1 bay leaf
- 1/4 cup cornstarch
- 1/2 cup cold water

■ Cut roast in half. Place onion in a 4- or 5-qt. slow cooker. Add pork. Drain pineapple, reserving juice; set pineapple aside. In a small bowl, combine the sugar, lime juice, soy sauce, brown sugar, teriyaki sauce, garlic, ginger, curry, salt, pepper, bay leaf and reserved juice. Pour over roast.

■ Cover and cook on low for 5-6 hours or until a meat thermometer reads 160°. Add pineapple during the last hour of cooking.

■ Remove the meat, onion and pineapple to a serving platter; keep warm. Discard bay leaf. Skim fat from cooking juices; transfer to a small saucepan. Bring liquid to a boil. Combine cornstarch and water until smooth; gradually stir into the pan. Bring to a boil; cook and stir for 2 minutes or until thickened. Serve with pork.

Yield: 10 servings.

The moisture in brown sugar tends to trap air between the crystals, so it should be firmly packed when measuring. This is why Taste of Home recipes specify packed brown sugar in ingredients lists.

Robust Italian Sausage & Pasta

LaDonna Reed
PONCA CITY, OKLAHOMA

Sit back and let the slow cooker do the hard work with this savory main dish. Since you don't cook the pasta separately, there's one less pot to wash after supper.

PREP: 15 min.
COOK: 6-1/2 hours

- 4 Italian sausage links (4 ounces *each*), halved
- 1 jar (25.6 ounces) Italian sausage spaghetti sauce
- 1 can (10 ounces) diced tomatoes and green chilies, undrained
- 1 large green pepper, julienned
- 1 medium onion, diced
- 2 garlic cloves, minced
- 1 teaspoon Italian seasoning
- 2 cups uncooked spiral pasta

■ In a large nonstick skillet, brown sausage links. Transfer to a 3-qt. slow cooker. Add the jar of spaghetti sauce, tomatoes, green pepper, onion, garlic and Italian seasoning.

■ Cover and cook on low for 6 hours. Stir in pasta. Cover and cook on high for about 30-40 minutes or until pasta is tender.

Yield: 4 servings.

Penny Hawkins
MEBANE, NORTH CAROLINA

Tender chunks of pork slowly cook in this well-seasoned, wine-infused sauce. Add some crushed red pepper flakes for a little added kick if you want.

Tuscan Pork Stew

Tuscan Pork Stew*

PREP: 15 min. ■ COOK: 8-1/2 hours

- 1 boneless whole pork loin roast (1-1/2 pounds), cut into 1-inch cubes
- 2 tablespoons olive oil
- 2 cans (14-1/2 ounces *each*) Italian diced tomatoes, undrained
- 2 cups reduced-sodium chicken broth
- 2 cups frozen pepper stir-fry vegetable blend, thawed
- 1/2 cup dry red wine *or* additional reduced-sodium chicken broth
- 1/4 cup orange marmalade
- 2 garlic cloves, minced
- 1 teaspoon dried oregano
- 1/2 teaspoon fennel seed
- 1/2 teaspoon pepper
- 1/8 teaspoon crushed red pepper flakes, optional
- 2 tablespoons cornstarch
- 2 tablespoons cold water
- Hot cooked fettuccine, optional

■ In a large skillet, brown pork in oil on all sides until no longer pink; drain. Place pork in a 5-qt. slow cooker.

■ In a large bowl, combine the tomatoes, broth, vegetable blend, wine, marmalade, garlic, oregano, fennel seed, pepper and pepper flakes if desired; pour over pork. Cover and cook on low for 8-10 hours or until meat is tender.

■ Mix the cornstarch and water until smooth; stir into stew. Cover and cook on high for 30 minutes or until gravy is thickened. Serve with fettuccine if desired.

Yield: 8 servings.

***Nutrition Facts:** 1 cup (calculated without fettuccine) equals 232 calories, 7 g fat (2 g saturated fat), 42 mg cholesterol, 614 mg sodium, 19 g carbohydrate, 1 g fiber, 19 g protein. **Diabetic Exchanges:** 2 lean meat, 1 starch, 1 vegetable, 1/2 fat.

Zippy Bean Stew*

Debbie Matthews
BLUEFIELD, WEST VIRGINIA

This bean stew is a staple for my coworkers and me once the weather turns cool. Although this is a low-fat dish, it definitely doesn't taste like it!

PREP: 10 min.
COOK: 4 hours

- 1 can (16 ounces) kidney beans, rinsed and drained
- 1 can (15 ounces) pinto beans, rinsed and drained
- 1 can (14-1/2 ounces) diced tomatoes and green chilies
- 1 can (14-1/2 ounces) vegetable broth *or* reduced-sodium chicken broth
- 2 cups frozen corn, thawed
- 1 can (4 ounces) chopped green chilies, undrained
- 3 cups water
- 2 medium carrots, sliced
- 1 large onion, chopped
- 2 garlic cloves, minced
- 2 teaspoons chili powder

■ In a 3-qt. slow cooker, combine the beans, tomatoes, broth, corn and green chilies. Stir in the water, carrots, onion, garlic and chili powder. Cover and cook on high for 4-5 hours or until vegetables are tender and flavors are blended.

Yield: 6 servings.

***Nutrition Facts:** 1-1/2 cups equals 218 calories, 1 g fat (trace saturated fat), 0 cholesterol, 964 mg sodium, 44 g carbohydrate, 10 g fiber, 11 g protein. **Diabetic Exchanges:** 2 starch, 2 vegetable, 1 lean meat.

Oktoberfest Pork Roast

Tonya Swain
SEVILLE, OHIO

This recipe was adapted from one my mom made when I was growing up. It has all of our favorite "fall" flavors, such as apples, pork roast, sauerkraut and potatoes.

Oktoberfest Pork Roast

PREP: 35 min. ■ COOK: 8 hours

- 16 small red potatoes
- 1 can (14 ounces) sauerkraut, rinsed and well drained
- 2 large tart apples, peeled and cut into wedges
- 1 pound smoked kielbasa or Polish sausage, cut into 16 slices
- 2 tablespoons brown sugar
- 1 teaspoon caraway seeds
- 1 teaspoon salt, *divided*
- 1 teaspoon pepper, *divided*
- 1 boneless pork loin roast (3 pounds)
- 3 tablespoons canola oil

■ Place potatoes in a greased 6-qt. slow cooker. Top with sauerkraut, apples and kielbasa. Sprinkle with brown sugar, caraway seeds, 1/2 teaspoon salt and 1/2 teaspoon pepper.

■ Cut roast in half. Combine remaining salt and pepper; rub over meat. In a large skillet, brown meat in oil on all sides. Transfer to the slow cooker. Cover and cook on low for 8-10 hours or until a meat thermometer reads 160° and vegetables are tender. Skim fat and thicken pan juices if desired.

Yield: 8 servings.

Red Clam Sauce

JoAnn Brown
LATROBE, PENNSYLVANIA

This recipe tastes like it's been slaved over all day. Instead, it cooks while you do other things. What a great way to jazz up a can of diced tomatoes.

PREP: 25 min.
COOK: 3 hours

- 1 medium onion, chopped
- 1 tablespoon canola oil
- 2 garlic cloves, minced
- 2 cans (6-1/2 ounces *each*) chopped clams, undrained
- 1 can (14-1/2 ounces) diced tomatoes, undrained
- 1 can (6 ounces) tomato paste
- 1/4 cup minced fresh parsley
- 1 bay leaf
- 1 teaspoon sugar
- 1 teaspoon dried basil
- 1/2 teaspoon dried thyme
- 6 ounces linguine, cooked and drained

■ In a small skillet, saute onion in oil until tender. Add garlic; cook 1 minute longer.

■ Transfer to a 1-1/2 or 2-qt. slow cooker. Stir in the clams, tomatoes, tomato paste, parsley, bay leaf, sugar, basil and thyme. Cover and cook on low for 3-4 hours or until heated through. Discard bay leaf. Serve with linguine.

Yield: 4 servings.

Pork Carnitas

Tracy Byers
CORVALLIS, OREGON

I set out all the toppings, and folks have fun assembling their own carnitas. Because I can prepare everything in advance, I get to spend more time with my guests.

Pork Carnitas

PREP: 10 min. ■ COOK: 9 hours

- 1 boneless pork shoulder butt roast *or* loin roast (2 to 3 pounds), cut into 3-inch cubes
- 1/2 cup lime juice
- 1 teaspoon salt
- 1/2 teaspoon pepper
- 1/2 teaspoon crushed red pepper flakes
- 12 flour tortillas (6 inches), warmed
- 2 cups (8 ounces) shredded cheddar *or* Monterey Jack cheese
- 2 medium avocados, peeled and diced
- 2 medium tomatoes, diced
- 1 medium onion, diced
- Shredded lettuce, minced fresh cilantro, optional and salsa

■ In a 3-qt. slow cooker, combine pork, lime juice, salt, pepper and pepper flakes. Cover and cook on high for 1 hour; stir. Reduce heat to low and cook 8-10 hours longer or until meat is tender.

■ Shred pork with two forks (it may look somewhat pink). Spoon about 1/3 cup of pork mixture down the center of each tortilla. Top with cheese, avocados, tomatoes, onion, lettuce and cilantro if desired. Fold in bottom and sides of tortilla. Serve with salsa.

Yield: 12 servings.

Creamy Ham & Potatoes

Wendy Rowley
GREEN RIVER, WYOMING

If you love scalloped potatoes, this downsized version with tender chunks of ham is just perfect for you.

PREP: 20 min.
COOK: 5 hours

- 2 large red potatoes, cubed
- 1/3 cup cubed process cheese (Velveeta)
- 3/4 cup cubed fully cooked ham
- 1 tablespoon dried minced onion
- 2/3 cup condensed cream of celery soup, undiluted
- 2/3 cup 2% milk
- 1 tablespoon all-purpose flour
- 1/4 teaspoon pepper

■ In a greased 1-1/2-qt. slow cooker, layer the potatoes, cheese, ham and onion.

■ In a small bowl, combine soup and milk; whisk in flour and pepper. Pour over potatoes. Cover and cook on low for about 5-6 hours or until potatoes are tender. Stir before serving.

Yield: 2 servings.

Italian Meat Sauce With Meatballs

Jane McMillan
DANIA BEACH, FLORIDA

My chunky, meaty sauce has a bit of heat from the sausage and red pepper. It's delicious served over pasta.

PREP: 25 min. ■ COOK: 4-1/4 hours

- 1 pound bulk hot Italian sausage
- 1 medium onion, chopped
- 1 small green pepper, chopped
- 12 frozen fully cooked Italian meatballs (1/2 ounce *each*), thawed and halved
- 2 cans (15 ounces *each*) tomato sauce
- 1 can (14-1/2 ounces) diced tomatoes, undrained
- 1/3 cup tomato paste
- 1/4 cup grated Parmesan and Romano cheese blend
- 1 tablespoon minced garlic
- 1 teaspoon dried oregano
- 1 teaspoon dried basil
- 1 teaspoon dried parsley flakes
- 1/4 teaspoon crushed red pepper flakes
- 1 cup (4 ounces) shredded part-skim mozzarella cheese
- Hot cooked pasta

■ In a large skillet, cook the sausage, onion and pepper over medium heat until sausage is no longer pink; drain. Transfer to a 4-qt. slow cooker. Add the meatballs, tomato sauce, tomatoes, tomato paste, Parmesan cheese blend, garlic and seasonings. Cover and cook on low for 4-5 hours or until hot and bubbly.

■ Sprinkle with mozzarella cheese. Cook 15 minutes longer or until cheese is melted. Serve with pasta.

Yield: 8 servings.

Whenever a Taste of Home recipe calls for Italian sausage, it is referring to sweet Italian sausage. Recipes which are using hot Italian sausage specifically call for that product.

Spicy Sausage Hash Browns*

Angela Sheridan
OPDYKE, ILLINOIS

I love to develop my own recipes and have people requesting them often. My family members and friends from our church tend to be my favorite critics.

PREP: 15 min.
COOK: 5 hours

- 1 pound bulk spicy pork sausage
- 1 package (30 ounces) frozen shredded hash brown potatoes, thawed
- 2 cups (16 ounces) sour cream
- 1 jar (16 ounces) double-cheddar cheese sauce
- 2 cans (4 ounces *each*) chopped green chilies
- 1/2 teaspoon crushed red pepper flakes

■ In a large skillet, cook sausage over medium heat until no longer pink; drain. Transfer to a 4-qt. slow cooker. Stir in the remaining ingredients. Cover and cook on low for 5-6 hours or until heated through.

Yield: 9 servings.

Editor's Note: This recipe was tested with Ragu double-cheddar cheese sauce.

***Nutrition Facts:** 1 cup equals 368 calories, 25 g fat (12 g saturated fat), 73 mg cholesterol, 723 mg sodium, 22 g carbohydrate, 2 g fiber, 10 g protein.

Soups, Sides & Sandwiches

74

69

72

The classic pairing of soup and sandwich never ceases to satisfy as a meal and the two are also great served alongside main courses. In addition, savory side dishes made in the slow cooker free up stovetop space and kitchen time. So simmer up a sandwich, soup or side dish today!

Brown Rice and Vegetables

Taste of Home Test Kitchen

This filling rice dish, featuring big chunks of butternut squash and colorful sweet potatoes, makes a great combination of sweet and savory flavors.

Brown Rice and Vegetables

PREP: 20 min. ■ COOK: 5 hours

- 1 cup uncooked brown rice
- 1 medium butternut squash (about 3 pounds), cubed
- 2 medium apples, coarsely chopped
- 1 medium sweet potato, peeled and cubed
- 1 medium onion, chopped
- 1 teaspoon salt
- 1/2 teaspoon pepper
- 1 can (14-1/2 ounces) reduced-sodium chicken broth
- 1/2 cup raisins
- 1 tablespoon minced fresh tarragon *or* 1 teaspoon dried tarragon

■ Place rice in a greased 4- or 5-qt slow cooker. In a large bowl, combine the squash, apples, sweet potato, onion, salt and pepper; add to slow cooker. Pour broth over vegetables. Cover and cook on low for 5-6 hours or until vegetables are tender. Stir in raisins and tarragon.

Yield: 12 servings.

Italian Beef Sandwiches

Carol Allen

MCLEANSBORO, ILLINOIS

Before leaving for work, I often put these ingredients in the slow cooker so supper is ready when I get home. This recipe is also good to take to a get-together.

PREP: 15 min.
COOK: 7 hours

- 1 boneless beef chuck roast (3 to 4 pounds)
- 3 tablespoons dried basil
- 3 tablespoons dried oregano
- 1 cup water
- 1 envelope onion soup mix
- 10 to 12 Italian rolls *or* sandwich buns

■ Cut roast in half; place in a 5-qt. slow cooker. Combine the basil, oregano and water; pour over roast. Sprinkle with soup mix.

■ Cover and cook on low for 7-9 hours or until meat is tender. Remove meat; shred with a fork and keep warm. Strain broth and skim fat. Serve meat on rolls; use broth for dipping if desired.

Yield: 10-12 servings.

To shred slow-cooked meat, simply use two forks to pull the meat in opposite directions. Keep shredding the meat to achieve the desired consistency.

Fall Garden Medley

Krystine Kercher
LINCOLN, NEBRASKA

I like to make this recipe in the fall and winter for special occasions because it's very colorful, tasty and healthy. It's a hearty side dish that complements many different meats.

Fall Garden Medley*

PREP: 20 min. ■ COOK: 5 hours

- 4 large carrots, cut into 1-1/2-inch pieces
- 3 fresh beets, peeled and cut into 1-1/2-inch pieces.
- 2 medium sweet potatoes, peeled and cut into 1-1/2-inch pieces
- 2 medium onions, peeled and quartered
- 1/2 cup water
- 2 teaspoons salt
- 1/2 teaspoon pepper
- 1/4 teaspoon dried thyme
- 1 tablespoon olive oil
- Fresh parsley *or* dried parsley flakes, optional

■ Place the carrots, beets, sweet potatoes, onions and water in a greased 3-qt. slow cooker. Sprinkle with salt, pepper and thyme. Drizzle with olive oil. Cover and cook on low for 5-6 hours or until tender.

■ Stir vegetables and sprinkle with parsley if desired.

Yield: 8 servings.

***Nutrition Facts:** 3/4 cup equals 83 calories, 2 g fat (trace saturated fat), 0 cholesterol, 633 mg sodium, 16 g carbohydrate, 3 g fiber, 2 g protein.

Shoepeg Corn Side Dish

Gloria Schutz
TRENTON, ILLINOIS

I took this dish to a potluck, and everyone asked for the recipe. If shoepeg corn isn't available in your region, then regular canned corn works well, too!

PREP: 20 min.
COOK: 3 hours

- 1 can (14-1/2 ounces) French-style green beans, drained
- 2 cans (7 ounces *each*) white *or* shoepeg corn
- 1 can (10-3/4 ounces) condensed cream of mushroom soup, undiluted
- 1 jar (4-1/2 ounces) sliced mushrooms, drained
- 1/2 cup shredded cheddar cheese
- 1/2 cup sour cream
- 1/2 cup slivered almonds
- 3/4 cup French-fried onions

■ In a 3-qt. slow cooker, combine the first seven ingredients. Cover and cook on low for 3-4 hours or until vegetables are tender, stirring occasionally. Sprinkle with the onions during the last 15 minutes of cooking.

Yield: 8 servings.

Penny Fagan
MOBILE, ALABAMA

Loaded with veggies, meatballs and spices, this meal-in-one soup is hearty enough to warm up any cold winter day. It's a recipe you'll make time and again!

Veggie Meatball Soup

Veggie Meatball Soup*

PREP: 20 min. ■ COOK: 6 hours

- 1 package (12 ounces) frozen fully cooked Italian meatballs
- 1 can (28 ounces) diced tomatoes, undrained
- 3 cups beef broth
- 2 cups shredded cabbage
- 1 can (16 ounces) kidney beans, rinsed and drained
- 1 medium zucchini, sliced
- 1 cup fresh green beans, cut into 1-inch pieces
- 1 cup water
- 2 medium carrots, sliced
- 1 teaspoon dried basil
- 1/2 teaspoon minced garlic
- 1/4 teaspoon salt
- 1/8 teaspoon dried oregano
- 1/8 teaspoon pepper
- 1 cup uncooked elbow macaroni
- 1/4 cup minced fresh parsley
- Grated Parmesan cheese, optional

■ In a 5-qt. slow cooker, combine the first 14 ingredients. Cover and cook on low for 5-6 hours or until vegetables are almost tender.

■ Stir in the macaroni and parsley; cook 30 minutes longer or until macaroni is tender. Serve with cheese if desired.

Yield: 6 servings (2-1/2 quarts).

***Nutrition Facts:** 1-2/3 cups equals 335 calories, 14 g fat (6 g saturated fat), 27 mg cholesterol, 1,295 mg sodium, 37 g carbohydrate, 9 g fiber, 19 g protein.

Black Bean Potato au Gratin

Erin Chilcoat
SMITHTOWN, NEW YORK

The addition of black beans and vegetables adds protein and fiber to this tasty side dish. For a fun, Southwestern twist, add a handful or two of chopped cooked ham or chorizo and replace the peas with 1 cup of frozen corn.

PREP: 25 min.
COOK: 8 hours

- 2 cans (15 ounces *each*) black beans, rinsed and drained
- 1 can (10-3/4 ounces) condensed cream of mushroom soup, undiluted
- 1 medium sweet red pepper, chopped
- 1 cup frozen peas
- 1 cup chopped sweet onion
- 1 celery rib, thinly sliced
- 2 garlic cloves, minced
- 1 teaspoon dried thyme
- 1/4 teaspoon coarsely ground pepper
- 1-1/2 pounds medium red potatoes, cut into 1/4-inch slices
- 1 teaspoon salt
- 1 cup (4 ounces) shredded cheddar cheese

■ In a large bowl, combine the beans, soup, red pepper, peas, onion, celery, garlic, thyme and pepper. Spoon half of mixture into a greased 3- or 4-qt. slow cooker. Layer with half of the potatoes, salt and cheese. Repeat layers. Cover and cook on low for 8-10 hours or until the potatoes are tender.

Yield: 6 servings.

Vegetable Beef Barley Soup*

Tara MacDonald
KANSAS CITY, MISSOURI

The barley helps to make this soup filling and robust. I like to eat it with a piece of crusty bread slathered in butter.

PREP: 45 min. ■ COOK: 7 hours

- 1 teaspoon seasoned salt
- 1 teaspoon onion powder
- 1 teaspoon garlic powder
- 1-1/2 pounds beef stew meat, cut into 1-inch cubes
- 2 tablespoons canola oil
- 3 cups water
- 3 medium potatoes, peeled and diced
- 1 cup sliced fresh carrots
- 1 cup chopped celery
- 1/2 cup chopped onion
- 1 teaspoon beef bouillon granules
- 1 can (15-1/4 ounces) whole kernel corn, drained
- 1 can (14-1/2 ounces) diced tomatoes, undrained
- 1 can (8-1/2 ounces) peas, drained
- 1 cup tomato juice
- 3/4 cup medium pearl barley
- 1/2 teaspoon salt
- 1/4 teaspoon pepper

■ In a large resealable plastic bag, combine the seasoned salt, onion powder and garlic powder. Add beef and toss to coat. In a large skillet, brown beef in oil until meat is no longer pink; drain. Transfer to a 5- or 6-qt. slow cooker. Add the water, potatoes, carrots, celery, onion and bouillon.

■ Cover and cook on low for 5-6 hours or until meat and vegetables are almost tender. Add corn, tomatoes, peas, tomato juice, barley, salt and pepper; cover and cook 2 hours longer or until barley is tender.

Yield: 8 servings (2-3/4 quarts).

***Nutrition Facts:** 1-1/3 cups equals 364 calories, 10 g fat (3 g saturated fat), 53 mg cholesterol, 852 mg sodium, 44 g carbohydrate, 8 g fiber, 22 g protein. **Diabetic Exchanges:** 2 starch, 2 medium-fat meat, 1 vegetable, 1/2 fat.

No-Bean Chili

PREP: 10 min.
COOK: 4 hours

- 1-1/2 pounds lean ground beef (90% lean)
- 1 can (14-1/2 ounces) stewed tomatoes
- 1 can (8 ounces) tomato sauce
- 1 small onion, chopped
- 1 small green pepper, chopped
- 1 can (4 ounces) chopped green chilies
- 1/2 cup minced fresh parsley
- 1 tablespoon chili powder
- 1 garlic clove, minced
- 1-1/4 teaspoons salt
- 1/2 teaspoon paprika
- 1/4 teaspoon pepper
- Hot cooked rice *or* pasta
- Shredded cheddar, sour cream *or* sliced green onions, optional

■ Crumble the beef into a 3-qt. slow cooker. Add the next 11 ingredients and mix well. Cover and cook on high for 4-5 hours or until heated through. Serve with rice or pasta. Serve with cheddar, sour cream or green onions if desired.

Yield: 6 servings.

To store celery, remove it from the bag it comes in, and wrap it in paper towel and aluminum foil, and store it in the refrigerator. When you need a stalk or two, simply take what you need and return the rest to the fridge.

Molly Butt
GRANVILLE, OHIO

I often combine the ingredients for this zesty chili the night before. In the morning I load up the slow cooker and let it go! It's that easy to prepare. You can use the toppings the recipe calls for, or use whatever you want, such as sliced avocado or corn chips.

Polynesian Ham Sandwiches

Jackie Smulski
LYONS, ILLINOIS

The sweetness of brown sugar and pineapple along with the tanginess of Dijon mustard make a perfect combination for my tasty, slow-cooked sandwich filling.

Polynesian Ham Sandwiches

PREP: 20 min. ■ **COOK:** 3 hours

- 2 pounds fully cooked ham, finely chopped
- 1 can (20 ounces) crushed pineapple
- 3/4 cup packed brown sugar
- 1/3 cup chopped green pepper
- 1/4 cup Dijon mustard
- 1 green onion, chopped
- 1 tablespoon dried minced onion
- 12 hamburger buns *or* kaiser rolls, split

■ In a 3-qt. slow cooker, combine the first seven ingredients. Cover and cook on low for 3-4 hours or until heated through. Using a slotted spoon, place 1/2 cup on each bun.

Yield: 12 servings.

Anything Goes Sausage Soup

Sheena Wellard
NAMPA, IDAHO

To chase away the winter chills, just throw together this soup and let the slow cooker do the work for you. It's hearty, flavorful and full of sausage and vegetables.

PREP: 40 min.
COOK: 9-1/2 hours

- 1 pound bulk pork sausage
- 4 cups water
- 1 can (10-3/4 ounces) condensed cream of mushroom soup, undiluted
- 1 can (10-3/4 ounces) condensed cheddar cheese soup, undiluted
- 5 medium red potatoes, cubed
- 4 cups chopped cabbage
- 3 large carrots, thinly sliced
- 4 celery ribs, chopped
- 1 medium zucchini, chopped
- 1 large onion, chopped
- 5 chicken bouillon cubes
- 1 tablespoon dried parsley flakes
- 3/4 teaspoon pepper
- 1 can (12 ounces) evaporated milk

■ In a large skillet, cook sausage over medium heat until no longer pink; drain. Transfer to a 6-qt. slow cooker. Stir in the water and soups until blended. Add the vegetables, bouillon, parsley and pepper.

■ Cover and cook on low for 9-10 hours or until vegetables are tender. Stir in milk; cover and cook 30 minutes longer.

Yield: 15 servings (about 4 quarts).

Wilda Bensenhaver
DELAND, FLORIDA

For a tasty twist on conventional chili, try this low-fat version. It's packed with plenty of beans, tender grilled chicken and a wonderfully zippy blend of spices.

Flavorful White Chili

Flavorful White Chili*

PREP: 10 min. + standing ■ COOK: 8 hours

- 1 pound dried great northern beans
- 4 cups chicken broth
- 2 cups chopped onions
- 3 garlic cloves, minced
- 2 teaspoons ground cumin
- 1-1/2 teaspoons dried oregano
- 1 teaspoon ground coriander
- 1/8 teaspoon ground cloves
- 1/8 teaspoon cayenne pepper
- 1 can (4 ounces) chopped green chilies
- 1/2 pound boneless skinless chicken breast, grilled and cubed
- 1 teaspoon salt
- 3/4 cup shredded reduced-fat Mexican cheese blend

■ Sort beans and rinse with cold water. Place beans in a Dutch oven; add water to cover by 2 in. Bring to a boil; boil for 2 minutes. Remove from the heat; cover and let stand for 1 hour. Drain and rinse beans, discarding liquid.

■ Place beans in a 3-qt. slow cooker. Add the broth, onions, garlic and seasonings. Cover and cook on low for 7-8 hours or until beans are almost tender. Add the chilies, chicken and salt; cover and cook for 1 hour or until the beans are tender. Serve with cheese.

Yield: 6 servings.

***Nutrition Facts:** 1-1/3 cups chili with 2 tablespoons cheese equals 384 calories, 5 g fat (2 g saturated fat), 37 mg cholesterol, 1,224 mg sodium, 53 g carbohydrate, 16 g fiber, 34 g protein. **Diabetic Exchanges:** 4 lean meat, 3 starch.

Glazed Spiced Carrots

Taste of Home Test Kitchen

Glazed carrots are a classic side dish for all kinds of entrees and special menus. This recipe is very easy to put together, leaving your oven and stove free for other cooking needs.

PREP: 10 min.
COOK: 6 hours

- 2 pounds fresh baby carrots
- 1/2 cup peach preserves
- 1/2 cup butter, melted
- 1/4 cup packed brown sugar
- 1 teaspoon vanilla extract
- 1/2 teaspoon ground cinnamon
- 1/4 teaspoon salt
- 1/8 teaspoon ground nutmeg
- 2 tablespoons cornstarch
- 2 tablespoons water
- Toasted chopped pecans, optional

■ Place carrots in a 3-qt. slow cooker. Combine the preserves, butter, brown sugar, vanilla, cinnamon, salt and nutmeg. Combine cornstarch and water until smooth; stir into preserves mixture. Pour over carrots. Cover and cook on low for 6-8 hours or until carrots are tender.

■ Stir carrots and sprinkle with pecans if desired.

Yield: 6 servings.

Spicy Meatless Chili

Jane McMillan
DANIA BEACH, FLORIDA

I'm retired now, but when I was working, this recipe was a mainstay! I could prepare the ingredients the night before, then on the way out the door, simply throw everything in the slow cooker. When I got home later, I prepared the toppings and supper was done.

PREP: 25 min. ■ COOK: 8 hours

- 2 cans (14-1/2 ounces *each*) Mexican diced tomatoes, undrained
- 1 can (15 ounces) black beans, rinsed and drained
- 2 cups frozen corn, thawed
- 1 cup salsa
- 1 medium zucchini, cut into 1/2-inch pieces
- 1 medium green pepper, coarsely chopped
- 1 small onion, coarsely chopped
- 1 celery rib, chopped
- 3 tablespoons chili powder
- 1 teaspoon dried oregano
- 2 garlic cloves, minced
- 3/4 teaspoon salt
- 3/4 teaspoon pepper
- 1/2 teaspoon ground cumin
- 1/4 teaspoon cayenne pepper
- Sour cream, chopped avocado, chopped onion *and/or* shredded cheddar cheese, optional

■ In a 4-qt. slow cooker, combine the first 15 ingredients. Cover and cook on low for 8-10 hours or until vegetables are tender. Garnish with sour cream, avocado, onion and/or cheese if desired.

Yield: 5 servings (2 quarts).

One of the advantages of a slow cooker is that it uses very little electricity due to low wattage. On average, it would cost just 25 cents to operate a slow cooker for a total of 10 hours. Multiply the cooking costs for a slow cooker versus an oven over an entire year, and you will experience real savings!

Praline Sweet Potatoes

Joanna Stanforth
SCOTT AIR FORCE BASE, ILLINOIS

I had a house full of relatives and was short on cooking space. I used the basic idea of the traditional sweet potato casserole and adapted it for the slow cooker. The recipe has been a huge hit ever since!

PREP: 15 min.
COOK: 4 hours

- 3 cups mashed sweet potatoes
- 1 cup sugar
- 3 eggs
- 1/2 cup 2% milk
- 1/4 cup butter, melted
- 1 teaspoon salt
- 1 teaspoon vanilla extract

TOPPING:

- 1/2 cup packed brown sugar
- 1/2 cup chopped pecans
- 1/4 cup all-purpose flour
- 2 tablespoons cold butter

■ In a large bowl, combine the sweet potatoes, sugar, eggs, milk, butter, salt and vanilla. Transfer to a greased 1-1/2-qt. slow cooker. Cover and cook on low for 3 hours.

■ In a small bowl, combine the brown sugar, pecans and flour; cut in butter until crumbly. Sprinkle over sweet potatoes. Cover and cook 1-2 hours longer or until a thermometer reads 160°.

Yield: 6 servings.

Slow Cooker Sloppy Joes

Joeanne Steras
GARRETT, PENNSYLVANIA

Slow cook your way to a crowd-pleasing entree! Here, ground beef is transformed into a classic sandwich filling with just a few pantry staples.

Slow Cooker Sloppy Joes

PREP: 15 min. ■ COOK: 4 hours

- 2 pounds ground beef
- 1 cup chopped green pepper
- 2/3 cup chopped onion
- 2 cups ketchup
- 2 envelopes sloppy joe mix
- 2 tablespoons brown sugar
- 1 teaspoon prepared mustard
- 12 hamburger buns, split

■ In a large skillet, cook the beef, pepper and onion over medium heat until meat is no longer pink; drain. Stir in the ketchup, sloppy joe mix, brown sugar and mustard.

■ Transfer to a 3-qt. slow cooker. Cover and cook on low for 4-5 hours or until flavors are blended. Spoon 1/2 cup onto each bun.

Yield: 12 servings.

Harvard Beets

Taste of Home Test Kitchen

Fresh beets are delicious when combined with aromatic spices and cooked until tender. These beets have a good balance of sweet and sour, and with just the right touch of spices they're a hit!

PREP: 15 min.
COOK: 7 hours

- 2 pounds small fresh beets, peeled and halved
- 1/2 cup sugar
- 1/4 cup packed brown sugar
- 2 tablespoons cornstarch
- 1/2 teaspoon salt
- 1/4 cup orange juice
- 1/4 cup cider vinegar
- 2 tablespoons butter
- 1-1/2 teaspoons whole cloves

■ Place beets in a 3-qt. slow cooker. In a small bowl, combine sugar, brown sugar, cornstarch and salt. Stir in orange juice and vinegar. Pour over the beets; dot with butter. Place cloves on a double thickness of cheesecloth; bring up corners of cloth and tie with string to form a bag. Place bag in slow cooker.

■ Cover and cook on low for 7-8 hours or until tender. Discard spice bag.

Yield: 6 servings.

Bridget Klusman
OTSEGO, MICHIGAN

After my sister spent a year in France as an au pair, I created this lighter, easier version of traditional French cassoulet for her. It uses chicken instead of the usual duck and comes together in a slow cooker.

Chicken Cassoulet Soup

PREP: 35 min. ■ COOK: 6 hours

- 1/2 pound bulk pork sausage
- 5 cups water
- 1/2 pound cubed cooked chicken
- 1 can (16 ounces) kidney beans, rinsed and drained
- 1 can (15 ounces) black beans, rinsed and drained
- 1 can (15 ounces) garbanzo beans *or* chickpeas, rinsed and drained
- 2 medium carrots, shredded
- 1 medium onion, chopped
- 1/4 cup dry vermouth
- 5 teaspoons chicken bouillon granules
- 4 garlic cloves, minced
- 1 teaspoon dried lavender flowers, optional
- 1/2 teaspoon dried thyme
- 1/4 teaspoon fennel seed, crushed
- 1/2 pound bacon strips, cooked and crumbled

■ In a large skillet, cook the sausage over medium heat until no longer pink; drain.

■ Transfer to a 4- or 5-qt. slow cooker. Add the water, chicken, beans, carrots, onion, vermouth, bouillon, garlic, lavender if desired, thyme and fennel. Cover and cook on low for 6-8 hours or until heated through. Divide among bowls; sprinkle with bacon.

Yield: 7 servings (2-3/4 quarts).

Editor's Note: Look for dried lavender flowers in spice shops. If using lavender from the garden, make sure it hasn't been treated with chemicals.

Always rinse and drain canned beans to remove the extra salt that is used in the canning process. If you choose to use the bean liquid, both the amount of salt and water in the recipe should be reduced for the best flavor possible.

Slow-Cooked Mac 'n' Cheese

Bernice Glascoe
ROXBORO, NORTH CAROLINA

This classic casserole is a rich and cheesy meatless main dish. I've never met anyone who didn't ask for second helpings of the all-time favorite.

PREP: 15 min.
COOK: 4-1/4 hours

- 1 package (16 ounces) elbow macaroni
- 1/2 cup butter, melted
- 2 eggs, beaten
- 4 cups (16 ounces) shredded cheddar cheese, *divided*
- 1 can (12 ounces) evaporated milk
- 1 can (10-3/4 ounces) condensed cheddar cheese soup, undiluted
- 1 cup 2% milk
- 1/8 teaspoon paprika

■ Cook macaroni according to package directions; drain. Place in a 5-qt. slow cooker; add butter. In a large bowl, combine the eggs, 3 cups cheese, evaporated milk, soup and 2% milk. Pour over macaroni mixture and stir to combine. Cover and cook on low for 4 hours.

■ Sprinkle with the remaining cheese. Cover and cook 15 minutes longer or until the cheese is melted. Sprinkle with paprika.

Yield: 10 servings.

Forgotten Minestrone

Marsha Ransom
SOUTH HAVEN, MICHIGAN

This soup gets its name because the broth simmers for hours, allowing me to work on my writing. After one taste, however, your family will agree this full-flavored soup is unforgettable!

Forgotten Minestrone*

PREP: 15 min. ■ COOK: 7-1/2 hours

- 1 pound beef stew meat, cut into 1/2-inch cubes
- 1 can (28 ounces) diced tomatoes, undrained
- 1 medium onion, chopped
- 2 tablespoons minced dried parsley
- 2-1/2 teaspoons salt, optional
- 1-1/2 teaspoons ground thyme
- 1 beef bouillon cube
- 1/2 teaspoon pepper
- 6 cups water
- 1 medium zucchini, halved and thinly sliced
- 2 cups chopped cabbage
- 1 can (15 ounces) garbanzo beans *or* chickpeas, rinsed and drained
- 1 cup uncooked elbow macaroni
- 1/4 cup grated Parmesan cheese, optional

■ In a 5-qt. slow cooker, combine the first nine ingredients. Cover and cook on low for 7-9 hours or until meat is tender.

■ Add the zucchini, cabbage, beans and macaroni; cover and cook on high for 30-45 minutes or until macaroni and vegetables are tender. Sprinkle each serving with cheese if desired.

Yield: 8 servings.

***Nutrition Facts:** 1 cup (calculated w/o added salt and Parmesan cheese) equals 246 calories, 6 g fat (0g saturated fat), 33 mg cholesterol, 453 mg sodium, 30 g carbohydrate, 0 fiber, 19 g protein. **Diabetic Exchanges:** 2 vegetable, 1-1/2 starch, 1 meat.

Get creative with Forgotten Minestrone. Don't like cabbage? Leave it out. Not a zucchini fan? Skip that, too. Toss in a handful of frozen peas or corn kernels. Replace the thyme with basil or whatever herb you and your family enjoy most.

Florence Robinson
LENOX, IOWA

When I want to impress guests, I put these satisfying sandwiches on the menu. I serve the au jus sauce in individual bowls for easy dipping.

French Dip Sandwiches

French Dip Sandwiches

PREP: 30 min. ■ COOK: 7 hours + standing

- 2 large onions, cut into 1/4-inch slices
- 1/4 cup butter, cubed
- 1 beef rump roast *or* bottom round roast (3 to 4 pounds)
- 5 cups water
- 1/2 cup soy sauce
- 1 envelope onion soup mix
- 1-1/2 teaspoons browning sauce, optional
- 1 garlic clove, minced
- 12 to 14 French rolls, split
- 1 cup (4 ounces) shredded Swiss cheese

■ In a large skillet, saute onions in butter until tender; transfer to a 5-qt. slow cooker. Cut the roast in half; place over onions.

■ In a large bowl, combine the water, soy sauce, soup mix, browning sauce if desired and garlic; pour over roast. Cover and cook on low for 7-9 hours or until the meat is tender.

■ Remove roast with a slotted spoon and let stand for 15 minutes. Thinly slice meat across the grain. Place on rolls; sprinkle with the Swiss cheese. Place on ungreased baking sheet.

■ Broil 3-4 in. from heat for 1 minute or until cheese is melted. Replace tops. Skim fat from cooking juices; strain. Serve as a dipping sauce.

Yield: 12-14 servings.

Coconut-Pecan Sweet Potatoes

Raquel Haggard
EDMOND, OKLAHOMA

These delicious sweet potatoes cook effortlessly in the slow cooker so you can tend to other things. Coconut gives this classic dish a fun, mouthwatering flavor.

PREP: 15 min.
COOK: 4 hours

- 4 pounds sweet potatoes, peeled and cut into chunks
- 1/2 cup chopped pecans
- 1/2 cup flaked coconut
- 1/3 cup sugar
- 1/3 cup packed brown sugar
- 1/4 cup reduced-fat butter, melted
- 1/2 teaspoon ground cinnamon
- 1/4 teaspoon salt
- 1/2 teaspoon coconut extract
- 1/2 teaspoon vanilla extract

■ Place sweet potatoes in a 5-qt. slow cooker coated with cooking spray. Combine the pecans, coconut, sugar, brown sugar, butter, cinnamon and salt; sprinkle over potatoes.

■ Cover and cook on low for 4 hours or until potatoes are tender. Stir in extracts.

Yield: 12 servings.

Editor's Note: This recipe was tested with Land O'Lakes light stick butter.

Stuffed Sweet Onions

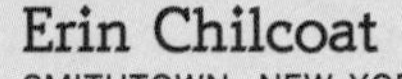

Erin Chilcoat

SMITHTOWN, NEW YORK

This is perfect to serve alongside grilled steak. Even if you're not an onion fan, the low heat and long cooking time of the dish mellows and sweetens the naturally sharp onion flavors.

Stuffed Sweet Onions

PREP: 45 min. ■ **COOK:** 4 hours

- 4 medium sweet onions
- 2 small zucchini, shredded
- 1 large garlic clove, minced
- 1 tablespoon olive oil
- 1 teaspoon dried basil
- 1 teaspoon dried thyme
- 1/4 teaspoon salt
- 1/4 teaspoon pepper
- 1/2 cup dry bread crumbs
- 4 thick-sliced bacon strips, cooked and crumbled
- 1/4 cup grated Parmesan cheese
- 1/4 cup reduced-sodium chicken broth

■ Peel onions and cut a 1/4-in. slice from the top and bottom. Carefully cut and remove the center of each onion, leaving a 1/2-in. shell; chop removed onion.

■ In a large skillet, saute the zucchini, garlic and chopped onions in oil until tender and juices are reduced. Stir in the basil, thyme, salt and pepper. Remove from the heat. Stir in the bread crumbs, bacon and Parmesan cheese. Fill onion shells with zucchini mixture. Place in a greased 3- or 4-qt. slow cooker. Add broth to the slow cooker.

■ Cover and cook on low for 4-5 hours or until onions are tender.

Yield: 4 servings.

Sauerkraut Sausage Soup

Yvonne Kett

APPLETON, WISCONSIN

My husband and I make our own sauerkraut and grow many of the vegetables found in this easy slow cooker soup. It cooks all day and smells delicious when we come home from work.

PREP: 20 min.
COOK: 5 hours

- 4 cups chicken broth
- 1 pound smoked Polish sausage, cut into 1/2-inch slices
- 1 can (16 ounces) sauerkraut, rinsed and well drained
- 2 cups sliced fresh mushrooms
- 1-1/2 cups cubed peeled potatoes
- 1 can (10-3/4 ounces) condensed cream of mushroom soup, undiluted
- 1-1/4 cups chopped onions
- 2 large carrots, sliced
- 2 celery ribs, chopped
- 2 tablespoons white vinegar
- 2 teaspoons dill weed
- 1 teaspoon sugar
- 1/4 teaspoon pepper

■ In a 5-qt. slow cooker, gently combine all ingredients. Cover and cook on low for 5-6 hours or until vegetables are tender.

Yield: 10 servings.

Southern Shredded BBQ Chicken

Angela Spengler
CLOVIS, NEW MEXICO

My family loves traditional pork barbecue served over mashed potatoes. I swapped the pork for chicken in honor of the delicious chicken barbecue my childhood church used to serve at its annual fundraiser. I also love cornbread and think that this yummy chicken is even better when served with a hot, buttery slice.

PREP: 30 min. ■ **COOK:** 6 hours

- 4 pounds bone-in chicken breast halves, skin removed
- 1 can (10-3/4 ounces) condensed tomato soup, undiluted
- 1/2 cup packed brown sugar
- 1/2 cup cider vinegar
- 1-1/2 teaspoons chili powder
- 1 teaspoon salt
- 1 teaspoon celery seed
- 1 teaspoon soy sauce
- 1/4 teaspoon cayenne pepper

CORN BREAD:

- 1 cup all-purpose flour
- 1 cup yellow cornmeal
- 2 tablespoons sugar
- 2 teaspoons baking powder
- 1/4 teaspoon salt
- 2 eggs
- 1 cup 2% milk
- 6 tablespoons butter, melted, *divided*

■ Place chicken in a 4-qt. slow cooker. In a small bowl, combine the tomato soup, brown sugar, vinegar, chili powder, salt, celery seed, soy sauce and cayenne. Pour over chicken. Cover and cook on low for 6-8 hours or until meat is tender.

■ Meanwhile, in a large bowl, combine the flour, cornmeal, sugar, baking powder and salt. Combine the eggs, milk and 4 tablespoons butter; stir into the dry ingredients just until combined.

■ Pour into a greased 8-in. square baking pan. Bake at 350° for 18-20 minutes or until a toothpick inserted near the center comes out clean. Drizzle remaining butter over warm bread.

■ Remove chicken from slow cooker. When cool enough to handle, remove meat from bones; discard bones. Shred meat with two forks; return to slow cooker. Using a slotted spoon, serve the chicken with corn bread.

Yield: 6 servings.

Slow-Cooker Vegetable Soup

Heather Thurmeier
PENSE, SASKATCHEWAN

After a long day, it's a real treat to come home to this savory dinner. It's a nice traditional beef soup with old-fashioned goodness. We pair it with crusty rolls topped with melted mozzarella cheese.

PREP: 15 min.
COOK: 8 hours

- 1 pound round steak, cut into 1/2-inch cubes
- 1 can (14-1/2 ounces) diced tomatoes, undrained
- 2 medium potatoes, peeled and cubed
- 2 medium onions, diced
- 3 celery ribs, sliced
- 2 carrots, sliced
- 3 beef bouillon cubes
- 1/2 teaspoon dried basil
- 1/2 teaspoon dried oregano
- 1/2 teaspoon salt
- 1/4 teaspoon pepper
- 3 cups water
- 1-1/2 cups frozen mixed vegetables

■ In a 3-qt. slow cooker, combine the first 12 ingredients. Cover and cook on high for 6 hours. Add vegetables; cover and cook 2 hours longer or until meat and vegetables are tender.

Yield: 8-10 servings (about 2-1/2 quarts).

Lentil Stew

Michelle Collins
SUFFOLK, VIRGINIA

This vegetarian stew is perfect when you want to take a break from meat. Adding the cream at the end gives it a smoother texture than expected.

PREP: 45 min. ■ COOK: 6 hours

- 2 large onions, thinly sliced, *divided*
- 2 tablespoons canola oil
- 2 tablespoons minced fresh gingerroot
- 3 garlic cloves, minced
- 8 plum tomatoes, chopped
- 2 teaspoons ground coriander
- 1-1/2 teaspoons ground cumin
- 1/4 teaspoon cayenne pepper
- 3 cups vegetable broth
- 2 cups water
- 2 cups dried lentils, rinsed
- 1 can (4 ounces) chopped green chilies
- 3/4 cup heavy whipping cream
- 2 tablespoons butter
- 1 teaspoon cumin seeds
- 6 cups cooked basmati *or* jasmine rice
- Sliced green onions *or* minced fresh cilantro, optional

■ In a large skillet, saute half of the onions in oil until tender. Add ginger and garlic; saute for 1 minute. Add the tomatoes, coriander, cumin and cayenne; cook and stir 5 minutes longer.

■ In a 4-or 5-qt. slow cooker, combine the vegetable broth, water, lentils, green chilies, tomato mixture and remaining onion. Cover and cook on low for 6-8 hours or until lentils are tender.

■ Just before serving, stir cream into slow cooker. In a small skillet, heat butter over medium heat. Add cumin seeds; cook and stir for 1-2 minutes or until golden brown. Add to lentil mixture.

■ To serve, spoon stew over rice. Sprinkle with green onions or cilantro if desired.

Yield: 8 servings (2-3/4 quarts).

Fresh gingerroot is available in the grocer's produce section. It should have a smooth skin. If it's wrinkled and cracked, the root is dry and past its prime. When stored in a heavy-duty resealable plastic bag, unpeeled gingerroot can be frozen for up to 1 year. When needed, simply peel and grate.

Loaded Mashed Potatoes

PREP: 25 min. + chilling
COOK: 3 hours

- 3 pounds potatoes (about 9 medium), peeled and cubed
- 1 package (8 ounces) cream cheese, softened
- 1 cup (8 ounces) sour cream
- 1/2 cup butter, cubed
- 1/4 cup 2% milk
- 1-1/2 cups (6 ounces) shredded cheddar cheese
- 1-1/2 cups (6 ounces) shredded pepper Jack cheese
- 1/2 pound bacon strips, cooked and crumbled
- 4 green onions, chopped
- 1/2 teaspoon onion powder
- 1/2 teaspoon garlic powder

■ Place potatoes in a Dutch oven and cover with water. Bring to a boil. Reduce heat; cover and cook for 10-15 minutes or until tender. Drain. Mash potatoes with cream cheese, sour cream, butter and milk. Stir in the cheeses, bacon, onions and seasonings. Transfer to a large bowl; cover and refrigerate overnight.

■ Transfer to a greased 3- or 4-quart slow cooker. Cover and cook on low for 3 to 3-1/2 hours.

Yield: 10 servings.

Ann Nolte
TAMPA, FLORIDA

Every year my mom made cream cheese mashed potatoes for Thanksgiving. I've tailored the recipe to my family and have carried on the tradition. I also make them in a slow cooker, which is convenient because I can prepare the potatoes a day ahead, freeing up oven space.

All-Day Red Beans & Rice

Celinda Dahlgren
NAPA, CALIFORNIA

My family loves New Orleans-style cooking, so I make this authentic dish often. Being a busy working woman, I appreciate how simple and scrumptious it is.

All-Day Red Beans & Rice

PREP: 20 min. + soaking ■ COOK: 8-1/2 hours

- 1 cup dried red beans
- 7 cups water, *divided*
- 2 smoked ham hocks
- 1 medium onion, chopped
- 1-1/2 teaspoons minced garlic
- 1 teaspoon ground cumin
- 1 medium tomato, chopped
- 1 medium green pepper, chopped
- 1 teaspoon salt
- 4 cups hot cooked rice

■ Sort beans and rinse in cold water. Place beans in a 3-qt. slow cooker. Add 4 cups water; cover and let stand overnight.

■ Drain and rinse beans, discarding liquid. Return beans to slow cooker; add the ham hocks, onion, garlic, cumin and remaining water. Cover and cook on low for 8-10 hours or until beans are tender.

■ Remove ham hocks; cool slightly. Remove meat from bones. Finely chop meat and return to slow cooker; discard bones. Stir in tomato, green pepper and salt; cover and cook on high for 30 minutes or until the pepper is tender. Serve with rice.

Yield: 6 servings.

Italian Turkey Sandwiches*

Carol Riley
OSSIAN, INDIANA

I hope you enjoy these yummy turkey sandwiches as much as our family does. The recipe makes plenty, so it's great for potlucks. Leftovers are just as good reheated the next day.

PREP: 10 min.
COOK: 5 hours

- 1 bone-in turkey breast (6 pounds), skin removed
- 1 medium onion, chopped
- 1 small green pepper, chopped
- 1/4 cup chili sauce
- 3 tablespoons white vinegar
- 2 tablespoons dried oregano *or* Italian seasoning
- 4 teaspoons beef bouillon granules
- 12 kaiser *or* hard rolls, split

■ Place turkey breast in a greased 5-qt. slow cooker. Add onion and green pepper.

■ Combine the chili sauce, vinegar, oregano and bouillon; pour over turkey and vegetables. Cover and cook on low for 5-6 hours or until a meat thermometer reads 170°.

■ Shred turkey with two forks and return to the slow cooker; heat through. Spoon 1/2 cup onto each roll.

Yield: 12 servings.

***Nutrition Facts:** 1 sandwich equals 374 calories, 4 g fat (1 g saturated fat), 118 mg cholesterol, 724 mg sodium, 34 g carbohydrate, 2 g fiber, 49 g protein. **Diabetic Exchanges:** 6 lean meat, 2 starch.

Bette Votral
BETHLEHEM, PENNSYLVANIA

My husband and father go crazy for this stuffing! It also freezes well so we can all enjoy it on a regular basis.

Everything Stuffing

Everything Stuffing*

PREP: 30 min. ■ COOK: 3 hours

- 1/2 pound bulk Italian sausage
- 4 cups seasoned stuffing cubes
- 1-1/2 cups crushed corn bread stuffing
- 1/2 cup chopped toasted chestnuts *or* pecans
- 1/2 cup minced fresh parsley
- 1 tablespoon minced fresh sage *or* 1 teaspoon rubbed sage
- 1/8 teaspoon salt
- 1/8 teaspoon pepper
- 1-3/4 cups sliced baby portobello mushrooms
- 1 package (5 ounces) sliced fresh shiitake mushrooms
- 1 large onion, chopped
- 1 medium apple, peeled and chopped
- 1 celery rib, chopped
- 3 tablespoons butter
- 1 can (14-1/2 ounces) chicken broth

■ In a large skillet, cook sausage over medium heat until no longer pink; drain. Transfer to a large bowl. Stir in the stuffing cubes, corn bread stuffing, chestnuts, parsley, sage, salt and pepper.

■ In the same skillet, saute the mushrooms, onion, apple and celery in butter until tender. Stir into stuffing mixture. Add enough broth to reach desired moistness. Transfer to a 5-qt. slow cooker. Cover and cook on low for 3 hours, stirring once.

Yield: 9 servings.

***Nutrition Facts:** 3/4 cup equals 267 calories, 13 g fat (4 g saturated fat), 21 mg cholesterol, 796 mg sodium, 30 g carbohydrate, 3 g fiber, 8 g protein.

Nacho Hash Brown Casserole

Pat Habiger
SPEARVILLE, KANSAS

This tasty slow cooker recipe will free up your oven and produce the best hash browns ever! Soft and super cheesy, they make a comforting side dish for meat, poultry or even pork.

PREP: 15 min.
COOK: 3-1/4 hours

- 1 package (32 ounces) frozen cubed hash brown potatoes, thawed
- 1 can (10-3/4 ounces) condensed cream of celery soup, undiluted
- 1 can (10-3/4 ounces) condensed nacho cheese soup, undiluted
- 1 large onion, finely chopped
- 1/3 cup butter, melted
- 1 cup (8 ounces) reduced-fat sour cream

■ In a greased 3-qt. slow cooker, combine the first five ingredients. Cover and cook on low for 3-4 hours or until potatoes are tender. Stir in sour cream. Cover and cook 15-30 minutes longer or until heated through.

Yield: 8 servings.

Sue Livermore
DETROIT LAKES, MINNESOTA

Bacon adds subtle smokiness to this hearty side that's loaded with flavor. Serve it over rice for an easy, yet tasty main dish.

Slow-Cooked Pork & Beans

Slow-Cooked Pork & Beans

PREP: 25 min. ■ COOK: 6 hours

- 1 package (1 pound) sliced bacon, chopped
- 1 cup chopped onion
- 2 cans (15 ounces *each*) pork and beans, undrained
- 1 can (16 ounces) kidney beans, rinsed and drained
- 1 can (15-1/4 ounces) lima beans, rinsed and drained
- 1 can (16 ounces) butter beans, rinsed and drained
- 1 can (15 ounces) black beans, rinsed and drained
- 1 cup packed brown sugar
- 1/2 cup cider vinegar
- 1 tablespoon molasses
- 2 teaspoons garlic powder
- 1/2 teaspoon ground mustard

■ In a large skillet, cook bacon and onion over medium heat until bacon is crisp. Remove to paper towels to drain.

■ In a 4-qt. slow cooker, combine the remaining ingredients; stir in bacon mixture. Cover and cook on low for 6-8 hours or until mixture is heated through.

Yield: 12 servings.

When a glass bottle of molasses is almost empty, take off the metal cap and warm the bottle in the microwave for a few seconds. This thins the remaining liquid so it runs out better. Also, be sure to spritz the measuring spoon or cup with nonstick cooking spray, so the molasses pours out easily.

Pineapple Baked Beans

Gladys De Boer
CASTLEFORD, IDAHO

Tangy pineapple dresses up these hearty baked beans. Brown the beef while you open the cans and chop the vegetables, and it won't take long to get this side dish ready for the slow cooker.

PREP: 10 min.
COOK: 4 hours

- 1 pound ground beef
- 1 can (28 ounces) baked beans
- 3/4 cup pineapple tidbits, drained
- 1 jar (4-1/2 ounces) sliced mushrooms, drained
- 1 large onion, chopped
- 1 large green pepper, chopped
- 1/2 cup barbecue sauce
- 2 tablespoons soy sauce
- 1 garlic clove, minced
- 1/2 teaspoon salt
- 1/4 teaspoon pepper

■ In a large skillet, cook beef over medium heat until no longer pink; drain. Transfer to a 5-qt. slow cooker. Add the remaining ingredients and mix well.

■ Cover and cook on low for 4-8 hours or until bubbly.

Yield: 12-16 side-dish serving (or 6-8 main-dish servings)

Teriyaki Pulled Pork Sandwiches

Taste of Home Test Kitchen

The aroma of pork roast slowly cooking in pineapple juice and teriyaki sauce is always a nice way to come home at the end of a busy day!

Teriyaki Pulled Pork Sandwiches

PREP: 10 min. ■ COOK: 8 hours

- 1 boneless pork shoulder butt roast (3 pounds)
- 2 teaspoons olive oil
- 1 cup finely chopped onion
- 1 cup teriyaki sauce, *divided*
- 1/2 cup unsweetened pineapple juice
- 3 tablespoons all-purpose flour
- 8 whole wheat hamburger buns, split
- 1 can (20 ounces) sliced pineapple, drained

■ Cut roast in half. In a large skillet, brown roast in oil. Transfer to a 5-qt. slow cooker. Add the onion, 1/2 cup teriyaki sauce and pineapple juice. Cover and cook on low for 7-9 hours or until meat is tender.

■ Remove roast; set aside. In a small bowl, combine the flour and remaining teriyaki sauce until smooth; stir into cooking juices. Cover and cook on high for 30-40 minutes or until thickened.

■ Shred meat with two forks; return to the slow cooker and heat through. Spoon 1/2 cup onto each bun; top with a pineapple slice.

Yield: 8 servings.

Potato Chowder*

Anna Mayer
FORT BRANCH, INDIANA

One of the ladies in our church quilting group brought this savory potato soup to a meeting, and everyone loved how the cream cheese and bacon made it so rich. It's easy to assemble in the morning, letting it simmer on its own all day.

PREP: 15 min.
COOK: 8 hours

- 8 cups diced potatoes
- 1/3 cup chopped onion
- 3 cans (14-1/2 ounces *each*) chicken broth
- 1 can (10-3/4 ounces) condensed cream of chicken soup, undiluted
- 1/4 teaspoon pepper
- 1 package (8 ounces) cream cheese, cubed
- 1/2 pound sliced bacon, cooked and crumbled, optional

Minced chives, optional

■ In a 5-qt. slow cooker, combine the first five ingredients. Cover and cook on low for 8-10 hours or until potatoes are tender.

■ Add cream cheese; stir until blended. Garnish with bacon and chives if desired.

Yield: 12 servings (3 quarts).

***Nutrition Facts:** One 1-cup serving (prepared with reduced-fat cream of chicken soup and reduced-fat cream cheese; calculated without bacon) equals 148 calories, 4 g fat (2 g saturated fat), 13 mg cholesterol, 655 mg sodium, 22 g carbohydrate, 2 g fiber, 6 g protein. **Diabetic Exchanges:** 1-1/2 starch, 1/2 fat.

Snacks & Sweets

When it's time to celebrate, let your slow cooker do the work for you. Whether you need a tempting dessert, tasty appetizer or terrific snack, this chapter offers easy-to-make ideas for your next party or get-together. Your guests will be impressed!

Sweet 'n' Spicy Meatballs

Genie Brown
ROANOKE, VIRGINIA

You'll usually find a batch of these meatballs in my freezer. The slightly sweet sauce nicely complements the spicy pork sausage. They're delicious!

Sweet 'n' Spicy Meatballs

PREP: 25 min. ■ BAKE: 15 min.

- 2 pounds bulk spicy pork sausage
- 1 egg, lightly beaten
- 1 cup packed brown sugar
- 1 cup red wine vinegar
- 1 cup ketchup
- 1 tablespoon soy sauce
- 1 teaspoon ground ginger

■ In a large bowl, combine sausage and egg. Shape into 1-in. balls. Place on a greased rack in a shallow baking pan. Bake at 400° for 15-20 minutes or until meat is no longer pink; drain.

■ Meanwhile, in a small saucepan, combine the brown sugar, vinegar, ketchup, soy sauce and ginger. Bring to a boil. Reduce heat; simmer, uncovered, until sugar is dissolved.

■ Transfer meatballs to a 3-qt. slow cooker. Add the sauce and stir gently to coat. Cover and keep warm on low until serving.

Yield: about 4 dozen.

Hot Mulled Wine

Taste of Home Test Kitchen

For a festive holiday drink or something to keep you warm during those cold winter months, you'll love this comforting wine.

PREP: 15 min.
COOK: 4 hours

- 2 cinnamon sticks (3 inches)
- 6 whole cloves
- 1 fresh rosemary sprig
- 1 bottle (750 milliliters) Cabernet Sauvignon *or* other dry red wine
- 1 cup fresh *or* frozen cranberries
- 2/3 cup sugar
- 1/3 cup bourbon
- 1/3 cup orange juice
- 4 teaspoons grated orange peel

■ Place cinnamon sticks, cloves and rosemary on a double thickness of cheesecloth; bring up corners of cloth and tie with string to form a bag.

■ In a 1-1/2-qt. slow cooker, combine the wine, cranberries, sugar, bourbon, orange juice and peel. Add spice bag. Cover and cook on low for 4-5 hours or until heated through. Discard the spice bag and serve warm.

Yield: 5 servings.

Bananas Foster

Crystal Bruns
ILIFF, COLORADO

The flavors of caramel, rum and walnut naturally complement fresh bananas in this classic dessert made easy! Flaked coconut makes this sweet treat even more scrumptious.

Bananas Foster

PREP: 10 min. ■ COOK: 2 hours

- 5 medium firm bananas
- 1 cup packed brown sugar
- 1/4 cup butter, melted
- 1/4 cup rum
- 1 teaspoon vanilla extract
- 1/2 teaspoon ground cinnamon
- 1/3 cup chopped walnuts
- 1/3 cup flaked coconut
- Ice cream *and/or* pound cake

■ Cut bananas in half lengthwise, then widthwise; layer in the bottom of a 1-1/2-qt. slow cooker. Combine the brown sugar, butter, rum, vanilla and cinnamon; pour over bananas. Cover and cook on low for 1-1/2 hours or until heated through.

■ Sprinkle with walnuts and coconut; cook 30 minutes longer. Serve with ice cream or pound cake.

Yield: 5 servings.

Fruit Salsa

Florence Buchkowsky
PRINCE ALBERT, SASKATCHEWAN

Serve this fruity salsa anywhere you'd use ordinary salsa. My son and I experimented with different ingredients to find the combination we liked best. Preparing it in a slow cooker not only minimizes prep time but it also maximizes flavor.

PREP: 10 min.
COOK: 2 hours

- 3 tablespoons cornstarch
- 4 teaspoons white vinegar
- 1 can (11 ounces) mandarin oranges, undrained
- 1 can (8-1/2 ounces) sliced peaches, undrained
- 3/4 cup pineapple tidbits
- 1 medium onion, chopped
- 1/2 *each* medium green, sweet red and yellow pepper, chopped
- 3 garlic cloves, minced
- Tortilla chips

■ In a 3-qt. slow cooker, combine cornstarch and vinegar until smooth. Stir in fruits, onion, peppers and garlic.

■ Cover and cook on high for 2-3 hours or until thickened and heated through, stirring occasionally. Serve with the tortilla chips.

Yield: 4 cups.

Pam Rohr
TROY, OHIO
You'll need only five ingredients to stir up my hearty dip that tastes like a Reuben sandwich. It's requested at all the get-togethers we attend.

Reuben Spread

Reuben Spread

PREP: 5 min. ■ COOK: 3 hours

- 2-1/2 cups cubed cooked corned beef
- 1 jar (16 ounces) sauerkraut, rinsed and well drained
- 2 cups (8 ounces) shredded Swiss cheese
- 2 cups (8 ounces) shredded cheddar cheese
- 1 cup mayonnaise
- Snack rye bread

■ In a 3-qt. slow cooker, combine the first five ingredients. Cover and cook on low for 3-4 hours or until heated through and cheese is melted, stirring occasionally. Serve warm with rye bread.

Yield: about 5 cups.

Editor's Note: Reduced-fat cheese and mayonnaise are not recommended for this recipe.

It's usually cheaper to buy cheese in blocks than in shredded form. Purchase large quantities of cheddar, Monterey Jack and mozzarella, then shred them in a food processor. Store the shredded cheese in the freezer in heavy-duty resealable plastic bags so you have it at your fingertips whenever it's needed

Warm Broccoli Cheese Dip

Barbara Maiol
CONYERS, GEORGIA

When my family gathers for a party, this flavorful, creamy dip is served. Everyone loves its zip from the jalapeno pepper and the crunch of the broccoli.

PREP: 15 min.
COOK: 2-1/2 hours

- 2 jars (8 ounces *each*) process cheese sauce
- 1 can (10-3/4 ounces) condensed cream of chicken soup, undiluted
- 3 cups frozen chopped broccoli, thawed and drained
- 1/2 pound fresh mushrooms, chopped
- 2 tablespoons chopped seeded jalapeno pepper
- Assorted fresh vegetables

■ In a 1-1/2-qt. slow cooker, combine cheese sauce and soup. Cover and cook on low for 30 minutes or until cheese is melted, stirring occasionally. Stir in the broccoli, mushrooms and jalapeno. Cover and cook on low for 2-3 hours or until vegetables are tender. Serve with assorted fresh vegetables.

Yield: 5-1/2 cups.

Editor's Note: We recommend wearing disposable gloves when cutting hot peppers. Avoid touching your face.

Taste of Home Test Kitchen

The slow cooker is the perfect cooking vessel for the classic dessert creme brulee. The crunchy brown sugar topping in this recipe is wonderful, and the custard is smooth and creamy. It'll also free up your oven space for other dishes.

Maple Creme Brulee

PREP: 20 min. ■ COOK: 2 hours + chilling

- 1-1/3 cups heavy whipping cream
- 3 egg yolks
- 1/2 cup packed brown sugar
- 1/4 teaspoon ground cinnamon
- 1/2 teaspoon maple flavoring

TOPPING:

- 1-1/2 teaspoons sugar
- 1-1/2 teaspoons brown sugar

■ In a small saucepan, heat cream until bubbles form around sides of pan. In a small bowl, whisk the egg yolks, brown sugar and cinnamon. Remove cream from heat; stir a small amount of hot cream into egg mixture. Return all to pan, stirring constantly. Stir in maple flavoring.

■ Transfer to three 6-oz. custard cups. Place in a 6-qt. slow cooker; add 1 in. of boiling water to slow cooker. Cover and cook on high for 2 to 2-1/2 hours or until centers are just set (mixture will jiggle). Carefully remove cups from slow cooker; cool for 10 minutes. Cover and refrigerate for at least 4 hours.

■ For topping, combine sugar and brown sugar. If using a creme brulee torch, sprinkle custards with sugar mixture. Heat sugar with the torch until caramelized. Serve immediately.

■ If broiling the custards, place ramekins on a baking sheet; let stand at room temperature for 15 minutes. Sprinkle with sugar mixture. Broil 8 in. from the heat for 3-5 minutes or until sugar is caramelized. Refrigerate for 1-2 hours or until firm.

Yield: 3 servings.

Hot Crab Dip

Terri Perrier
SIMONTON, TEXAS

One batch of this slow-cooker appetizer isn't enough for my family, so I often double the recipe. Bits of sweet onion give the creamy dip a bit of a crunch.

PREP: 10 min. ■ COOK: 2 hours

- 1 package (8 ounces) cream cheese, softened
- 1/2 cup finely chopped sweet onion
- 1/4 cup grated Parmesan cheese
- 1/4 cup mayonnaise
- 2 garlic cloves, minced
- 2 teaspoons sugar
- 1 can (6 ounces) crabmeat, drained, flaked and cartilage removed
- Assorted crackers

■ In a 1-1/2-qt. slow cooker, combine the first six ingredients; stir in crab. Cover and cook on low for 2-3 hours or until heated through. Serve with crackers.

Yield: 2 cups.

Blueberry Grunt

Cleo Gonske
REDDING, CALIFORNIA

If you love blueberries, then you can't go wrong with my easy slow-cooked dessert. For a special treat, serve it warm with vanilla ice cream.

PREP: 20 min.
COOK: 2-1/2 hours

- 4 cups fresh *or* frozen unsweetened blueberries
- 3/4 cup sugar
- 1/2 cup water
- 1 teaspoon almond extract

DUMPLINGS:

- 2 cups all-purpose flour
- 4 teaspoons baking powder
- 1 teaspoon sugar
- 1/2 teaspoon salt
- 1 tablespoon cold butter
- 1 tablespoon shortening
- 3/4 cup 2% milk
- Vanilla ice cream, optional

■ In a 3-qt. slow cooker, combine the blueberries, sugar, water and extract. Cover and cook on high for 2-3 hours or until bubbly.

■ For dumplings, in a small bowl, combine the flour, baking powder, sugar and salt. Cut in butter and shortening until crumbly. Add milk; stir just until moistened. Drop by tablespoonfuls onto hot blueberry mixture. Cover and cook 30 minutes longer or until a toothpick inserted in a dumpling comes out clean.

■ Serve warm with ice cream if desired.

Yield: 6 servings.

Spiced Ambrosia Punch

Aysha Schurman
AMMON, IDAHO

Inspired by the spices in Chai, I created this unique twist on basic spiced cider punch. It's so easy to make and everyone seems wonderfully surprised by the apricot and peach twist.

Spiced Ambrosia Punch

PREP: 15 min. ■ COOK: 3 hours

- 3-1/2 cups apple cider *or* juice
- 3 cups apricot nectar
- 1 cup peach nectar *or* additional apricot nectar
- 1/4 cup water
- 3 tablespoons lemon juice
- 1/2 teaspoon ground cardamom
- 1/2 teaspoon ground nutmeg
- 2 cinnamon sticks (3 inches)
- 1 teaspoon thinly sliced fresh gingerroot
- 1 teaspoon grated orange peel
- 8 whole cloves
- Lemon *or* orange slices, optional

■ In a 3- or 4-qt. slow cooker, combine the first seven ingredients. Place the cinnamon, ginger, orange peel and cloves on a double thickness of cheesecloth; bring up corners of cloth and tie with string to form a bag. Place bag in slow cooker.

■ Cover and cook on low for 3-4 hours or until heated through. Remove and discard spice bag. Garnish with lemon or orange slices if desired.

Yield: 10 servings (3/4 cup each).

Tropical Compote Dessert

PREP: 15 min.
COOK: 2-1/4 hours

- 1 jar (24 ounces) mixed tropical fruit
- 1 jalapeno pepper, seeded and chopped
- 1/4 cup sugar
- 1 tablespoon chopped crystallized ginger
- 1/4 teaspoon ground cinnamon
- 1 can (15 ounces) mandarin oranges, drained
- 1 jar (6 ounces) maraschino cherries, drained
- 1 medium firm banana, sliced
- 6 individual round sponge cakes
- 6 tablespoons flaked coconut, toasted

■ Drain tropical fruit, reserving 1/4 cup liquid. Combine tropical fruit and jalapeno in a 1-1/2-qt. slow cooker. Combine the sugar, ginger, cinnamon and reserved juice; pour over fruit. Cover and cook on low for 2 hours. Stir in the mandarin oranges, cherries and banana; cook 15 minutes longer.

■ Place sponge cakes on dessert plates; top with compote. Sprinkle with coconut.

Yield: 6 servings.

Editor's Note: We recommend wearing disposable gloves when cutting hot peppers. Avoid touching your face.

Taste of Home Test Kitchen

For a simple yet satisfying dessert, try the assorted fruit warmed up in a slow cooker. Crystallized ginger and jalapeno give it a tasty twist. To make a more adult version of this recipe, use brandy instead of the extra tropical fruit juice.

Sweet & Spicy Peanuts

Taste of Home Test Kitchen
With a caramel-like coating, these crunchy peanuts have a touch of heat from the hot sauce. They make a tasty snack any time of day.

Sweet & Spicy Peanuts

PREP: 10 min. ■ COOK: 1-1/2 hours

- 3 cups salted peanuts
- 1/2 cup sugar
- 1/3 cup packed brown sugar
- 2 tablespoons butter, melted
- 2 tablespoons hot water
- 1 tablespoon sriracha Asian hot chili sauce or hot pepper sauce
- 1 teaspoon chili powder

■ Place peanuts in a greased 1-1/2 qt. slow cooker. In a small bowl, combine the sugars, butter, water, hot sauce and chili powder. Pour over peanuts. Cover and cook on high for 45 minutes; stir. Cover and cook 45 minutes longer.

■ Spread on waxed paper to cool. Store in an airtight container.

Yield: 4 cups.

Taco Joe Dip

Lang Secrest
SIERRA VISTA, ARIZONA

This recipe was given to us by our daughter. My husband and I love the taste of it, and because it's made in a slow cooker, it's great for parties or busy days.

PREP: 5 min.
COOK: 5 hours

- 1 can (16 ounces) kidney beans, rinsed and drained
- 1 can (15-1/4 ounces) whole kernel corn, drained
- 1 can (15 ounces) black beans, rinsed and drained
- 1 can (14-1/2 ounces) stewed tomatoes
- 1 can (8 ounces) tomato sauce
- 1 can (4 ounces) chopped green chilies, drained
- 1 envelope taco seasoning
- 1/2 cup chopped onion

Tortilla chips

■ In a 5-qt. slow cooker, combine the first eight ingredients. Cover and cook on low for 5-7 hours. Serve with tortilla chips.

Yield: about 7 cups.

Paige Arnette
LAWRENCEVILLE, GEORGIA

For a rich, fudgy dessert that's a cross between pudding and cake, stop right here! Serve it warm with a scoop of vanilla ice cream.

Chocolate Pudding Cake

Chocolate Pudding Cake

PREP: 10 min. ■ COOK: 6 hours

- 1 package (18-1/4 ounces) chocolate cake mix
- 1 package (3.9 ounces) instant chocolate pudding mix
- 2 cups (16 ounces) sour cream
- 4 eggs
- 1 cup water
- 3/4 cup canola oil
- 1 cup (6 ounces) semisweet chocolate chips
- Whipped cream *or* ice cream, optional

■ In a large bowl, combine the first six ingredients; beat on low speed for 30 seconds. Beat on medium for 2 minutes. Stir in chocolate chips. Pour into a greased 5-qt. slow cooker.

■ Cover and cook on low for 6-8 hours or until a toothpick inserted near the center comes out with moist crumbs. Serve in bowls with whipped cream or ice cream if desired.

Yield: 10-12 servings.

Plain yogurt can be substituted in equal amounts for sour cream in baking recipes as well as in casseroles, dips and sauces.

Nacho Salsa Dip

Sally Hull
HOMESTEAD, FLORIDA

This zesty dip is great for any get-together and allows me to spend more time with my guests. I always have requests to bring it when my husband and I attend potluck parties.

PREP: 15 min.
COOK: 3 hours

- 1 pound ground beef
- 1/3 cup chopped onion
- 2 pounds process cheese (Velveeta), cubed
- 1 jar (16 ounces) chunky salsa
- 1/4 teaspoon garlic powder
- Tortilla chips *or* cubed French bread

■ In a large skillet, cook beef and onion over medium heat until meat is no longer pink; drain well.

■ Transfer to a greased 3-qt. slow cooker; stir in the cheese, salsa and garlic powder. Cover and cook on low for 3-4 hours or until heated through. Stir and serve with tortilla chips or cubed bread.

Yield: 7 cups.

Peppered Meatballs

Darla Schroeder

STANLEY, NORTH DAKOTA

Plenty of ground pepper gives these saucy meatballs their irresistible zest. They're so hearty, I sometimes serve them over noodles as a main course.

PREP: 35 min. ■ COOK: 2 hours

- 1/2 cup sour cream
- 2 teaspoons grated Parmesan *or* Romano cheese
- 2 to 3 teaspoons pepper
- 1 teaspoon salt
- 1 teaspoon dry bread crumbs
- 1/2 teaspoon garlic powder
- 1-1/2 pounds ground beef

SAUCE:

- 1 can (10-3/4 ounces) condensed cream of mushroom soup, undiluted
- 1 cup (8 ounces) sour cream
- 2 teaspoons dill weed
- 1/2 teaspoon sugar
- 1/2 teaspoon pepper
- 1/4 teaspoon garlic powder

■ In a large bowl, combine the sour cream and cheese. Add the pepper, salt, bread crumbs and garlic powder. Crumble meat over mixture and mix well. Shape into 1-in. balls.

■ Place meatballs on a greased rack in a shallow baking pan. Bake at 350° for 20-25 minutes or until no longer pink; drain.

■ Transfer meatballs to a 1-1/2-qt. slow cooker. Combine the sauce ingredients; pour over meatballs. Cover and cook on high for 2-3 hours or until heated through.

Yield: 1-1/2 dozen (2 cups sauce).

Slow-Cooked Smokies

Sundra Hauck

BOGALUSA, LOUISIANA

I like to include these little smokies smothered in barbecue sauce on all my appetizer buffets since they're popular with both children and adults.

PREP: 5 min. ■ COOK: 6 hours

- 1 package (1 pound) miniature smoked sausages
- 1 bottle (28 ounces) barbecue sauce
- 1-1/4 cups water
- 3 tablespoons Worcestershire sauce
- 3 tablespoons steak sauce
- 1/2 teaspoon pepper

■ In a 3-qt. slow cooker, combine all ingredients. Cover and cook on low for 5-6 hours or until heated through. Serve with a slotted spoon.

Yield: 8 servings.

Amaretto Cherries With Dumplings

PREP: 15 min.
COOK: 7-3/4 hours

- 2 cans (14-1/2 ounces *each*) pitted tart cherries
- 3/4 cup sugar
- 1/4 cup cornstarch
- 1/8 teaspoon salt
- 1/4 cup Amaretto

DUMPLINGS:

- 1 cup all-purpose flour
- 1/4 cup sugar
- 1 teaspoon baking powder
- 1/2 teaspoon grated lemon peel
- 1/8 teaspoon salt
- 1/3 cup 2% milk
- 3 tablespoons butter, melted

Vanilla ice cream, optional

■ Drain cherries, reserving 1/4 cup juice. Place cherries in a 3-qt. slow cooker.

■ In a small bowl, combine the sugar, cornstarch and salt. Stir in reserved juice until smooth. Add to slow cooker. Cover and cook on high for 7 hours. Drizzle Amaretto over cherry mixture.

■ For dumplings, combine the flour, sugar, baking powder, lemon peel and salt. Stir in milk and butter just until moistened. Drop by tablespoonfuls onto hot cherry mixture. Cover and cook for 45 minutes or until a toothpick inserted in dumplings comes out clean. Serve warm with ice cream if desired.

Yield: 5 servings.

Amaretto Cherries with Dumplings

Taste of Home Test Kitchen

You can't beat the flavor combination of almond with tart cherries. These light and fluffy dumplings are heavenly, and topped with the luscious sauce and a scoop or two of cool, creamy ice cream, it makes for a scrumptious dessert.

Buffalo Wing Dip

Taste of Home Test Kitchen

If you love spicy wings, you'll adore this dip. It's super cheesy, full of rich flavor and really has the taste of buffalo wings! I like to serve it at tailgate parties.

Buffalo Wing Dip

PREP: 20 min. ■ COOK: 2 hours

- 2 packages (8 ounces *each*) cream cheese, softened
- 1/2 cup ranch salad dressing
- 1/2 cup sour cream
- 5 tablespoons crumbled blue cheese
- 2 cups shredded cooked chicken
- 1/2 cup buffalo wing sauce
- 2 cups (8 ounces) shredded cheddar cheese, *divided*
- 1 green onion, sliced

Tortilla chips

■ In a small bowl, combine the cream cheese, dressing, sour cream and blue cheese. Transfer to a 3-qt. slow cooker. Layer with chicken, wing sauce and 1 cup cheese. Cover and cook on low for 2-3 hours or until heated through. Sprinkle with remaining cheese and onion. Serve with tortilla chips.

Yield: 6 cups.

Hot Cocoa For a Crowd*

Deborah Canaday

MANHATTAN, KANSAS

This is a simple, delicious and comforting hot cocoa with a hint of cinnamon. It has just the right amount of sweetness.

PREP: 10 min.

COOK: 3 hours

- 5 cups nonfat dry milk powder
- 3/4 cup sugar
- 3/4 cup baking cocoa
- 1 teaspoon vanilla extract
- 1/4 teaspoon ground cinnamon
- 11 cups water

Miniature marshmallows and peppermint candy sticks, optional

■ In a 5- or 6-qt. slow cooker, combine the milk powder, sugar, cocoa, vanilla and cinnamon; gradually whisk in water until smooth. Cover and cook on low for 3-4 hours or until heated through.

■ Garnish with marshmallows and use peppermint sticks for stirrers if desired.

Yield: 12 servings (1 cup each).

***Nutrition Facts:** 1 cup (calculated without optional ingredients) equals 164 calories, 1 g fat (0g saturated fat), 5 mg cholesterol, 156 mg sodium, 31 g carbohydrate, 1 g fiber, 11 g protein. **Diabetic Exchanges:** 1 starch, 1 fat-free milk.

Marinated Chicken Wings

Janie Botting

SULTAN, WASHINGTON

I've made these nicely flavored chicken wings many times for social gatherings. They're so moist and tender.

PREP: 5 min. + marinating ■ COOK: 3-1/2 hours

- 20 whole chicken wings (about 4 pounds)
- 2 cups soy sauce
- 1/2 cup white wine *or* chicken broth
- 1/2 cup canola oil
- 2 to 3 garlic cloves, minced
- 2 tablespoons sugar
- 2 teaspoons ground ginger

■ Cut chicken wings into three sections; discard wing tips. In a large bowl, combine remaining ingredients. Pour half the sauce into a large resealable plastic bag. Add wings, seal and toss to coat. Refrigerate overnight. Cover and refrigerate remaining marinade.

■ Drain and discard marinade. Place chicken in a 5-qt. slow cooker; top with reserved sauce. Cover and cook on low for 3-4 hours or until chicken juices run clear.

■ Transfer wings to a serving dish; discard cooking juices.

Yield: 18-20 servings.

Editor's Note: Uncooked chicken wing sections (wingettes) may be substituted for whole chicken wings.

Caramel Pears

Taste of Home Test Kitchen

The crystallized ginger and cinnamon add a yummy flavor to this decadent desert made with fresh pears.

PREP: 15 min. ■ COOK: 2 hours

- 6 medium pears, peeled and sliced
- 3/4 cup packed brown sugar
- 1/4 cup heavy whipping cream
- 2 teaspoons lemon juice
- 2 tablespoons butter, melted
- 1 tablespoon chopped crystallized ginger
- 1 teaspoon cornstarch
- 1/2 teaspoon ground cinnamon
- Grilled pound cake, whipped topping and toasted almond slices

■ In a 1-1/2-qt. slow cooker, combine the first eight ingredients. Cover and cook on low for 2-3 hours or until heated through. Serve warm over pound cake. Top with whipped topping; sprinkle with almonds.

Yield: 6 servings.

Saucy Cocktail Meatballs

Susie Snyder

BOWLING GREEN, OHIO

I received this recipe from my grandmother many years ago. She would serve it every year at Christmas while I was growing up. Now I serve it every year.

PREP: 10 min.
COOK: 3 hours

- 1 package (32 ounces) frozen fully cooked homestyle meatballs, thawed
- 1 can (10-3/4 ounces) condensed tomato soup, undiluted
- 1/3 cup chopped onion
- 1/3 cup chopped green pepper
- 2 tablespoons brown sugar
- 4 teaspoons Worcestershire sauce
- 1 tablespoon white vinegar
- 1 tablespoon prepared mustard

■ Place meatballs in a 3-qt. slow cooker. In a small bowl, combine the remaining ingredients. Pour over meatballs.

■ Cover and cook on low for 3-4 hours or until heated through.

Yield: about 6 dozen.

STOVETOP SUPPERS

Beef & Ground Beef

A single-skillet or one-pot supper is an easy way to get a quick meal on the table so that you spend less time in the kitchen and more time with the ones you love. Choose from any of the hearty beef and ground beef dishes in this chapter. You may even find a new family favorite!

Hamburger Chop Suey

Beth Pisula
FREEPORT, ILLINOIS

Fast, hearty and colorful, this chop suey uses up those summer garden peppers and spinach. If you are able to get them, pea pods are delicious thrown into the mix.

Hamburger Chop Suey*

PREP/TOTAL TIME: 30 min.

- 1 tablespoon cornstarch
- 2 teaspoons minced fresh gingerroot
- 1 teaspoon reduced-sodium beef bouillon granules
- 3/4 cup water
- 1/3 cup reduced-sodium soy sauce

CHOP SUEY:

- 1 pound lean ground beef (90% lean)
- 2 celery ribs, sliced
- 1 cup sliced fresh mushrooms
- 1 medium green pepper, sliced
- 1 medium sweet red pepper, sliced
- 1 medium onion, halved and thinly sliced
- 1 can (14 ounces) bean sprouts, drained
- 1 can (8 ounces) sliced water chestnuts, drained
- 1 cup fresh spinach, torn
- 3 cups hot cooked rice

■ In a small bowl, combine the cornstarch, ginger and bouillon; stir in water and soy sauce until blended. Set aside.

■ In a large nonstick skillet or wok, stir-fry the beef, celery, mushrooms, peppers and onion until the meat is no longer pink and vegetables are tender. Drain. Stir in the bean sprouts, water chestnuts and spinach.

■ Stir reserved sauce mixture; add to the pan. Bring to a boil; cook and stir for 1-2 minutes or until thickened. Serve with cooked rice.

Yield: 6 servings.

***Nutrition Facts:** 1-1/3 cups chop suey with 1/2 cup rice equals 287 calories, 6 g fat (2 g saturated fat), 37 mg cholesterol, 679 mg sodium, 37 g carbohydrate, 4 g fiber, 20 g protein. **Diabetic Exchanges:** 2 lean meat, 2 vegetable, 1-1/2 starch.

Be sure to select a wok or skillet that is large enough to accommodate the volume of food you'll be stir-frying. If the food is crowded in the pan, it may steam. You may need to stir-fry the food in batches.

Meghan Crihfield
RIPLEY, WEST VIRGINIA

Thanks to no-cook lasagna noodles, this skillet lasagna makes a filling, flavorful and fast Italian meal. Your family will love it!

Saucy Skillet Lasagna

Saucy Skillet Lasagna

PREP/TOTAL TIME: 30 min.

- 1 pound ground beef
- 1 can (14-1/2 ounces) diced tomatoes, undrained
- 2 eggs, lightly beaten
- 1-1/2 cups ricotta cheese
- 4 cups Italian baking sauce
- 1 package (9 ounces) no-cook lasagna noodles
- 1 cup (4 ounces) shredded part-skim mozzarella cheese, optional

■ In a large skillet, cook beef over medium heat until no longer pink; drain. Transfer to a large bowl; stir in tomatoes. In a small bowl, combine eggs and ricotta cheese.

■ Return 1 cup meat mixture to the skillet; spread evenly. Layer with 1 cup ricotta mixture, 1-1/2 cups sauce and half of the noodles. Repeat layers. Top with remaining sauce.

■ Bring to a boil. Reduce heat; cover and simmer for 15-17 minutes or until noodles are tender and a thermometer reads 160°. Remove from the heat. Sprinkle with mozzarella cheese if desired; let stand for 2 minutes or until cheese is melted.

Yield: 6-8 servings.

Editor's Note: This recipe was tested with Barilla Al Forno Italian Baking Sauce.

Meatball Skillet Meal

Donna Smith
VICTOR, NEW YORK

With colorful vegetables and nicely seasoned meatballs, this tasty meal-in-one dish offers a delicious dinner. And it won't break the bank!

PREP/TOTAL TIME: 30 min.

- 1/2 cup finely chopped fresh mushrooms
- 1/3 cup quick-cooking oats
- 2 tablespoons finely chopped green pepper
- 2 tablespoons finely chopped onion
- 2 tablespoon dried parsley flakes
- 1 teaspoon dried basil
- 1 teaspoon dried oregano
- 1/2 teaspoon dried thyme
- 1/2 teaspoon salt
- 1/4 teaspoon pepper
- 1 pound ground beef
- 4 medium carrots, sliced
- 1 small zucchini, sliced
- 1 can (14-1/2 ounces) diced tomatoes, undrained
- 4 cups hot cooked rice

■ In a large bowl, combine the first 10 ingredients. Crumble beef over mixture and mix well. Shape into 1-1/4-in. balls.

■ In a large skillet, cook meatballs over medium heat until no longer pink; drain. Add carrots and zucchini; cook, uncovered, for 5 minutes or until tender. Stir in tomatoes; heat through. Serve with rice.

Yield: 6 servings.

West African Beef Stew

Rhonda Hunter
IVORY COAST, WEST AFRICA

My husband and I run a dorm for missionaries' children, who live with us while their parents work. This traditional African dish is easy to Americanize and tastes great.

West African Beef Stew

PREP: 30 min. ■ COOK: 50 min.

- 1-1/2 pounds beef top sirloin steak, cut into 1-inch cubes
- 2 medium onions, sliced
- 2 teaspoons canola oil
- 1 garlic clove, minced
- 1 cup water
- 4 teaspoons beef bouillon granules
- 4 cups shredded cabbage
- 2 medium green peppers, julienned
- 1 medium zucchini, cut into 1/4-inch slices
- 3 tablespoons creamy peanut butter
- Cayenne pepper
- Hot cooked rice, optional

■ In a Dutch oven, brown steak and onions in oil. Add garlic; cook 1 minute longer. Add water and bouillon; bring to a boil. Reduce heat; cover and simmer for 40-45 minutes or until meat is tender.

■ Stir in cabbage, green peppers and zucchini. Bring to a boil. Reduce heat; cover and simmer for 8-10 minutes or until vegetables are tender.

■ Just before serving, stir in peanut butter and sprinkle with cayenne. Serve with rice if desired.

Yield: 6 servings.

Six-Layer Dinner

Charlotte McDaniel
WILLIAMSVILLE, ILLINOIS

This recipe was originally a five-layer dish, but I increased the amount of ground beef and added the celery, which suited my family's palates.

PREP: 5 min.
COOK: 1 hour 20 min.

- 1-1/2 pounds ground beef
- 2 medium onions, thinly sliced
- 3 medium potatoes, peeled and thinly sliced
- 1 large green pepper, chopped
- 1-1/2 teaspoons salt
- 1/2 teaspoon pepper
- 2 celery ribs, chopped
- 1 can (14-1/2 ounces) stewed tomatoes
- 1/4 teaspoon dried basil

■ In a Dutch oven, cook beef over medium heat until no longer pink; drain. Layer beef with onions, potatoes and green pepper, seasoning each layer lightly with salt and pepper. Top with celery, tomatoes and basil.

■ Bring to a boil. Reduce heat; cover and simmer for 1 hour or until vegetables are tender.

Yield: 6-8 servings.

Family-Favorite Cheeseburger Pasta

Raquel Haggard
EDMOND, OKLAHOMA

I created this recipe to satisfy a cheeseburger craving. It really did the trick, but without the extra calories. What a delicious, healthy classic!

Family-Favorite Cheeseburger Pasta*

PREP/TOTAL TIME: 30 min.

- 1-1/2 cups uncooked whole wheat penne pasta
- 3/4 pound lean ground beef (90% lean)
- 2 tablespoons finely chopped onion
- 1 can (14-1/2 ounces) no-salt-added diced tomatoes
- 2 tablespoons dill pickle relish
- 2 tablespoons prepared mustard
- 2 tablespoons ketchup
- 1 teaspoon steak seasoning
- 1/4 teaspoon seasoned salt
- 3/4 cup shredded reduced-fat cheddar cheese
- Chopped green onions, optional

■ Cook pasta according to package directions. Meanwhile, in a large skillet, cook beef and onion over medium heat until meat is no longer pink; drain. Drain the pasta; add to meat mixture.

■ Stir in the tomatoes, relish, mustard, ketchup, steak seasoning and seasoned salt. Bring to a boil. Reduce the heat; simmer, uncovered, for 5 minutes.

■ Sprinkle with cheese. Remove from the heat; cover and let stand until cheese is melted. Garnish with green onions if desired.

Yield: 4 servings.

Editor's Note: This recipe was tested with McCormick's Montreal Steak Seasoning. Look for it in the spice aisle.

***Nutrition Facts:** 1-1/2 cups equals 391 calories, 12 g fat (6 g saturated fat), 57 mg cholesterol, 759 mg sodium, 43 g carbohydrate, 4 g fiber, 28 g protein. **Diabetic Exchanges:** 3 lean meat, 2 starch, 1 vegetable, 1/2 fat.

Reduced-fat cheese products contain at least 25% less fat than the original version. These items can be used in most of the recipes that are heated or where the cheese is melted.

Karen Dunn
KANSAS CITY, MISSOURI
I found this recipe in a magazine some 20 years ago. Its great flavor and the fact that leftovers just get better have made it a real family favorite!

Sirloin Strips over Rice

Sirloin Strips over Rice*

PREP: 15 min. ■ COOK: 30 min.

- 1-1/2 pounds beef top sirloin steak, cut into thin strips
- 1 teaspoon salt
- 1/4 teaspoon pepper
- 2 teaspoons olive oil, *divided*
- 2 medium onions, thinly sliced
- 1 garlic clove, minced
- 1 can (14-1/2 ounces) diced tomatoes, undrained
- 1/2 cup reduced-sodium beef broth
- 1/3 cup dry red wine *or* additional reduced-sodium beef broth
- 1 bay leaf
- 1/2 teaspoon dried basil
- 1/2 teaspoon dried thyme
- 3 cups hot cooked rice

■ Sprinkle beef strips with salt and pepper. In a large nonstick skillet coated with cooking spray, brown beef in 1 teaspoon oil. Remove and keep warm.

■ In the same skillet, saute onions in remaining oil until tender. Add the garlic; cook 1 minute longer. Stir in the tomatoes, broth, wine, bay leaf, basil and thyme. Bring to a boil. Reduce the heat; simmer, uncovered, for 10 minutes.

■ Return beef to the pan; cook for 2-4 minutes or until tender and the mixture is heated through. Discard bay leaf. Serve with rice.

Yield: 6 servings.

***Nutrition Facts:** 2/3 cup beef mixture with 1/2 cup rice equals 299 calories, 7 g fat (2 g saturated fat), 63 mg cholesterol, 567 mg sodium, 31 g carbohydrate, 3 g fiber, 25 g protein. **Diabetic Exchanges:** 3 lean meat, 1-1/2 starch, 1 vegetable, 1/2 fat.

Dijon Mushroom Beef*

Judith McGhan
PERRY HALL, MARYLAND

Coated in a mild Dijon mustard sauce, the beef strips and sliced mushrooms in this dish are delicious over noodles or rice.

PREP/TOTAL TIME: 20 min.

- 1/2 pound fresh mushrooms, sliced
- 1 medium onion, sliced
- 2 teaspoons olive oil
- 1 pound beef top sirloin steak, thinly sliced
- 1 can (10-3/4 ounces) reduced-fat reduced-sodium condensed cream of mushroom soup, undiluted
- 3/4 cup fat-free milk
- 2 tablespoons Dijon mustard

Hot cooked yolk-free noodles, optional

■ In a large nonstick skillet, saute mushrooms and onion in oil until tender. Remove and set aside. In the same skillet, cook beef until no longer pink. Add soup, milk, mustard and mushroom mixture. Bring to a boil. Reduce heat; cook and stir until thickened. Serve with hot cooked noodles if desired.

Yield: 4 servings.

***Nutrition Facts:** 1 cup beef mixture (calculated without noodles) equals 261 calories, 9 g fat (3 g saturated fat), 50 mg cholesterol, 541 mg sodium, 16 g carbohydrate, 2 g fiber, 28 g protein. **Diabetic Exchanges:** 3 lean meat, 1 fat-free milk, 1/2 fat.

June Bridges
FRANKLIN, INDIANA

One year, when St. Patrick's Day was near, I knew my family wouldn't like it if I served plain cabbage again, so I tried this recipe. It's become a family tradition for us.

Dilly Corned Beef and Cabbage

Dilly Corned Beef and Cabbage

PREP: 2-1/2 hours ■ BROIL: 5 min.

- 1 corned beef brisket (2-1/2 to 3-1/2 pounds)
- 1/4 cup honey
- 3 teaspoons Dijon mustard, *divided*
- 1 medium head cabbage (3 pounds)
- 2 tablespoons butter
- 1 tablespoon minced fresh dill *or* 1 teaspoon dill weed

■ Place brisket with its seasoning packet in a Dutch oven; add enough water to cover. Cover and simmer for 2-1/2 hours or until tender. Remove the brisket and place on a broiling pan; reserve the cooking liquid in a Dutch oven. Combine the honey and 1 teaspoon mustard; brush half over meat.

■ Broil 4 in. from the heat for 3 minutes. Brush with the remaining honey mixture; broil 2 minutes more or until glazed. Meanwhile, cut cabbage into eight wedges; simmer in cooking liquid for 10-15 minutes or until tender.

■ Combine butter, dill and remaining mustard; serve with cabbage wedges and sliced corned beef.

Yield: 6-8 servings.

Steak Diane

Phoebe Carre
MULLICA HILL, NEW JERSEY

When I want to provide a memorable dinner but don't want to spend hours in the kitchen, this is the recipe I rely on.

PREP/TOTAL TIME: 15 min.

- 4 beef ribeye steaks (1/2 inch thick and 8 ounces *each*)
- 1/4 teaspoon pepper
- 1/8 teaspoon salt
- 2 tablespoons finely chopped green onion
- 1/2 teaspoon ground mustard
- 4 tablespoons butter, *divided*
- 1 tablespoon lemon juice
- 1-1/2 teaspoons Worcestershire sauce
- 1 tablespoon minced fresh parsley
- 1 tablespoon minced chives

■ Sprinkle steaks on both sides with pepper and salt; set aside. In a large skillet, cook onion and mustard in 2 tablespoons butter for 1 minute. Add steaks; cook for 2-5 minutes on each side or until the meat reaches desired doneness (for medium-rare, a meat thermometer should read 145°; medium 160°; well-done 170°).

■ Remove steaks to a serving platter and keep warm. In the same skillet, add the lemon juice, Worcestershire sauce and remaining butter; cook and stir for 2 minutes or until thickened. Add parsley and chives. Serve with steaks.

Yield: 4 servings.

Savory Beef Stew

Margaret McCully
ST. JOHN, NEW BRUNSWICK

Wine lends a warm background flavor for this satisfying take on a traditional French stew. I use low-fat mashed beans to thicken the broth and boost the nourishment.

Savory Beef Stew*

PREP: 25 min. ■ COOK: 1-1/4 hours

- 1/4 cup all-purpose flour
- 1 pound beef stew meat, cut into 1-inch cubes
- 1 small onion, chopped
- 1 tablespoon canola oil
- 1-1/2 cups water
- 1 can (10-1/2 ounces) condensed beef consomme, undiluted
- 1/2 cup sherry *or* reduced-sodium beef broth
- 1 teaspoon Worcestershire sauce
- 1 teaspoon dried parsley flakes
- 1/4 teaspoon salt
- 1/4 teaspoon garlic powder
- 1/8 teaspoon pepper
- 2 medium carrots, chopped
- 2 medium parsnips, peeled and chopped
- 1 large potato, peeled and chopped
- 1 medium turnip, peeled and chopped

■ Place flour in a large resealable plastic bag; add beef, a few pieces at a time, and shake to coat.

■ In a large saucepan coated with cooking spray, cook beef and onion in oil over medium-high heat until beef is browned on all sides. Stir in the water, consomme, sherry, Worcestershire sauce and seasonings. Bring to a boil. Reduce the heat; cover and simmer for 1 hour.

■ Stir in the carrots, parsnips, potato and turnip. Bring to a boil. Reduce heat; cover and simmer for 30-45 minutes or until the meat and vegetables are tender.

Yield: 4 servings.

***Nutrition Facts:** 1-1/4 cups equals 349 calories, 12 g fat (3 g saturated fat), 73 mg cholesterol, 742 mg sodium, 29 g carbohydrate, 5 g fiber, 27 g protein. **Diabetic Exchanges:** 3 lean meat, 2 vegetable, 1 starch, 1/2 fat.

Any dish prepared by simmering food in liquid for a long period of time in a covered pot can be considered stew. Stew most often refers to a main dish that contains meat, vegetables and a thick broth made from the stewing juices.

Creamy Beef and Onions*

Jennifer Rahe
ST. CLOUD, MINNESOTA

If your family leans toward beef recipes, be sure to give this one a try. The stick-to-your-ribs mainstay gets its tang from a low-fat sauce of yogurt and gravy. Add a tossed salad and a basket of biscuits for a complete meal.

PREP/TOTAL TIME: 20 min.

- 1 pound lean ground beef (90% lean)
- 2 cups sliced fresh mushrooms
- 2 medium onions, cut into thin wedges
- 1 garlic clove, minced
- 1 jar (12 ounces) fat-free beef gravy
- 2/3 cup reduced-fat plain yogurt
- 1 tablespoon Worcestershire sauce
- 1/4 teaspoon dried thyme
- 1/8 teaspoon pepper
- Hot cooked noodles
- 4 teaspoons minced fresh parsley

■ In a nonstick skillet, cook the beef, mushrooms and onions over medium heat until meat is no longer pink. Add garlic; cook 1 minute longer. Drain.

■ In a small bowl, combine the gravy, yogurt, Worcestershire sauce, thyme and pepper; pour over beef. Cook until heated through. Serve with noodles; sprinkle with parsley.

Yield: 4 servings.

***Nutrition Facts:** One serving (1 cup beef mixture, calculated without noodles) equals 266 calories, 9 g fat (4 g saturated fat), 65 mg cholesterol, 588 mg sodium, 19 g carbohydrate, 2 g fiber, 26 g protein. **Diabetic Exchanges:** 3 lean meat, 1 starch, 1 vegetable.

To prepare mushrooms, gently remove any dirt by rubbing with a mushroom brush or damp paper towel. Or quickly rinse the mushrooms under cold water, drain and pat dry with paper towels. Do not peel the mushrooms but do trim the stems.

Spicy Tomato Steak

Anne Landers
LOUISVILLE, KENTUCKY

I came up with this dish 25 years ago after eating something similar on vacation in New Mexico. The results were delicious!

PREP: 15 min. + marinating
COOK: 45 min.

- 2 tablespoons cider vinegar
- 1 teaspoon salt
- 1 teaspoon pepper
- 1 pound beef round steak, trimmed and cut into 1/4-inch strips
- 1/4 cup all-purpose flour
- 2 tablespoons olive oil
- 3 medium tomatoes, peeled, seeded and cut into wedges
- 2 medium potatoes, peeled and thinly sliced
- 2 cans (4 ounces *each*) chopped green chilies
- 1 garlic clove, minced
- 1 teaspoon dried basil

■ In a large resealable bag, combine the vinegar, salt and pepper. Add the beef; seal bag and turn to coat. Refrigerate for 30 minutes.

■ Drain marinade. Place flour in another large resealable bag; add beef and toss to coat. In a large skillet, cook beef in oil over medium heat for 15-20 minutes or until tender.

■ Add remaining ingredients. Cover and simmer about 20-30 minutes or until the potatoes are tender, stirring occasionally.

Yield: 6 servings.

Moo Shu Sloppy Joes

Mike Tchou
PEPPER PIKE, OHIO

Asian-style sloppy joes made with hoisin sauce, barbecue sauce and coleslaw mix are a nice change from the ordinary! It's just the ticket when you are hungry for something new.

Moo Shu Sloppy Joes

PREP/TOTAL TIME: 30 min.

- 2 teaspoons cornstarch
- 1/2 cup cold water
- 1/4 cup barbecue sauce
- 1/4 cup hoisin sauce
- 2 tablespoons reduced-sodium soy sauce
- 2 teaspoons minced fresh gingerroot
- 1 teaspoon minced garlic
- 1/4 teaspoon salt
- 1 small onion, sliced
- 1 small sweet red pepper, sliced
- 2 teaspoons canola oil
- 1 pound lean ground beef (90% lean)
- 3 cups coleslaw mix
- 8 flour tortillas (6 inches), warmed

■ Combine the cornstarch, water, barbecue sauce, hoisin sauce, soy sauce, ginger, garlic and salt until blended; set aside.

■ In a large skillet, saute onion and red pepper in oil until crisp-tender; remove and set aside. In the same skillet, cook beef over medium heat until meat is no longer pink; drain.

■ Stir cornstarch mixture and add to the skillet. Bring to a boil; cook and stir for 1-2 minutes or until thickened. Add coleslaw mix; stir to coat. Spoon meat mixture into the center of each tortilla; top with onion mixture. Roll up tightly.

Yield: 4 servings.

Cajun Macaroni

June Ellis
ERIE, ILLINOIS

When I prepare my favorite meat loaf, I usually end up with an extra half pound of ground beef. I created this Cajun-flavored dish as a way to use it up.

PREP: 15 min.
COOK: 20 min.

- 1/2 pound ground beef
- 1/3 cup chopped onion
- 1/3 cup chopped green pepper
- 1/3 cup chopped celery
- 1 can (14-1/2 ounces) diced tomatoes, undrained
- 1-1/2 teaspoons Cajun seasoning
- 1 package (7-1/4 ounces) macaroni and cheese dinner mix
- 2 tablespoons milk
- 1 tablespoon butter

■ In a large saucepan, cook the beef, onion, green pepper and celery over medium heat until meat is no longer pink; drain. Add tomatoes and Cajun seasoning. Cook, uncovered, for 15-20 minutes, stirring occasionally.

■ Meanwhile, prepare macaroni and cheese according to package directions, using 2 tablespoons milk and 1 tablespoon butter. Stir in beef mixture; cook for 2-3 minutes or until heated through.

Yield: 4 servings.

Barbara White
CROSS PLAINS, WISCONSIN

My whole family used to help prepare this sauerbraten. The aroma as it cooks is wonderful.

Sauerbraten

Sauerbraten

PREP: 10 min. ■ COOK: 4-1/4 hours + chilling

- 1 tablespoon whole peppercorns
- 1 tablespoon whole allspice
- 1 tablespoon salt
- 1 beef rump roast *or* bottom round roast (4 to 5 pounds)
- 4 bacon strips, diced
- 1 cup vinegar
- 1 cup water
- 12 whole peppercorns
- 12 whole allspice
- 1 large onion, sliced
- 2 bay leaves
- 1 jar (12 to 13 ounces) plum preserves *or* preserves of your choice
- 2 gingersnaps, crushed
- 1 cup beef broth *or* port wine
- 1/2 cup all-purpose flour

■ Place tablespoons of peppercorns and allspice in a cloth bag; crush. Mix in salt; rub over roast. Set aside. In a large Dutch oven, cook bacon over medium heat until crisp. Transfer to paper towels.

■ In the same pan, brown roast in drippings, over medium heat, on all sides. Add the vinegar, water, whole peppercorns, whole allspice, onion, bay leaves and reserved bacon; bring to a boil. Reduce heat; cover and simmer for 2 hours. Stir in preserves and gingersnaps; cook 1 hour longer or until meat is tender.

■ Chill roast overnight in cooking liquid. Skim off fat. Heat roast slowly in cooking liquid until heated through, about 1 hour.

■ Remove roast and keep warm. Strain cooking liquid; return 3-1/2 cups to pan. Combine broth and flour; stir into cooking liquid. Bring to a boil. Reduce heat, cook and stir for 1-2 minutes or until thickened and bubbly. Slice roast; serve with gravy.

Yield: 12-14 servings.

Garlic-Mushroom Ribeyes

PREP/TOTAL TIME: 25 min.

- 4 beef ribeye steaks (1 inch thick and 8 ounces *each*)
- 1/4 teaspoon pepper
- 1/8 teaspoon salt
- 4 tablespoons butter, *divided*
- 4 to 8 garlic cloves, peeled and sliced
- 1 pound sliced fresh mushrooms
- 3 tablespoons beef broth

■ Sprinkle steaks with pepper and salt. In a large skillet, saute the steaks for 2 minutes on each side in 1 tablespoon butter or until meat reaches desired doneness (for medium-rare, a meat thermometer should read 145°; medium, 160°; well-done, 170°). Remove and keep warm.

■ In the same skillet, cook garlic in 1 tablespoon butter for 1 minute. Remove garlic and set aside. Add mushrooms to skillet; saute in remaining butter for 5 minutes or until tender. Stir in the broth. Bring to a boil; cook and stir over high heat until liquid is absorbed. Add reserved garlic. Serve with steaks.

Yield: 4 servings.

Kelly Ward-Hartman
CAPE CORAL, FLORIDA

It's easy to dress up delicious ribeyes with mushrooms and garlic sauteed in butter for a special steak dinner. The dish is simple and the flavor tremendous. This recipe uses a stovetop method, but you can also try grilling them!

Beef Rouladen

Helga Schlape
FLORHAM PARK, NEW JERSEY

Until I entered kindergarten, we spoke German in our home and kept many old-world customs. We always enjoyed the food of our family's homeland. Mom usually prepared this for my birthday dinner.

PREP: 30 min. ■ COOK: 1-1/2 hours

- 3 pounds beef top round steak (1/2 inch thick)
- 1/2 teaspoon salt
- 1/4 teaspoon pepper
- 6 bacon strips
- 3 whole dill pickles, halved lengthwise
- 2 tablespoons canola oil
- 2 cups water
- 1 medium onion, chopped
- 2 tablespoons minced fresh parsley
- 2 teaspoons beef bouillon granules, optional
- 1/4 cup all-purpose flour
- 1/2 cup cold water
- 1/2 teaspoon browning sauce, optional

■ Cut steak into six serving-size pieces; pound to 1/4-in. thickness. Sprinkle with salt and pepper. Place a bacon strip down the center of each piece; arrange a pickle half on one edge. Roll up and secure with a toothpick.

■ In a large skillet, heat oil over medium-high heat. Brown beef on all sides. Add the water, onion, parsley and bouillon if desired. Bring to a boil. Reduce heat; cover and simmer for 1-1/2 to 2 hours or until meat is tender. Remove to a serving platter and keep warm.

■ For gravy, skim fat from drippings. Combine the flour, water and browning sauce if desired; stir into drippings. Bring to a boil; cook and stir for 2 minutes or until thickened. Serve with beef.

Yield: 6 servings.

To keep fresh parsley in the refrigerator for several weeks, wash the entire bunch in warm water, shake off all excess moisture, wrap in paper towels and seal in a plastic bag.

Stuffed Green Pepper

Helen Engelhart
MAPLEWOOD, MINNESOTA

My family looks forward to this in the summer when fresh tomatoes and green peppers are available.

PREP: 10 min.
COOK: 55 min.

- 6 medium fresh tomatoes, peeled, seeded and chopped
- 1 medium onion, chopped
- 3 celery ribs, diced
- 1 can (8 ounces) tomato sauce
- 1 cup water
- 2 teaspoons salt, *divided*
- 1/2 teaspoon pepper, *divided*
- 4 medium green peppers
- 1 pound lean ground beef (90% lean)
- 1 cup instant rice, cooked
- 1 teaspoon dried basil

■ In a large saucepan, combine the freshly-chopped tomatoes, onion, celery, tomato sauce, water, 1 teaspoon salt and1/4 teaspoon pepper. Bring to a boil. Reduce heat and simmer 10-15 minutes. Meanwhile, cut tops off of green peppers and remove seeds; set aside.

■ In a large bowl, combine the ground beef, rice, basil and remaining salt and pepper. Fill peppers with beef mixture. Carefully place peppers in tomato sauce. Spoon some sauce over tops of peppers.

■ Cover and simmer for 40-45 minutes or until beef is cooked and peppers are tender.

Yield: 4 servings.

Pot Roast with Vegetables

National Livestock and Meat Board

This old-fashioned favorite uses an economical cut of beef that's simmered to perfection. The addition of veggies makes it a meal in one.

Pot Roast with Vegetables*

PREP: 10 min. ■ COOK: 2-1/4 hours

- 1 garlic clove, minced
- 1 teaspoon dried oregano
- 1/2 teaspoon lemon-pepper seasoning
- 1 boneless beef chuck pot roast (3 pounds)
- 1 tablespoon canola oil
- 3/4 cup plus 1 tablespoon water, *divided*
- 16 small new potatoes, halved
- 4 medium carrots, cut into 2-1/2 inch pieces
- 4 medium parsnips, cut into 2-1/2 inch pieces
- 2 small leeks, cut into 1-1/2 inch pieces
- 2 teaspoons cornstarch

■ Combine the garlic, oregano and lemon-pepper; rub over roast. In a Dutch oven, brown roast in oil on all sides. Pour off drippings. Add 3/4 cup water; bring to a boil. Reduce heat; cover and simmer for 1-3/4 hours.

■ Add vegetables; cover and simmer for 30-35 minutes or until beef and vegetables are tender. Remove to a serving platter and keep warm.

■ Strain cooking liquid; skim off fat. Return 1 cup liquid to pan and bring to a boil over medium high heat.

■ Combine cornstarch and remaining water until smooth; add to pan. Cook and stir for 1 minute or until gravy is thickened and bubbly. Serve with roast and vegetables.

Yield: 8 servings.

***Nutrition Facts:** 1 serving equals 287 calories, 7 g fat (0 saturated fat), 64 mg cholesterol, 48 mg sodium, 28 g carbohydrate, 0 fiber, 27 g protein. **Diabetic Exchanges:** 4 lean meat, 1-1/2 starch, 1 vegetable.

Bacon Cheeseburger Pasta

Melissa Stevens
ELK RIVER, MINNESOTA

I try to make all my dinners not only kid friendly, but easy to reheat since my husband works long hours and often eats later than our children. Here's a great example!

Bacon Cheeseburger Pasta

PREP/TOTAL TIME: 20 min.

- 8 ounces uncooked penne pasta
- 1 pound ground beef
- 6 bacon strips, diced
- 1 can (10-3/4 ounces) condensed tomato soup, undiluted
- 1 cup (4 ounces) shredded cheddar cheese
- Barbecue sauce and prepared mustard, optional

■ Cook the pasta according to package directions. Meanwhile, in a large skillet, cook the beef over medium heat until no longer pink; drain and set aside.

■ In the same skillet, cook the bacon until crisp; remove with a slotted spoon to paper towels. Discard drippings. Drain the pasta; add to the skillet. Stir in the soup, beef and bacon; heat through. Remove from the heat and sprinkle with cheese. Cover and let stand for 2-3 minutes or until the cheese is melted. Serve with barbecue sauce and mustard if desired.

Yield: 4-6 servings.

Swiss Steak

Linda Stiles
BALTIMORE, OHIO

This is one of my family's favorite recipes. I sometimes serve it with white or wild rice. You can also substitute venison for the beef.

PREP: 15 min.
COOK: 1-1/2 hours

- 2 pounds beef top round steak (1 inch thick)
- 3 tablespoons all-purpose flour
- 1/2 teaspoon salt
- 1/4 teaspoon pepper
- 2 tablespoons canola oil
- 2 medium onions, sliced
- 2 celery ribs, chopped
- 1 can (14-1/2 ounces) diced tomatoes, undrained
- 2 tablespoons Worcestershire sauce
- 1/4 teaspoon dried oregano
- Hot cooked noodles, optional

■ Cut meat into serving-size pieces. In a large resealable plastic bag, combine the flour, salt and pepper. Add beef, a few pieces at a time, and shake to coat.

■ In a large skillet, brown meat in oil on both sides. Top with onions and celery. Combine the tomatoes, Worcestershire sauce and oregano; spoon over vegetables. Cover and simmer for 1-1/2 to 2 hours or until meat is tender. Serve with noodles if desired.

Yield: 6 servings.

Mexican Steak and Beans

Edie Farm
FARMINGTON, NEW MEXICO

For a super hearty supper, I head south of the border for this stovetop dish that's easy to prepare.

PREP: 10 min. ■ COOK: 1 hour 5 min.

- 1 tablespoon all-purpose flour
- 1/2 to 1 teaspoon chili powder
- 1/4 teaspoon salt
- 1/8 teaspoon ground cumin
- 1/8 teaspoon pepper
- 1 boneless beef round steak (1/2 pound), cut into 1-inch cubes
- 1 tablespoon canola oil
- 3/4 cup thinly sliced celery
- 1 medium onion, chopped
- 1/2 cup water
- 1/4 cup chili sauce
- 1 medium carrot, cut into 1/2 inch slices
- 1 small green pepper, cut into 1-1/2 inch strips
- 3/4 cup kidney beans, rinsed and drained
- Hot cooked rice, optional

■ In a resealable plastic bag, combine the first five ingredients. Add the steak; shake to coat.

■ In a large skillet, cook steak in oil until browned on all sides; drain. Add the celery, onion, water and chili sauce. Bring to a boil. Reduce heat; cover and simmer for 30 minutes.

■ Add carrot; cover and simmer for 15 minutes. Stir in green pepper and beans. Cover and simmer 10 minutes longer or until meat and vegetables are tender. Serve with rice if desired.

Yield: 2 servings.

When stacking non-stick skillets on cupboard shelves, place a paper plate between each to prevent scratches. This prolongs the life of the skillets.

Pizza Spaghetti

Robert Smith
LAS VEGAS, NEVADA

This recipe came to me when I saw someone dip a slice of pizza into a pasta dish. My wife and kids love it and so do my friends!

PREP: 20 min.
COOK: 30 min.

- 1/2 pound lean ground beef (90% lean)
- 1/2 pound Italian turkey sausage links, casings removed, crumbled
- 1/2 cup chopped sweet onion
- 4 cans (8 ounces *each*) no-salt-added tomato sauce
- 3 ounces sliced turkey pepperoni
- 1 tablespoon sugar
- 2 teaspoons minced fresh parsley *or* 1/2 teaspoon dried parsley flakes
- 2 teaspoons minced fresh basil *or* 1/2 teaspoon dried basil
- 9 ounces uncooked whole wheat spaghetti
- 3 tablespoons grated Parmesan cheese

■ In a large nonstick skillet, cook the beef, sausage and onion over medium heat until meat is no longer pink; drain.

■ Stir in the tomato sauce, pepperoni, sugar, parsley and basil. Bring to a boil. Reduce heat; simmer, uncovered, for 20-25 minutes or until thickened. Meanwhile, cook spaghetti according to package directions.

■ Drain spaghetti; toss with sauce. Sprinkle with cheese.

Yield: 6 servings.

Poultry

It's easy to find a meal that satisfies everyone with this collection of quick-cooking recipes featuring versatile chicken or turkey. Best of all, the one-dish wonders cook up quickly on the stovetop, so there's always time for a wholesome meal.

Chicken and Artichoke Pasta

Laurel Johnson
STERLING HEIGHTS, MICHIGAN

Without a doubt, this is the meal my husband requests most often. I like to serve it with a loaf of crusty French bread. It makes a speedy weeknight dinner.

Chicken and Artichoke Pasta

PREP/TOTAL TIME: 30 min.

- 4 cups uncooked bow tie pasta
- 1 pound chicken tenderloins, cut into 1-inch pieces
- 2 tablespoons olive oil, *divided*
- 1/2 pound sliced fresh mushrooms
- 1/2 cup chopped green onions
- 2 tablespoons white wine *or* chicken broth
- 1 can (14-1/2 ounces) diced tomatoes with roasted garlic, undrained
- 1 can (14 ounces) water-packed quartered artichoke hearts, rinsed and drained
- 1/4 teaspoon salt
- 2 teaspoons cornstarch
- 2 teaspoons cold water
- 1 tablespoon thinly sliced fresh basil *or* 1 teaspoon dried basil
- 1/2 cup shaved Parmesan cheese

■ Cook the pasta according to package directions. Meanwhile, in a large skillet, saute chicken in 1 tablespoon oil until no longer pink. Remove and keep warm.

■ In the same skillet, saute mushrooms and onions in remaining oil until tender; add wine, stirring to loosen the browned bits from pan. Reduce heat to medium. Stir in the tomatoes, artichokes, salt and chicken. Cook and stir for 4-5 minutes or until heated through.

■ Combine cornstarch and water until smooth. Gradually stir into pan. Bring to a boil; cook and stir for 1 minute or until thickened. Stir in the basil. Drain pasta; serve with chicken mixture and cheese.

Yield: 5 servings.

To quickly chop a lot of basil and end up with attractive results, create basil chiffonade, or thin shredded strips. Sprinkle a few drops of canola oil on the leaves and gently rub to evenly coat. This will prevent them from darkening. Stack several leaves and roll them into a tight tube, then thinly slice widthwise.

Turkey with Mushrooms and Cream

Emma Rea
COLUMBIA, SOUTH CAROLINA

My mom serves this savory French dish for holidays, special occasions and when she entertains out-of-town company. The turkey is moist, and the sour cream sauce delicious.

PREP/TOTAL TIME: 30 min.

- 1 package (17.6 ounces) turkey breast cutlets
- 1 tablespoon canola oil
- 3 tablespoons butter, *divided*
- 3/4 cup water, *divided*
- 1/4 cup unsweetened apple juice
- 2 teaspoons chicken bouillon granules, *divided*
- 1/4 teaspoon pepper
- 1 cup (8 ounces) sour cream
- 1 pound fresh mushrooms, chopped
- Hot cooked rice

■ In a large skillet over medium-high heat, cook turkey in oil and 2 tablespoons butter until golden brown and no pink remains; drain. Remove and keep warm.

■ In the same skillet, combine 1/2 cup water, apple juice, 1 teaspoon bouillon and pepper; cook and stir over medium heat until bouillon is dissolved. Stir in sour cream; heat through.

■ Meanwhile, in another skillet, combine remaining butter, water and bouillon; cook and stir over medium heat until bouillon is dissolved. Add mushrooms; cook for 10 minutes or until liquid has evaporated. Serve turkey over rice; top with cream sauce and mushrooms.

Yield: 4 servings.

To cut down on side dish preparation time, cook whole packages of rice or noodles and freeze the extra portions in resealable plastic bags. Later it's easy to take them out of the bag, pop in the microwave and have fresh hot rice or noodles in a snap!

Peanutty Chicken

Mary Kay Dixson
DECATUR, ALABAMA

We use peanuts in a variety of dishes. This tender chicken, covered in a tasty gravy and sprinkled with peanuts, has a zip that perks up taste buds.

PREP: 10 min.
COOK: 45 min.

- 1 teaspoon chili powder
- 1 teaspoon salt
- 1/4 teaspoon pepper
- 1 broiler/fryer chicken (3-1/2 to 4 pounds), cut up
- 5 tablespoons butter
- 1 cup orange juice
- 2/3 to 1 cup salted peanuts
- Orange slices *or* minced fresh cilantro, optional

■ Combine the chili powder, salt and pepper; rub over the chicken. In a large skillet, saute the chicken in butter until golden brown. Reduce the heat; cover and cook for about 30 minutes or until the juices run clear.

■ Transfer chicken to a serving platter and keep warm. Add orange juice to skillet, stirring to loosen browned bits from the pan; simmer for 5 minutes. Pour over chicken. Sprinkle with peanuts. Garnish with orange slices and cilantro if desired.

Yield: 4 servings.

Taste of Home Test Kitchen
Jalapeno pepper gives a little kick to the fruit salsa in this recipe. Preparing this tropical-tasting dish in a skillet keeps your kitchen cool, which is especially nice on a summer day.

Chicken Breasts with Fruit Salsa

Chicken Breasts with Fruit Salsa

PREP/TOTAL TIME: 30 min.

- 1 tablespoon canola oil
- 1/4 teaspoon salt
- 1/4 teaspoon pepper
- 1 garlic clove, minced
- 4 boneless skinless chicken breast halves (4 ounces *each*)
- 2 tablespoons butter
- 3/4 cup pineapple tidbits, drained
- 1/2 cup quartered fresh strawberries
- 1 kiwifruit, peeled, quartered and sliced
- 1/4 cup chopped red onion
- 1 jalapeno pepper, seeded and chopped
- 1 teaspoon cornstarch
- 1/4 cup orange juice

■ In a small bowl, combine the oil, salt, pepper and garlic. Spread over one side of each chicken breast.

■ In a large skillet, saute the chicken seasoned side down in butter for 4-6 minutes on each side or until a meat thermometer reads 170°. Remove chicken to serving platter; keep warm.

■ Meanwhile, for salsa, in a small bowl, combine the fruit, onion and pepper; set aside. Combine the cornstarch and juice until smooth; gradually stir into skillet. Bring to a boil; cook and stir for 1-2 minutes or until thickened. Remove from the heat; pour over fruit mixture and gently toss to coat. Serve with chicken.

Yield: 4 servings.

Editor's Note: We recommend wearing disposable gloves when cutting hot peppers. Avoid touching your face.

Chicken Pasta Primavera

Raelynn Bulkley
PLEASANT GROVE, UTAH

This colorful combination of chicken, pasta and vegetables is very popular at my house. Coated in a creamy sauce, the made-in-minutes meal is sure to be well-received at your house, too.

PREP/TOTAL TIME: 30 min.

- 2 cups uncooked spiral pasta
- 1 pound boneless skinless chicken breasts, cubed
- 2 tablespoons butter
- 2 garlic cloves, minced
- 1 package (16 ounces) frozen broccoli-cauliflower blend, thawed
- 3/4 cup heavy whipping cream
- 3/4 cup grated Parmesan cheese
- 1 teaspoon salt
- 1/4 teaspoon pepper

■ Cook pasta according to package directions. Meanwhile, in a large skillet, saute chicken in butter until chicken is no longer pink. Add garlic; cook 1 minute longer. Add the vegetables and cream; cook until vegetables are tender.

■ Drain pasta. Add the pasta, cheese, salt and pepper to skillet; cook and stir until heated through.

Yield: 4 servings.

C.W. Steve Stevenson
NEWFOUNDLAND, PENNSYLVANIA

I came up with this recipe in my attempt to re-create a meal at a European restaurant. The hearty Gorgonzola sauce pairs well with the chicken and pasta. It's a rich dish and is great with a crisp, green salad that has a light, lemony vinaigrette.

Gorgonzola Chicken Penne

PREP/TOTAL TIME: 30 min.

- 2 cups uncooked penne pasta
- 2 cups fresh broccoli florets
- 1 tablespoon water
- 1 pound boneless skinless chicken breasts, cut into 1-inch cubes
- 9 tablespoons butter, *divided*
- 1 large onion, chopped
- 6 tablespoons all-purpose flour
- 2 cups chicken broth
- 3/4 cup white wine *or* additional chicken broth
- 1-1/2 cups (6 ounces) crumbled Gorgonzola cheese
- Pepper to taste

■ Cook the pasta according to package directions. Meanwhile, place the broccoli and water in a small microwave-safe bowl. Cover and microwave on high for 2 to 2-1/2 minutes or until crisp-tender. Set aside.

■ In a large skillet, saute chicken in 3 tablespoons butter until no longer pink. Remove and keep warm. In the same skillet, saute onion in remaining butter until tender.

■ Stir in flour until blended. Gradually add broth and wine. Bring to a boil; cook and stir for 2 minutes or until thickened. Reduce heat to low; stir in cheese until blended.

■ Drain pasta and broccoli; add to onion mixture. Add chicken; heat through. Season with pepper.

Yield: 6 servings.

Cola Chicken

Jean Jarvis
WAUTOMA, WISCONSIN

Everyone who tries this chicken asks for the recipe. They're surprised to hear that soda is the secret ingredient!

PREP: 5 min. ■ COOK: 70 min.

- 1 can (12 ounces) diet cola
- 1/2 cup ketchup
- 2 to 4 tablespoons finely chopped onion
- 1/4 teaspoon dried oregano
- 1/4 teaspoon garlic powder
- 8 bone-in chicken thighs, skin removed

■ In a large skillet, combine first five ingredients. Bring to a boil; boil for 1 minute. Add chicken; stir to coat. Reduce heat to medium; cover and simmer for 20 minutes.

■ Uncover and simmer for 45 minutes or until a meat thermometer reads 180°.

Yield: 4 servings.

Mac and Cheese Chicken Skillet

Margaret Wilson
SUN CITY, CALIFORNIA

This is a wonderful and speedy Italian-style entree. Just open your pantry and you'll discover a quick-fix for dinner!

PREP/TOTAL TIME: 30 min.

- 1 pound boneless skinless chicken breasts, cut into 1-inch cubes
- 1 teaspoon olive oil
- 1 package (7-1/4 ounces) macaroni and cheese dinner mix
- 2-1/2 cups chicken broth
- 1 cup chopped zucchini
- 1/2 cup chopped onion
- 1 teaspoon dried oregano
- 1 can (14-1/2 ounces) Italian stewed tomatoes

■ In a large skillet, cook chicken in oil over medium-high heat until no longer pink.

■ Set aside the cheese packet from the macaroni dinner mix. Stir in the pasta, broth, zucchini, onion and oregano. Bring to a boil. Reduce heat; cover and simmer for 7-8 minutes or until pasta is tender, stirring occasionally.

■ Stir in the tomatoes and contents of the reserved cheese packet. Cook and stir for 3-4 minutes or until heated through.

Yield: 6 servings.

Smothered Ginger Chicken

Iva Smith

WILMINGTON, MASSACHUSETTS

Liven up ordinary chicken with this simple, saucy skillet dish. No one in my family can resist the moist chicken and old-fashioned gravy.

PREP: 10 min. ■ COOK: 70 min.

- 1/2 cup plus 3 tablespoons all-purpose flour, *divided*
- 1-1/2 teaspoons salt, *divided*
- 1/4 teaspoon pepper, *divided*
- 1 broiler/fryer chicken (3-1/2 to 4 pounds), cut up
- 3 tablespoons canola oil
- 1 cup chopped onion
- 1/4 cup *each* chopped green and sweet red pepper
- 3 garlic cloves, minced
- 1/2 teaspoon ground ginger
- 3 cups chicken broth

■ In a large resealable plastic bag, combine 1/2 cup flour, 1 teaspoon salt and 1/4 teaspoon pepper. Add chicken, a few pieces at a time, and shake to coat.

■ In a large skillet, fry chicken, a few pieces at a time, in oil until well browned. Remove from skillet; set aside and keep warm. Add onion and peppers to drippings; saute until tender. Add the garlic and cook 1 minute longer.

■ In a large bowl, combine the remaining flour, remaining salt and pepper, ginger and chicken broth until smooth. Stir into vegetable mixture; bring to a boil. Cook and stir for 2-3 minutes or until thickened. Return chicken to pan; cover and simmer for 45 minutes or until chicken juices run clear.

Yield: 4 servings.

To mince or chop, hold the handle of a chef's knife with one hand, and rest the finger of your other hand on the top of the blade near the tip. Using the handle to guide and apply pressure, move knife in an arc across the food with a rocking motion until pieces of food are the desired size. Mincing results in pieces no larger than 1/8 in., and chopping can produce 1/4-in. to 1/2-in. pieces.

Creamy Curried Turkey

Maureen Dufraimont

GUELPH, ONTARIO

A subtle hint of curry and a snappy crunch from apple and celery make this a fun variation on the classic creamed turkey.

PREP: 20 min. COOK: 15 min.

- 2 cups fat-free milk
- 1 tablespoon lemon juice
- 1 tablespoon reduced-fat sour cream
- 1 tablespoon reduced-fat mayonnaise
- 1 teaspoon salt
- 1/2 teaspoon curry powder
- 1/8 teaspoon pepper
- 1 cup sliced fresh mushrooms
- 1 medium apple, peeled and chopped
- 1 celery rib, chopped
- 1/4 cup chopped green pepper
- 2 tablespoons butter
- 1/4 cup all-purpose flour
- 3 cups cubed cooked turkey breast
- 1/2 cup frozen peas
- 5 toasted reduced-fat biscuits, split

■ Combine the first seven ingredients; set aside. In a large nonstick skillet, saute mushrooms, apple, celery and green pepper in butter until tender. Stir in flour until blended; gradually add milk mixture. Bring to a boil; cook and stir for 1-2 minutes or until thickened. Add turkey and peas; heat through. Serve with biscuits.

Yield: 5 servings.

Lorraine Caland
THUNDER BAY, ONTARIO
If you're looking for Italian comfort food, this is it! By using store-bought spaghetti sauce, you save time when preparing this creamy dish. You'll enjoy every bite!

Chicken & Tomato Risotto

Chicken & Tomato Risotto

PREP: 25 min. ■ COOK: 25 min.

- 3 cups chicken broth
- 1 pound boneless skinless chicken breasts, cut into 1-inch cubes
- 1 tablespoon olive oil
- 1-1/2 cups sliced fresh mushrooms
- 1 medium onion, chopped
- 2 tablespoons butter
- 1 garlic clove, minced
- 1 cup uncooked arborio rice
- 1 cup meatless spaghetti sauce
- 1/4 cup grated Parmesan cheese

■ In a small saucepan, heat broth and keep warm. In a large skillet, saute chicken in oil until no longer pink. Remove and keep warm.

■ In the same skillet, saute mushrooms and onion in butter until crisp-tender. Add garlic; cook 1 minute longer. Add rice; cook and stir for 3 minutes. Carefully stir in 1 cup warm broth. Cook and stir until all of the liquid is absorbed.

■ Add remaining broth, 1/2 cup at a time, stirring constantly. Allow the liquid to absorb between additions. Cook until risotto is creamy and rice is almost tender. (Cooking time is about 20 minutes.)

■ Stir in the spaghetti sauce, cheese and reserved chicken; cook and stir until thickened.

Yield: 4 servings.

Chicken Fajita Spaghetti*

Heather Brown
FRISCO, TEXAS
This tasty dinner has been a great time-saver for me.

PREP/TOTAL TIME: 20 min.

- 8 ounces uncooked spaghetti
- 1 pound boneless skinless chicken breasts, cut into strips
- 1 tablespoon canola oil
- 1 small onion, sliced
- 1 small sweet red pepper, julienned
- 1 small sweet yellow pepper, julienned
- 1 can (4 ounces) chopped green chilies
- 1/2 cup water
- 1/2 cup taco sauce
- 1 envelope fajita seasoning mix

■ Cook the spaghetti according to package directions. Meanwhile, in a large skillet, cook chicken over medium heat in oil for 4-5 minutes on each side or until meat is no longer pink; remove and keep warm.

■ In the same skillet, saute onion and peppers until tender. Add the chicken, chilies, water, taco sauce and fajita seasoning; heat through. Drain spaghetti; toss with chicken mixture.

Yield: 6 servings.

***Nutrition Facts:** 1-1/4 cups equals 282 calories, 5 g fat (1 g saturated fat), 42 mg cholesterol, 722 mg sodium, 37 g carbohydrate, 2 g fiber, 21 g protein. **Diabetic Exchange:** 2 starch, 2 lean meat, 1 vegetable.

Chicken with Cucumber Sauce

Sheryl Ann Houghton
SPRING GROVE, PENNSYLVANIA

I've served this chicken to nearly all our friends and relatives, and it's been met with many "Mmmms!" I sometimes prepare extra sauce to serve over steamed fresh carrots.

PREP/TOTAL TIME: 20 min.

- 1/4 cup yellow cornmeal
- 1-1/2 teaspoons ground mustard
- 1/4 teaspoon ground nutmeg
- 1/8 to 1/4 teaspoon cayenne pepper
- 1/2 teaspoon seafood seasoning, optional
- 8 boneless skinless chicken breast halves (4 ounces *each*)
- 2 tablespoons canola oil

CUCUMBER SAUCE:

- 1 bottle (8 ounces) ranch salad dressing
- 1 cup chopped peeled cucumber
- 1 tablespoon sliced green onion
- 1/2 teaspoon dill weed

■ In a large resealable plastic bag, combine the cornmeal, mustard, nutmeg, cayenne pepper and seafood seasoning if desired. Add chicken, a few pieces at a time, and shake to coat.

■ In a large skillet, cook chicken in oil over medium heat for 5-7 minutes on each side or until a meat thermometer reads 170°.

■ Meanwhile, in a large saucepan, combine the sauce ingredients; cook over low heat until heated through. Serve with chicken.

Yield: 8 servings.

Editor's Note: Chicken may also be served as a sandwich on buns topped with warm or chilled cucumber sauce.

Cornmeal can be either white, yellow or blue depending on which strain of corn is used. Traditionally, white cornmeal is more popular in the South and yellow is preferred in the North. Blue cornmeal can be found in specialty stores. All three types can be used interchangeably in recipes.

Creamy Shells And Chicken

PREP/TOTAL TIME: 30 min.

- 1/2 pound boneless skinless chicken breasts, cut into 1-inch strips
- 1/4 teaspoon salt
- 1/4 teaspoon pepper
- 2 tablespoons canola oil, *divided*
- 2 tablespoons butter, *divided*
- 1/2 cup chopped onion
- 1/2 cup chopped green pepper
- 1/2 cup chopped sweet red pepper
- 1-1/3 cups water
- 1/2 cup milk
- 1 package (4.9 ounces) creamy garlic shells
- Shredded Parmesan cheese

■ Sprinkle chicken with salt and pepper. In a large skillet, cook chicken over medium heat in 1 tablespoon oil and 1 tablespoon butter for 4-5 minutes or until no longer pink. Remove and keep warm.

■ In same skillet, saute onion and peppers in remaining oil and butter until crisp-tender. Stir in the water, milk and shells. Bring to a boil. Reduce heat; simmer, uncovered, for 10-12 minutes or until pasta is tender, stirring occasionally. Add the chicken; cook 2-3 minutes longer or until heated through. Sprinkle with cheese.

Yield: 3 servings.

Editor's Note: This recipe was prepared with Lipton Italian Sides creamy garlic shells.

Creamy Shells and Chicken

Trisha Kruse
EAGLE, IDAHO

This is a great weeknight chicken dish. While it simmers I can throw together a salad or steam some broccoli, and I have a tasty dinner ready in a flash. If you have a large group of people to feed, double or triple the recipe—just be sure to use a larger skillet to accommodate the increase in ingredients.

Sausage 'n' Chicken Skillet

Joanna Iovino
KINGS PARK, NEW YORK

Chicken and rice was a staple at my parents' house, but the chicken never turned out quite right. I enjoy this recipe much more now that I use tasty skinless chicken and kielbasa.

Sausage 'n' Chicken Skillet*

PREP: 15 min. ■ COOK: 40 min.

- 1/2 pound boneless skinless chicken breasts, cubed
- 1/2 teaspoon dried thyme, *divided*
- 1/4 teaspoon pepper, *divided*
- 1-1/2 teaspoons canola oil
- 1/4 pound smoked turkey kielbasa, cut into 1/4-inch slices
- 1 small onion, finely chopped
- 1 small green pepper, finely chopped
- 2 garlic cloves, minced
- 2 cups water
- 1 cup uncooked long grain rice
- 1/2 teaspoon reduced-sodium chicken bouillon granules
- 1/2 teaspoon hot pepper sauce

■ Sprinkle chicken with 1/4 teaspoon thyme and 1/8 teaspoon pepper. In a large nonstick skillet, saute chicken in oil until no longer pink. Remove and keep warm.

■ In the same skillet, saute the kielbasa, onion and green pepper until vegetables are tender. Add the garlic; cook 1 minute longer. Stir in water, rice, bouillon, hot pepper sauce, and remaining thyme and pepper. Bring to a boil. Reduce the heat; cover and simmer for 18-20 minutes or until liquid is absorbed and rice is tender.

■ Return chicken to the pan; heat through.

Yield: 4 servings.

***Nutrition Facts:** 1-1/4 cups equals 296 calories, 5 g fat (1 g saturated fat), 49 mg cholesterol, 352 mg sodium, 41 g carbohydrate, 1 g fiber, 20 g protein. **Diabetic Exchanges:** 2-1/2 starch, 2 lean meat, 1/2 fat.

When a recipe calls for thinly sliced boneless chicken or beef steak, such as for a stir-fry or casserole, the meat is much easier to slice if it is slightly frozen first.

Italian Turkey Cutlets*

Janet Bumb

BEALLSVILLE, MARYLAND

Because I'm watching my weight, I turn to this recipe regularly. Served with a flavorful tomato sauce, these cutlets taste so good that my son, who is thin and doesn't need to worry about his weight, requests them for his birthday dinner!

PREP/TOTAL TIME: 30 min.

- 1 small onion, finely chopped
- 5 teaspoons olive oil, *divided*
- 2 garlic cloves, minced
- 1 can (14-1/2 ounces) Italian stewed tomatoes
- 1 teaspoon dried basil
- 1 teaspoon dried oregano
- 1/2 teaspoon dried rosemary, crushed
- 1-1/4 pounds turkey breast cutlets
- 1/2 teaspoon salt
- 1/8 teaspoon pepper
- 2 tablespoons shredded Parmesan cheese

■ In a large saucepan, saute onion in 2 teaspoons oil until tender. Add garlic; cook 1 minute longer. Stir in the tomatoes, basil, oregano and rosemary. Bring to a boil. Reduce the heat; cook, uncovered, over medium heat for 15-20 minutes or until sauce thickens.

■ Meanwhile, sprinkle both sides of turkey cutlets with salt and pepper. In a large nonstick pan over medium heat, cook turkey in batches in remaining oil until no longer pink. Serve with tomato sauce. Sprinkle with cheese.

Yield: 4 servings.

***Nutrition Facts:** 1 serving equals 263 calories, 7 g fat (2 g saturated fat), 90 mg cholesterol, 750 mg sodium, 11 g carbohydrate, 3 g fiber, 37 g protein. **Diabetic Exchanges:** 5 lean meat, 2 vegetable, 1/2 fat.

If using home-canned tomatoes for the recipe above, use the same amount as the canned variety called for, but add 3 tablespoons finely chopped celery, 2 tablespoons finely chopped onion, 1 tablespoon finely chopped green pepper, 1/2 teaspoon sugar and 1/8 teaspoon salt.

Turkey Sweet Potato Supper

Margaret Wilson

SUN CITY, CALIFORNIA

This streamlined but elegant version of a traditional turkey dinner is a quick meal that's sure to brighten any table.

PREP/TOTAL TIME: 30 min.

- 2 turkey breast tenderloins (8 ounces *each*)
- 1 tablespoon butter
- 1 can (2 pounds, 8 ounces) sweet potatoes, drained
- 1/3 cup dried cranberries
- 1/3 cup maple syrup
- 1/4 cup orange juice
- 1/4 teaspoon ground cinnamon
- 1/2 teaspoon cornstarch
- 1 tablespoon cold water

■ In a large skillet, brown the turkey in butter on each side. Arrange sweet potatoes around turkey. Combine the cranberries, maple syrup, orange juice and cinnamon; pour over sweet potatoes. Bring to a boil. Reduce heat; cover and simmer for 15-20 minutes or until a meat thermometer reads 170°.

■ Remove turkey and sweet potatoes to a serving platter. Combine the cornstarch and water until smooth; add to skillet. Bring to a boil. Cook and stir for 1 minute or until thickened. Serve with turkey and sweet potatoes.

Yield: 4 servings.

Taste of Home Test Kitchen

Ramen noodles get a big pick-me-up with a simple but flavorful 4-ingredient sauce that goes perfectly with this tender chicken. The peanut butter and soy sauce add a delicious, Asian-inspired flavor to the entree that is quick-to-make but offers irresistible flavor.

Chicken over Curly Noodles

PREP/TOTAL TIME: 30 min.

- 1/4 cup packed brown sugar
- 1/4 cup creamy peanut butter
- 1/4 cup soy sauce
- 1 teaspoon minced garlic
- 1/2 cup dry bread crumbs
- 3 packages (3 ounces *each*) chicken ramen noodles
- 4 boneless skinless chicken breast halves (5 ounces *each*)
- 1 tablespoon olive oil
- 1 can (14 ounces) bean sprouts, drained

■ In a small bowl, combine the brown sugar, peanut butter, soy sauce and garlic; set aside. In a large resealable plastic bag, combine bread crumbs and contents of two noodle seasoning packets (discard the remaining packet or save for another use). Add chicken, one piece at a time, and shake to coat.

■ In a large skillet, cook chicken in oil over medium heat for 5-6 minutes on each side or until a meat thermometer reads 170°. Meanwhile, cook noodles according to package directions.

■ Remove chicken and keep warm. Add peanut butter mixture to skillet; cook and stir until heated through. Drain noodles. Add noodles and bean sprouts to skillet; toss to coat. Serve with chicken.

Yield: 4 servings.

Gnocchi Chicken Skillet

Taste of Home Test Kitchen

Potato gnocchi are little dumplings made from a potatoes, flour and eggs. Look for gnocchi in the pasta or frozen section of your grocery store.

PREP/TOTAL TIME: 25 min.

- 1 package (10 ounces) potato gnocchi
- 1 pound ground chicken
- 1/2 cup chopped onion
- 2 tablespoons olive oil
- 1 jar (26 ounces) spaghetti sauce
- 1/4 to 1/2 teaspoon dried oregano
- 1/4 teaspoon salt
- Shredded Parmesan cheese, optional

■ Prepare gnocchi according to package directions. Meanwhile, in a large skillet, cook chicken and onion in oil over medium heat until chicken is no longer pink; drain if necessary. Stir in the spaghetti sauce, oregano and salt.

■ Drain gnocchi; add to skillet. Cover and cook for 10-15 minutes or until heated through. Serve with cheese if desired.

Yield: 4 servings.

Chicken Rice Dish*

ReBecca Vandiver

BETHANY, OKLAHOMA

Spring asparagus and lemon dress up this tasty chicken entree.

PREP/TOTAL TIME: 25 min.

- 2 cups water
- 2 cups cut fresh asparagus (1-inch diagonal pieces)
- 1 package (6 ounces) long grain and wild rice mix
- 1/4 cup butter, *divided*
- 3/4 pound boneless skinless chicken breasts, cut into 1-inch strips
- 1/4 teaspoon salt
- 1 medium carrot, shredded
- 2 tablespoons lemon juice
- 1 teaspoon minced garlic
- 1/2 teaspoon grated lemon peel, optional

■ In a large saucepan, combine water, asparagus and rice mix with seasoning packet and 2 tablespoons butter. Bring to a boil; reduce heat. Cover and simmer for 10-15 minutes or until water is absorbed.

■ Meanwhile, in large skillet, saute chicken and salt in remaining butter until chicken is no longer pink. Add carrot, lemon juice, garlic and peel if desired; cook and stir for 1-2 minutes until carrot is crisp-tender. Stir into rice mixture.

Yield: 4 servings.

***Nutrition Facts:** 1-1/4 cups (prepared with reduced-fat butter) equals 247 calories, 7 g fat (4 g saturated fat), 54 mg cholesterol, 668 mg sodium, 29 g carbohydrate, 2 g fiber, 20 g protein. **Diabetic Exchanges:** 2 lean meat, 1-1/2 starch, 1 vegetable.

Easy Chicken Cacciatore

Rachel Greenawalt Keller
ROANOKE, VIRGINIA

We love this combination of chicken and tomatoes. For a tasty final touch, I like to top the chicken with a little grated Parmesan cheese or part-skim mozzarella.

Easy Chicken Cacciatore*

PREP: 10 min. ■ COOK: 25 min.

- 3 tablespoons all-purpose flour
- 1-1/2 teaspoons Italian seasoning
- 6 boneless skinless chicken breast halves (4 ounces *each*)
- 2 teaspoons olive oil, *divided*
- 1/2 cup chopped onion
- 1/2 pound sliced fresh mushrooms
- 1 cup sliced zucchini
- 2 cans (14-1/2 ounces *each*) Italian stewed tomatoes
- 1 can (6 ounces) tomato paste
- 1 teaspoon salt
- 8 ounces uncooked spaghetti

■ In a large resealable plastic bag, combine flour and Italian seasoning. Add chicken, a few at a time; seal and shake to coat. In a large nonstick skillet coated with cooking spray, cook chicken in 1 teaspoon oil for 4-5 minutes on each side or until browned. Remove the chicken from the skillet and keep warm.

■ In same skillet, cook onion in remaining oil for 2 minutes. Add mushrooms and zucchini; cook until onion is tender. Stir in the tomatoes, tomato paste and salt. Bring to a boil.

■ Return chicken to skillet. Reduce heat; cover and simmer 10-14 minutes or until a meat thermometer reads 160°. Cook pasta according to package directions; drain. Serve the chicken mixture with spaghetti.

Yield: 6 servings.

***Nutrition Facts:** 1 each equals 366 calories, 5 g fat (1 g saturated fat), 63 mg cholesterol, 931 mg sodium, 49 g carbohydrate, 6 g fiber, 32 g protein. **Diabetic Exchanges:** 3 lean meat, 3 vegetable, 2 starch, 1/2 fat.

Quick Skillet Chicken

LaVonne Elsbernd

FORTUNA, NORTH DAKOTA

Our teenagers' many activities keep me going right up until dinnertime. So I welcome foods like this that can be made in a hurry. Plus it's a great way to use leftover chicken.

PREP/TOTAL TIME: 30 min.

- 3 cups diced cooked chicken
- 1 egg, lightly beaten
- 1/2 cup crushed saltines
- 1/2 cup ground almonds
- 1/2 teaspoon salt
- 3 tablespoons butter
- 1 cup sliced celery
- 2 medium tomatoes, cut into thin wedges
- 1/2 medium green pepper, julienned
- 1/2 cup sugar
- 3 tablespoons cornstarch
- 1/2 cup water
- 1/2 cup lemon juice
- 1 can (6 ounces) pineapple juice
- 2 tablespoons soy sauce
- Hot cooked rice
- Chow mein noodles

■ In a large bowl, combine chicken and egg. Add the saltines, almonds and salt; toss well.

■ In a large skillet over medium heat, cook and stir chicken mixture in butter for 10 minutes, stirring occasionally. Add vegetables; saute for 2-3 minutes or until vegetables are crisp-tender. Remove from the heat and set aside.

■ In a large saucepan, combine sugar and cornstarch; stir in the water, juices and soy sauce until smooth. Bring to a boil over medium heat; cook for 1 minute or until thickened. Pour over chicken and vegetable mixture; heat through. Serve with rice and chow mein noodles.

Yield: 6 servings.

When lemons are in season or you have excess lemons on hand, juice them and freeze the juice in ice cube trays. Measure 1 or 2 tablespoons of juice into each compartment. When frozen, remove the cubes and place them in resealable freezer bags. This way you can have fresh lemon juice on hand whenever you need it.

Chicken Carrot Pilaf

Frances Musser

NEWMANSTOWN, PENNSYLVANIA

While this colorful stovetop supper is perfect for everyday family meals, it makes a lovely company dinner, too.

PREP: 20 min.
COOK: 20 min.

- 1 pound boneless skinless chicken breasts, cut into thin strips
- 1/4 cup butter, cubed
- 1-1/2 cups uncooked long grain rice
- 5 medium carrots, sliced
- 1 medium onion, chopped
- 1/2 cup sliced fresh mushrooms
- 1/4 cup chopped sweet red pepper
- 4 cups chicken broth
- 2 tablespoons minced fresh parsley

■ In a large skillet, brown chicken in butter until no longer pink. Remove and keep warm. In the same skillet, add the rice, carrots, onion, mushrooms and red pepper. Cook and stir until rice is browned and onion is tender.

■ Stir in broth. Place chicken over rice mixture. Bring to a boil. Reduce heat; cover and simmer for 20-25 minutes or until rice is tender. Stir in parsley. Let stand for 5 minutes before serving.

Yield: 6 servings.

Pork

136

135

134

Whether you need a quick family supper or something special for dinner guests, these one-dish meals sizzle with the bold flavor of pork. Choose from mouthwatering pork chops, irresistible plates of pasta, family-friendly sausage specialties and more. Each one is sure to please!

Pork Chops with Cranberry Sauce

Stephanie Homme
BATON ROUGE, LOUISIANA

Moist and tender pork chops are treated to a sweet, light cranberry glaze in this weeknight-friendly entree. It's one of my husband's favorites, quite suitable for company, too.

Pork Chops with Cranberry Sauce*

PREP/TOTAL TIME: 30 min.

- 6 boneless pork loin chops (4 ounces *each*)
- 1/4 teaspoon coarsely ground pepper
- 1/8 teaspoon salt
- 2 teaspoons cornstarch
- 1 cup cranberry-apple juice
- 2 teaspoons honey
- 3/4 cup dried cranberries
- 1 tablespoon minced fresh tarragon
- 1 tablespoon minced fresh parsley
- 3 cups hot cooked brown rice

- Sprinkle pork chops with pepper and salt. In a large nonstick skillet coated with cooking spray, cook chops over medium heat for 3-4 minutes on each side or until lightly browned. Remove and keep warm.
- In a small bowl, combine the cornstarch, juice and honey until smooth. Add to pan, stirring to loosen browned bits. Stir in the cranberries, tarragon and parsley. Bring to a boil; cook 2 minutes longer or until thickened and bubbly.
- Return pork chops to the pan. Reduce the heat; cover and simmer for 4-6 minutes or until a meat thermometer reads 160°. Serve with rice.

Yield: 6 servings.

***Nutrition Facts:** 1 pork chop with 3 tablespoons sauce and 1/2 cup rice equals 336 calories, 7 g fat (3 g saturated fat), 55 mg cholesterol, 92 mg sodium, 43 g carbohydrate, 3 g fiber, 24 g protein. **Diabetic Exchanges:** 3 lean meat, 2 starch, 1/2 fruit.

An herb with slender, green leaves that has a distinctive anise-like flavor, tarragon is widely used in French cooking. It pairs quite well with fish, chicken and vegetables, and it is most well-known for flavoring Bearnaise sauce and for making flavored vinegar.

Green Chili Burritos

Joy Margaret Gilbert
CORPUS CHRISTI, TEXAS

My husband introduced me to this recipe when we were engaged. It's become our family's favorite dish for birthday meals, informal get-togethers and everyday dinners.

Green Chili Burritos

PREP: 15 min. ■ COOK: 70 min.

- 1 pound boneless pork, cut into 3/4-inch cubes
- 1 tablespoon olive oil
- 1 can (10 ounces) diced tomatoes and green chilies, undrained
- 2 garlic cloves, minced
- 1 cup water
- 1 cup diced fresh tomato
- 1/2 cup chopped onion
- 1/4 cup chopped green pepper
- 1/2 teaspoon dried oregano
- 1/2 teaspoon salt
- 1/4 teaspoon pepper
- 1/4 teaspoon ground cumin
- 5 teaspoons cornstarch
- 2 tablespoons cold water
- 1 can (16 ounces) refried beans
- 10 flour tortillas (6 inches), warmed

■ In a skillet over medium heat, brown pork in oil; drain. Add the next 10 ingredients; bring to a boil. Reduce heat; cover and simmer for 1 hour or until pork is tender.

■ Combine cornstarch and water until smooth; gradually stir into pork mixture. Bring to a boil; cook and stir for 2 minutes or until thickened.

■ In a small saucepan, cook refried beans until heated through; spread evenly on tortillas. Spoon pork mixture down center of each tortilla. Fold the sides and ends over filling and roll up.

Yield: 4-6 servings.

To easily mince fresh garlic, crush a garlic clove with the blade of a chef's knife. Then peel away the skin and mince as directed.

Kim Gillis
HIGH FALLS, NEW YORK

Wine and fresh mushrooms lend elegance to this oh-so-simple meal. Use pre-sliced mushrooms and minced garlic rather than fresh to shave more time off of the preparation.

Elegant Pork Marsala

Elegant Pork Marsala*

PREP/TOTAL TIME: 30 min.

- 5 teaspoons cornstarch
- 2/3 cup reduced-sodium chicken broth
- 1/3 cup whole wheat flour
- 1/2 teaspoon pepper
- 6 boneless pork loin chops (4 ounces *each*)
- 1 tablespoon olive oil
- 2 cups sliced fresh mushrooms
- 1/3 cup chopped onion
- 2 turkey bacon strips, diced
- 1/4 teaspoon minced garlic
- 1 cup marsala wine *or* additional reduced-sodium chicken broth

■ In a small bowl, combine the cornstarch and broth until smooth; set aside.

■ Place the flour and pepper in a large resealable plastic bag. Add the pork, a few pieces at a time, and shake to coat. In a large nonstick skillet coated with cooking spray, cook the chops in oil for 4-5 minutes on each side or until a meat thermometer reads 160°. Remove and keep warm.

■ In the same skillet, saute the mushrooms, onion and bacon in drippings for 3 minutes or until bacon is crisp-tender. Add garlic; cook about 1 minute longer. Add wine, stirring to loosen browned bits from pan. Stir cornstarch mixture; add to pan. Bring to a boil; cook and stir for about 2 minutes or until slightly thickened. Serve with pork.

Yield: 6 servings.

***Nutrition Facts:** 1 pork chop with 1/3 cup sauce equals 232 calories, 10 g fat (3 g saturated fat), 60 mg cholesterol, 161 mg sodium, 7 g carbohydrate, 1 g fiber, 24 g protein. **Diabetic Exchanges:** 3 lean meat, 1/2 starch, 1/2 fat.

Snap Peas & Ham Alfredo

Taste of Home Test Kitchen

This fast-to-fix entree comes together in a jiffy with help from a frozen pasta and veggie medley. Using ham and fresh sugar snap peas really jazzes it up. Add some red pepper flakes to the creamy mixture for an extra kick.

PREP/TOTAL TIME: 20 min.

- 1 package (24 ounces) frozen pasta, broccoli and Alfredo sauce
- 2 cups fresh sugar snap peas
- 1/4 cup water
- 2 cups cubed fully cooked ham
- 1/2 teaspoon dried oregano
- 1/8 teaspoon pepper

■ Prepare pasta and sauce according to package directions. Meanwhile, place peas and water in a microwave-safe dish. Cover and microwave on high for 2-3 minutes or until crisp-tender; drain.

■ Stir the peas, ham, oregano and pepper into the pasta mixture; cook and stir for 3-4 minutes or until heated through.

Yield: 4 servings.

Creamy Dijon Pork Chops

Jan Briggs

GREENFIELD, WISCONSIN

These chops come together quickly. The combination of the white wine, cream and mustard makes a delicious sauce.

PREP: 10 min. ■ **COOK:** 35 min.

- 4 bone-in pork loin chops (1/4 to 1/2 inch thick)
- 1 tablespoon olive oil
- 1 medium onion, thinly sliced
- 1 teaspoon paprika
- 1/4 teaspoon salt
- 1/8 teaspoon pepper
- 1/2 cup dry white wine
- 1/2 cup heavy whipping cream
- 1 tablespoon Dijon mustard

■ In a large skillet, cook pork chops in oil over medium heat for 5 minutes on each side. Add onion; cook for 5 minutes or until onion is lightly browned and a meat thermometer reads 160°. Sprinkle with paprika, salt and pepper. Remove pork and onions; keep warm.

■ In the same skillet, cook wine over high heat until reduced to 1-2 tablespoons, stirring constantly. Reduce heat to low; add cream. Cook for 4-5 minutes or until thickened, stirring constantly. Remove from the heat; stir in mustard. Serve with pork and onions.

Yield: 4 servings.

Taco Mac

JoLynn Fribley

NOKOMIS, ILLINOIS

Pork sausage, taco seasoning and taco sauce add plenty of zip to easy macaroni and cheese. This zesty dish is just as yummy the next day. Just warm it up and top with shredded lettuce, diced tomatoes and cheese.

PREP/TOTAL TIME: 30 min.

- 1 package (24 ounces) shells and cheese dinner mix
- 1/2 pound bulk pork sausage, cooked and drained
- 1/3 cup taco sauce
- 1 tablespoon taco seasoning
- 4 cups shredded lettuce
- 2 medium tomatoes, chopped
- 1 cup (4 ounces) shredded cheddar cheese, optional

■ Prepare shells and cheese mix according to package directions. Stir in the sausage, taco sauce and seasoning. Garnish with lettuce, tomatoes and cheddar cheese if desired.

Yield: 6 servings.

Editor's Note: This recipe was tested with Kraft Velveeta Family-Size Shells & Cheese.

Pork Chop Supper

Ruth Andrewson

LEAVENWORTH, WASHINGTON

You can let this simmer while you do other chores. My mother often made it on laundry day.

PREP: 25 min.
COOK: 40 min.

- 1/2 cup all-purpose flour
- 6 bone-in pork loin chops (3/4 inch thick and 8 ounces *each*)
- 2 tablespoons olive oil
- 2 teaspoons dried thyme
- 2 teaspoons salt
- 1/4 teaspoon pepper
- 4 large potatoes (about 2-1/4 pounds)
- 5 medium carrots, sliced 1/4 inch thick
- 1 medium onion, cut into wedges
- 3 cups beef broth

■ Place flour in a large resealable plastic bag. Add chops, a few at a time, and shake to coat. In a large skillet; brown the chops in oil on both sides. Sprinkle with thyme, salt and pepper.

■ Peel potatoes and cut into 3/4-in. cubes. Add the potatoes, carrots and onion to the skillet. Pour broth over all; bring to a boil. Reduce heat; cover and simmer for 40-50 minutes or until a meat thermometer reads 160°.

Yield: 6 servings.

Ham & Sun-Dried Tomato Alfredo

Taste of Home Test Kitchen
This quick Alfredo favorite seems decadent and special. No one will guess it's prepared with just five ingredients! Sun-dried tomatoes add an elegant touch.

Ham & Sun-Dried Tomato Alfredo

PREP/TOTAL TIME: 20 min.

- 8 ounces uncooked linguine
- 1/4 cup chopped oil-packed sun-dried tomatoes
- 1 cup heavy whipping cream
- 1/2 cup grated Parmesan cheese
- 1 cup cubed fully cooked ham

■ Cook the linguine according to package directions.

■ Meanwhile, in a large skillet coated with cooking spray, saute the tomatoes for 1 minute. Reduce heat; stir in cream and cheese. Bring to a gentle boil over medium heat. Simmer, uncovered, for 5-7 minutes or until thickened.

■ Drain linguine; stir into sauce mixture. Add the ham and heat through.

Yield: 4 servings.

Polish Sausage And Veggies

Rita Kodet
CHULA VISTA, CALIFORNIA
Looking for something different to prepare with Polish sausage, I created this entree one afternoon. My family liked it so well that I've made it time and again since.

PREP/TOTAL TIME: 30 min.

- 4 cups cubed peeled potatoes (about 2-1/2 pounds)
- 1 pound smoked Polish sausage *or* smoked kielbasa, cut into 1/4-inch slices
- 1/2 cup chopped onion
- 1/2 cup julienned sweet yellow pepper
- 1/2 cup julienned sweet red pepper
- 1-1/2 teaspoons Cajun seasoning
- 1 tablespoon canola oil
- 1 tablespoon butter

■ In a large skillet over medium heat, cook the potatoes, sausage, onion, peppers and Cajun seasoning in oil and butter for 15-20 minutes or until potatoes are tender, stirring occasionally.

Yield: 6 servings.

Taste of Home Test Kitchen

These crispy pork medallions are treated to a refreshing strawberry sauce that's ideal for a summer meal.

Pork Medallions with Garlic-Strawberry Sauce

Pork Medallions with Garlic-Strawberry Sauce

PREP: 15 min. ■ COOK: 20 min.

- 1 pork tenderloin (1 pound), cut into 1/2-inch slices
- 1/4 teaspoon salt
- 1/4 teaspoon pepper
- 1/2 cup all-purpose flour
- 2 eggs, lightly beaten
- 2/3 cup seasoned bread crumbs
- 1/2 cup butter, *divided*
- 2 cups fresh strawberries
- 1 teaspoon minced garlic
- 1/4 cup hot water
- 1 teaspoon chicken bouillon granules
- Sliced fresh strawberries, optional

■ Flatten pork to 1/4-in. thickness; sprinkle with salt and pepper. Place the flour, eggs and bread crumbs in separate shallow bowls. Dip pork in the flour, eggs, then bread crumbs.

■ In a large skillet over medium heat, cook pork in 1/4 cup butter until juices run clear; remove and keep warm. Meanwhile, place strawberries in a food processor. Cover and process until pureed; set aside.

■ In the same skillet, saute garlic in remaining butter for 1 minute. Add the pureed strawberries, water and bouillon; heat through. Serve pork with sauce. Garnish with sliced strawberries if desired.

Yield: 4 servings.

Sausage Pierogi Skillet

Susan Held
COOKSVILLE, MARYLAND

I made this simple recipe one night with items I usually have on hand. It's convenient and tasty.

PREP/TOTAL TIME: 30 min.

- 1 package (16.9 ounces) frozen potato and onion pierogies
- 1 package (14 ounces) smoked turkey sausage, cut in half lengthwise and sliced into 1/2-inch pieces
- 2 tablespoons butter, *divided*
- 2 tablespoons canola oil, *divided*
- 1 medium onion, sliced
- 1 package (14 ounces) coleslaw mix
- 1/2 teaspoon garlic powder
- 1/4 teaspoon celery salt
- 1/4 teaspoon pepper
- 1 bay leaf

■ Cook pierogies according to package directions. Meanwhile, in a large skillet over medium heat, cook sausage in 1 tablespoon butter and 1 tablespoon oil; cook and stir for 2 minutes. Add the remaining ingredients; cook and stir for 1-2 minutes longer or until coleslaw is wilted. Remove from heat; keep warm.

■ In another large skillet, heat remaining butter and oil. Drain pierogies; add to skillet. Cook and stir until browned; add the sausage mixture and toss to coat. Discard bay leaf.

Yield: 5 servings.

Triple Pork with Rice

Margaret Pache
MESA, ARIZONA

Any meat lovers you know are bound to enjoy this special meal-in-one dish featuring pork, ham and bacon. The easy recipe makes for a satisfying dinner.

Triple Pork with Rice

PREP: 10 min. + marinating ■ COOK: 40 min.

- 1/2 pound lean boneless pork, cut into 1/2-inch cubes
- 4 ounces fully cooked ham, diced
- 4 bacon strips, diced
- 1 medium onion, sliced
- 1 medium sweet red pepper, julienned
- 1/2 cup lemon juice
- 1 to 2 jalapeno peppers, seeded and minced
- 1 teaspoon ground cumin
- 1/2 teaspoon caraway seeds
- 1/2 teaspoon salt
- 2 tablespoons canola oil
- 1-1/2 cups uncooked long grain rice
- 2 cans (14-1/2 ounces *each*) beef broth
- 1 can (14-1/2 ounces) diced tomatoes, undrained
- 1 can (8 ounces) kidney beans, rinsed and drained
- 1 medium ripe avocado, peeled and sliced, optional

■ In a large resealable plastic bag, combine the first 10 ingredients. Seal bag and turn to coat. Refrigerate for 1-2 hours.

■ Drain and discard marinade. In a large skillet, cook pork mixture in oil over medium heat for 5-6 minutes. Stir in rice; cook for 3 minutes. Add broth and tomatoes; bring to a boil. Reduce heat; cover and simmer for 20 minutes or until pork is tender.

■ Stir in beans; bring to a boil. Reduce heat; cover and simmer 5 minutes longer or until rice is tender. Garnish with avocado if desired.

Yield: 8 servings.

Editor's Note: We recommend wearing disposable gloves when cutting hot peppers. Avoid touching your face.

The easiest

avocados to peel and slice are those that are ripe yet firm. Cut the avocado in half lengthwise and twist the halves in opposite directions to separate. Scoop the seed out with a large spoon. To remove the peel, scoop out the flesh from each half with a large metal spoon, staying close to the peel. Slice, then dip slices in lemon juice to prevent them from turning brown.

Roasted Pepper Tortellini

Taste of Home Test Kitchen

This recipe calls for refrigerated tortellini, which cooks quickly, but you can also use dried tortellini. You'll love the bold flavors of this simple dish.

Roasted Pepper Tortellini

PREP/TOTAL TIME: 25 min.

- 1 package (20 ounces) refrigerated cheese tortellini
- 5 Italian sausage links
- 2 tablespoons olive oil
- 2 jars (7 ounces *each*) roasted sweet red peppers, drained
- 1 can (15 ounces) pizza sauce
- 1 cup (4 ounces) shredded part-skim mozzarella cheese
- 2 tablespoons shredded Parmesan cheese

■ Cook tortellini according to package directions. Meanwhile, in a large skillet, cook sausage in oil over medium heat until no longer pink; drain. Cut into 1/4-in. slices and return to skillet.

■ Place the red peppers in a blender; cover and process until smooth. Drain tortellini. Add the tortellini, pureed peppers and pizza sauce to the skillet; stir to combine. Cook for 5 minutes or until heated through. Sprinkle with cheeses; cover and heat until cheese is melted.

Yield: 6 servings.

Campfire Hash

Janet Danilow

WINKLEMAN, ARIZONA

In our area, we're able to camp almost all year-round. My family invented this recipe using ingredients we love so we could enjoy them on the campfire. This hearty meal tastes so good after a full day of outdoor activities.

PREP: 15 min.
COOK: 40 min.

- 1 large onion, chopped
- 2 tablespoons canola oil
- 2 garlic cloves, minced
- 4 large potatoes, peeled and cubed (about 2 pounds)
- 1 pound smoked kielbasa *or* Polish sausage, halved and sliced
- 1 can (4 ounces) chopped green chilies
- 1 can (15-1/4 ounces) whole kernel corn, drained

■ In a large ovenproof skillet, over medium heat, cook and stir onion in oil until tender. Add garlic; cook 1 minute longer. Add potatoes. Cook, uncovered, for 20 minutes, stirring occasionally.

■ Add kielbasa; cook and stir until potatoes are tender and well browned, about 10 minutes longer. Stir in chilies and corn; heat through.

Yield: 6 servings.

Taste of Home Test Kitchen

Spinach-stuffed chops with walnuts and lemon gravy make for a surprising twist on a down-home meal. It might feel elegant, but it really couldn't be any easier.

Spinach Pork Chops with Lemon Gravy

Spinach Pork Chops With Lemon Gravy

PREP: 20 min. ■ COOK: 20 min.

- 1/2 cup chopped onion
- 1 tablespoon butter
- 1 package (6 ounces) fresh baby spinach
- 3 teaspoons minced garlic
- 1/4 cup chopped walnuts, *divided*
- 4 boneless pork loin chops (1 inch thick and 6 ounces *each*)
- 1/4 teaspoon pepper
- 1 tablespoon olive oil
- 2 tablespoons all-purpose flour
- 1/4 teaspoon salt
- 3/4 cup chicken broth
- 1 tablespoon lemon juice

■ In a large skillet, saute onion in butter until tender. Add the spinach, garlic and 2 tablespoons walnuts; cook and stir just until spinach is wilted. Remove from the heat; set aside.

■ Cut a deep slit in each pork chop, forming a pocket. Stuff 1/4 cup spinach mixture into each chop; secure with toothpicks. Sprinkle with pepper. In the same skillet, cook chops in oil for 8-10 minutes on each side until a meat thermometer reads 160°. Remove and keep warm.

■ Stir flour and salt into the skillet until blended. Gradually stir in broth and lemon juice, stirring to loosen browned bits from pan. Bring to a boil; cook and stir for 2 minutes or until thickened. Serve over pork chops; sprinkle with remaining walnuts.

Yield: 4 servings.

Sweet-and-Sour Pork

Eleanor Dunbar

PEORIA, ILLINOIS

I stir up a homemade sweet-and-sour sauce for this colorful combination. Serve it with rice, chow mein noodles or both!

PREP: 15 min.
COOK: 20 min.

- 2/3 cup packed brown sugar
- 2/3 cup cider vinegar
- 2/3 cup ketchup
- 2 teaspoons soy sauce
- 1 pound boneless pork loin, cut into 1-inch cubes
- 1 tablespoon canola oil
- 1 medium onion, cut into chunks
- 2 medium carrots, sliced
- 1 medium green pepper, cut into 1-inch pieces
- 1/2 teaspoon minced garlic
- 1/4 teaspoon ground ginger
- 1 can (8 ounces) pineapple chunks, drained

Hot cooked rice, optional

■ Combine brown sugar, vinegar, ketchup, and soy sauce. Pour half into a large resealable plastic bag; add pork. Seal bag and turn to coat; refrigerate 30 minutes. Set remaining marinade aside.

■ Drain and discard marinade from pork. In a large skillet, cook pork in oil for 3 minutes. Add vegetables, garlic and ginger; saute until pork is no longer pink. Add reserved marinade. Bring to a boil; cook 1 minute or until heated through. Stir in pineapple. Serve with rice if desired.

Yield: 4 servings.

Dawn Goodison
ROCHESTER, NEW YORK

I enjoy this one-pan skillet supper because it's quick, and the cleanup is easy. But best of all, my family enjoys flavorful and nutritious dinners.

Pork 'n' Penne Skillet

Pork 'n' Penne Skillet

PREP/TOTAL TIME: 30 min.

- 2 tablespoons all-purpose flour
- 1 teaspoon chili powder
- 3/4 teaspoon salt
- 3/4 teaspoon pepper
- 1 pound boneless pork loin chops, cut into strips
- 2 cups sliced fresh mushrooms
- 1 cup chopped onion
- 1 cup chopped sweet red pepper
- 1 teaspoon dried oregano
- 1 tablespoon canola oil
- 1 tablespoon butter
- 1 teaspoon minced garlic
- 3 cups 2% milk
- 1 can (15 ounces) tomato sauce
- 2 cups uncooked penne

■ In a large resealable plastic bag, combine the flour, chili powder, salt and pepper. Add pork, a few pieces at a time, and shake to coat.

■ In a large skillet, cook the pork, mushrooms, onion, red pepper and oregano in oil and butter over medium heat for 4-6 minutes or until pork is browned. Add garlic; cook 1 minute longer.

■ Add the milk, tomato sauce and pasta. Bring to a boil. Reduce heat; simmer, uncovered, for 15-20 minutes or until meat is tender.

Yield: 8 servings.

Chili Spaghetti With Hot Dogs

Karen Tausend
BRIDGEPORT, MICHIGAN

I've been making this recipe for 35 years. It's one of my husband's favorite dishes. Low-fat franks and reduced-fat cheese can be used and it still tastes great.

PREP/TOTAL TIME: 30 min.

- 8 ounces uncooked spaghetti
- 1 package (1 pound) hot dogs, halved lengthwise and sliced
- 1/2 cup chopped onion
- 1/2 cup chopped celery
- 2 tablespoons canola oil
- 1 can (15 ounces) tomato sauce
- 1 tablespoon prepared mustard
- 1 teaspoon chili powder
- 1/2 teaspoon Worcestershire sauce
- 1/4 teaspoon salt
- 1/4 teaspoon pepper
- 1 cup (4 ounces) shredded cheddar cheese

■ Cook spaghetti according to package directions. Meanwhile, in a large skillet, saute the hot dogs, onion and celery in oil until tender. Stir in the tomato sauce, mustard, chili powder, Worcestershire sauce, salt and pepper. Cook, uncovered, for 5-8 minutes or until heated through, stirring occasionally.

■ Drain spaghetti; toss with hot dog mixture. Sprinkle with cheese.

Yield: 6 servings.

Saucy Ham and Rice

Janice Christofferson
EAGLE RIVER, WISCONSIN

This recipe is a tasty takeoff on beef Stroganoff. It is my husband's favorite way to eat leftover ham, so I prepare it for him at least once a month.

PREP/TOTAL TIME: 20 min.

- 1-1/2 pounds fully cooked ham, julienned
- 1 tablespoon butter
- 1 cup chopped celery
- 1 cup julienned green pepper
- 1 small onion, cut into thin wedges
- 1 can (10-3/4 ounces) condensed cream of mushroom soup, undiluted
- 2 tablespoons prepared mustard
- 3/4 teaspoon dill weed
- 1/8 teaspoon celery salt
- 1 cup (8 ounces) sour cream
- Hot cooked rice

■ In a large skillet, saute ham in butter for 2 minutes. Add the celery, green pepper and onion; saute until tender.

■ Stir in the soup, mustard, dill and celery salt; stir until smooth. Stir in sour cream; heat through (do not boil). Serve with rice.

Yield: 4-6 servings.

Kielbasa Tortellini Alfredo

Taste of Home Test Kitchen

We combined just six ingredients to create this hearty and colorful main dish. The stovetop supper is easy to put together and sure to please the whole family.

PREP/TOTAL TIME: 20 min.

- 1 package (9 ounces) refrigerated cheese *or* spinach tortellini
- 1/2 pound smoked kielbasa *or* Polish sausage, sliced
- 1 medium sweet red pepper, julienned
- 2 teaspoons canola oil
- 1 jar (16 ounces) Alfredo sauce
- 1 cup chopped tomato

■ Cook tortellini according to package directions. Meanwhile, in a large skillet, saute kielbasa and red pepper in oil for 3 minutes or until the pepper is crisp-tender.

■ Drain tortellini. Stir tortellini and Alfredo sauce into skillet; heat through. Garnish with tomato.

Yield: 4 servings.

Fire-Roasted Ziti with Sausage

Jean Komlos
PLYMOUTH, MICHIGAN

Escape from the ordinary! Smoked sausage and fire-roasted spaghetti sauce add nice flavor to this pasta dish. Look for fire-roasted sauce on the shelf with traditional spaghetti sauces.

PREP/TOTAL TIME: 30 min.

- 1 package (8 ounces) ziti *or* small tube pasta
- 1 can (28 ounces) Italian diced tomatoes, undrained
- 1 jar (26 ounces) fire-roasted tomato and garlic spaghetti sauce
- 1 package (16 ounces) smoked sausage, sliced
- 2 cups (8 ounces) shredded part-skim mozzarella cheese, *divided*
- 1 cup (8 ounces) 4% cottage cheese

■ In a large saucepan, cook pasta according to package directions; drain and return to the pan. Stir in the tomatoes, spaghetti sauce and sausage; heat through.

■ Stir in 1 cup mozzarella cheese and cottage cheese. Top with remaining mozzarella cheese. Cover and heat over medium heat for 2-5 minutes or until mozzarella cheese is melted.

Yield: 8 servings.

Nicole Werner
CLEVELAND, OHIO
This hearty pork-and-noodle mainstay has plenty of family-pleasing flavor. Just serve a simple vegetable side dish to round out the meal.

Golden Pork 'n' Noodles

Golden Pork 'n' Noodles

PREP/TOTAL TIME: 30 min.

- 4 cups uncooked egg noodles
- 1 pound ground pork
- 1/2 pound sliced fresh mushrooms
- 1 cup chopped green pepper
- 1/2 cup chopped onion
- 2 tablespoons canola oil
- 1 can (10-3/4 ounces) condensed golden mushroom soup, undiluted
- 1/2 cup milk
- 1 package (3 ounces) cream cheese, cubed
- 1 jar (4 ounces) sliced pimientos, drained
- 1-1/2 teaspoons dried marjoram
- 3/4 teaspoon salt
- 1/2 teaspoon pepper

■ Cook noodles according to package directions. Meanwhile, in a large skillet, cook the pork over medium heat until no longer pink. Drain; set aside.

■ In the same skillet, saute the mushrooms, green pepper and onion in oil until crisp-tender. Stir in the soup, milk, cream cheese, pimientos, marjoram, salt and pepper. Bring to a boil; cook and stir for 2 minutes or until cheese is melted.

■ Drain noodles; stir into skillet. Add pork; heat through.

Yield: 6 servings.

Mushroom Prosciutto Pasta

Taste of Home Test Kitchen
If prosciutto is not available at your deli counter, you can use diced ham instead.

PREP/TOTAL TIME: 30 min.

- 4 cups uncooked penne pasta
- 1/2 pound sliced fresh mushrooms
- 1/4 cup chopped onion
- 2 tablespoons butter
- 10 thin slices prosciutto, chopped
- 2 teaspoons cornstarch
- 2 cups heavy whipping cream
- 1/2 cup minced fresh parsley
- 1/4 teaspoon pepper
- Shredded Parmesan cheese, optional

■ Cook pasta according to package directions. Meanwhile, in a large skillet, saute mushrooms and onion in butter until tender. Add prosciutto; saute for 3 minutes.

■ In a small bowl, combine cornstarch and cream until smooth; stir into the skillet. Add parsley and pepper. Bring to a boil; cook and stir for 2 minutes or until thickened. Drain pasta; add to the skillet and stir to coat. Sprinkle with cheese if desired.

Yield: 6 servings.

Pork and Sweet Potatoes

Mary Relyea
CANASTOTA, NEW YORK

Sweet potatoes, sliced apple and moist pork tenderloin blend perfectly in this simple meal-in-one. Dried cranberries lend a burst of color, making the entree look just as good as it tastes!

Pork and Sweet Potatoes*

PREP/TOTAL TIME: 30 min.

- 1 pork tenderloin (1 pound), cut into 12 slices
- 1/2 cup all-purpose flour
- 1/2 teaspoon salt
- 1/4 teaspoon pepper
- 1 tablespoon canola oil
- 1 can (14-1/2 ounces) reduced-sodium chicken broth
- 2 medium sweet potatoes, peeled and cubed
- 1/2 cup dried cranberries
- 1 tablespoon Dijon mustard
- 1 medium apple, sliced
- 4 green onions, chopped

- Flatten pork to 1/4-in. thickness. In a large resealable plastic bag, combine the flour, salt and pepper; add pork, a few pieces at a time, and shake to coat.
- In a large nonstick skillet coated with cooking spray, brown pork in oil in batches. Remove and keep warm. Add the broth, sweet potatoes and cranberries to the skillet. Bring to a boil. Reduce heat; cover and simmer for 4-6 minutes or until potatoes are crisp-tender. Stir in mustard.
- Return pork to the pan; add apple and onions. Cover and simmer for 4-6 minutes or until meat juices run clear.

Yield: 4 servings.

***Nutrition Facts:** 3 slices pork with 1 cup potato mixture equals 352 calories, 8 g fat (2 g saturated fat), 63 mg cholesterol, 496 mg sodium, 45 g carbohydrate, 5 g fiber, 27 g protein. **Diabetic Exchanges:** 3 starch, 3 lean meat, 1/2 fat.

To core an apple, use an apple corer. Push the apple corer down into the center of a washed apple. Twist and remove the center seeds and membranes. You can also easily core an apple by cutting it into quarters, then removing the core from each quarter with a sharp knife.

Fish & Seafood

151

154

145

Creating a meal with fish or seafood means not having to spend much time in the kitchen. That's because dinners cook up fast when shrimp, fish or scallops are on the menu. The stovetop entrees in this chapter are a delightful change of pace from everyday meat-and-potatoes fare, so serve one up tonight!

Spanish-Style Paella

Taste of Home Test Kitchen
If you enjoy cooking ethnic foods, this hearty rice dish will be a favorite. It's brimming with generous chunks of sausage, shrimp and veggies.

Spanish-Style Paella

PREP: 10 min. ■ COOK: 35 min.

- 1/2 pound bulk Italian sausage
- 1/2 pound boneless skinless chicken breasts, cubed
- 1 tablespoon olive oil
- 1 garlic clove, minced
- 1 cup uncooked long grain rice
- 1 cup chopped onion
- 1-1/2 cups chicken broth
- 1 can (14-1/2 ounces) stewed tomatoes, undrained
- 1/2 teaspoon paprika
- 1/4 teaspoon ground cayenne pepper
- 1/4 teaspoon salt
- 10 strands saffron, crushed *or* 1/8 teaspoon ground saffron
- 1/2 pound uncooked medium shrimp, peeled and deveined
- 1/2 cup sweet red pepper strips
- 1/2 cup green pepper strips
- 1/2 cup frozen peas

■ In a large saucepan over medium-high heat, cook sausage and chicken in oil for 5 minutes or until sausage is lightly browned and chicken is no longer pink, stirring frequently. Add the garlic; cook 1 minute longer. Drain if necessary.

■ Stir in the rice and onion. Cook until onion is tender and rice is lightly browned, stirring frequently. Add broth, tomatoes, paprika, cayenne, salt and saffron. Bring to a boil. Reduce heat to low; cover and cook for about 10 minutes.

■ Stir in the shrimp, peppers and peas. Cover and cook 10 minutes longer or until the rice is tender, shrimp turn pink and liquid is absorbed.

Yield: 6-8 servings.

Saffron is a rare herb with a pungent flavor made from the stigmata of the saffron flower. It is harvested by hand, and it takes at least 4,000 stigmatas to produce 1 ounce. Don't have any saffron on hand? Lots of cooks use ground turmeric instead to add a similar flavor and the same bright yellow hue.

Shrimp 'n' Spinach Risotto

Jennifer Neilsen
WILLIAMSTON, NORTH CAROLINA

I enjoy concocting new, healthy recipes, and spinach is one of the few vegetables that my husband will eat. This creamy risotto makes a great meal-in-one or hearty side dish.

Shrimp 'n' Spinach Risotto*

PREP: 20 min. ■ **COOK:** 35 min.

- 3-1/4 to 3-3/4 cups reduced-sodium chicken broth
- 1-1/2 cups chopped fresh mushrooms
- 1 small onion, chopped
- 1 tablespoon butter
- 3 garlic cloves, minced
- 1 cup uncooked arborio rice
- 1 package (6 ounces) fresh baby spinach, coarsely chopped
- 1 pound cooked medium shrimp, peeled and deveined
- 1/2 cup shredded Parmesan cheese
- 1/4 teaspoon pepper

■ In a small saucepan, heat broth and keep warm. In a large nonstick skillet, saute mushrooms and onion in butter until tender, about 3 minutes. Add garlic; cook 1 minute longer. Add rice; cook and stir for 2-3 minutes. Carefully stir in 1 cup heated broth. Cook and stir until all of the liquid is absorbed.

■ Add remaining broth, 1/2 cup at a time, stirring constantly. Allow the liquid to absorb between additions. Cook just until risotto is creamy and rice is almost tender, about 20 minutes.

■ Add the spinach, shrimp, cheese and pepper; cook and stir until spinach is wilted and shrimp are heated through. Serve immediately.

Yield: 4 servings.

***Nutrition Facts:** 1-1/4 cups equals 405 calories, 8 g fat (4 g saturated fat), 187 mg cholesterol, 906 mg sodium, 47 g carbohydrate, 2 g fiber, 35 g protein. **Diabetic Exchanges:** 4 lean meat, 2-1/2 starch, 1 vegetable, 1 fat.

Arborio rice is a medium grain rice used for making risottos. In risottos, this rice has a creamy texture with a chewy center.

Bill Saul
MACON, MISSISSIPPI

My family owns a catfish processing plant, so we eat it on a regular basis. This colorful, zippy main dish is a great favorite of ours.

Catfish Jambalaya

Catfish Jambalaya*

PREP/TOTAL TIME: 30 min.

- 2 cups chopped onion
- 1/2 cup chopped celery
- 1/2 cup chopped green pepper
- 1/4 cup butter, cubed
- 2 garlic cloves, minced
- 1 can (10 ounces) diced tomatoes and green chilies, undrained
- 1 cup sliced fresh mushrooms
- 1/4 teaspoon cayenne pepper
- 1/2 teaspoon salt
- 1 pound catfish fillets, cubed
- Hot cooked rice, optional
- Sliced green onions, optional

■ In a large saucepan, saute onion, celery and green pepper in butter until tender, about 10 minutes. Add garlic; cook 1 minute longer. Add tomatoes, mushrooms, cayenne and salt; bring to a boil. Add catfish.

■ Reduce heat; cover and simmer until fish flakes easily with a fork, about 10 minutes. Serve with hot rice and garnish with sliced green onions if desired.

Yield: 4 servings.

***Nutrition Facts:** 1 serving (calculated without rice and green onions; prepared with non-stick cooking spray instead of butter and without salt) equals 161 calories, 4 g fat (0 saturated fat), 66 mg cholesterol, 395 mg sodium, 12 g carbohydrate, 0 fiber, 21 g protein. **Diabetic Exchanges:** 3 lean meat, 2 vegetable.

Citrus Garlic Shrimp

Diane Jackson
LAS VEGAS, NEVADA

Garlic is paired with sunny citrus in my special shrimp and linguine combination. It's pretty enough for company.

PREP/TOTAL TIME: 25 min.

- 1 package (16 ounces) linguine
- 1/2 cup olive oil
- 1/2 cup orange juice
- 1/3 cup lemon juice
- 3 to 4 garlic cloves, minced
- 5 teaspoons grated lemon peel
- 4 teaspoons grated orange peel
- 1 teaspoon salt
- 1/4 teaspoon pepper
- 1 pound uncooked medium shrimp, peeled and deveined
- Shredded Parmesan cheese and minced fresh parsley, optional

■ Cook linguine according to package directions. Meanwhile, in a blender, combine the next eight ingredients; cover and process until blended. Pour into a large skillet; bring to boil. Reduce heat, stir in the shrimp; simmer, uncovered for 3-4 minutes or until shrimp turn pink.

■ Drain linguine; toss with shrimp mixture. Sprinkle with cheese and parsley if desired.

Yield: 6 servings.

Scallops with Sun-Dried Tomatoes*

Jennifer Warzynak
ERIE, PENNSYLVANIA

A half-hour is all you need for this delightful stir-fry. I combine scallops with broccoli, pasta and sun-dried tomatoes for the main course, and a hint of lime juice makes it a natural addition to summer menus. It's a great, healthy way to serve seafood.

PREP/TOTAL TIME: 30 min.

- 6 ounces uncooked penne pasta
- 1/4 cup chopped sun-dried tomatoes (not packed in oil)
- 3/4 cup hot water
- 4 cups fresh broccoli florets
- 1/2 cup reduced-sodium chicken broth
- 3 garlic cloves, minced
- 2 tablespoons olive oil
- 1 pound bay scallops
- 1 teaspoon lime juice
- 1 teaspoon minced fresh basil
- 1/4 teaspoon salt
- 1/4 cup shredded Parmesan cheese

■ Cook pasta according to package directions. Meanwhile, in a small bowl, combine sun-dried tomatoes and hot water. Let stand for 5 minutes; drain and set aside.

■ Place the broccoli and broth in a microwave-safe bowl. Cover and microwave on high for 2-4 minutes or until broccoli is crisp-tender; set aside.

■ In a large nonstick skillet coated with cooking spray, cook garlic in oil over medium heat for 1 minute. Add scallops; cook for 2 minutes. Stir in lime juice, basil, salt, and reserved tomatoes and broccoli mixture; cook 2-3 minutes longer or until scallops are firm and opaque.

■ Drain the pasta; stir into scallop mixture and heat through. Sprinkle with cheese.

Yield: 4 servings.

***Nutrition Facts:** 2 cups equals 367 calories, 10 g fat (2 g saturated fat), 41 mg cholesterol, 585 mg sodium, 40 g carbohydrate, 4 g fiber, 30 g protein. **Diabetic Exchanges:** 3 lean meat, 2 starch, 1-1/2 fat, 1 vegetable.

Italian Shrimp And Pasta

PREP: 15 min.
COOK: 30 min.

- 1 garlic clove, minced
- 2 tablespoons olive oil
- 2 cans (14-1/2 ounces *each*) diced tomatoes, undrained
- 1/2 cup chicken broth
- 1/2 teaspoon dried basil
- 1/2 teaspoon dried oregano
- 1/4 teaspoon pepper
- 1 pound uncooked medium shrimp, peeled and deveined
- 6 ounces uncooked angel hair pasta

■ In a large skillet, saute garlic in oil for 1 minute or until crisp-tender. Add the tomatoes, broth, basil, oregano and pepper. Bring to a boil over medium heat. Reduce heat; simmer, uncovered, for 15 minutes.

■ Meanwhile, cook the pasta according to package directions. Add the shrimp to the tomato mixture; cook for 5-6 minutes or until shrimp turn pink. Drain pasta; toss with shrimp mixture.

Yield: 4 servings.

Frank Fader
PAYSON, ARIZONA

We like pasta with Italian tomato sauces, and this recipe is one we make often. It's heavy on the shrimp and light on the pasta, and that's the way we like it...we can remember when shrimp was unheard of in our budget, so I guess we're making up for it now!

Becky Armstrong
DECATUR, ALABAMA

This dish is a pleasure to serve because it's attractive as well as tasty. Crawfish speaks to my Southern heritage, and this etouffee is a tradition.

Crawfish Etouffee

Crawfish Etouffee

PREP: 5 min. ■ COOK: 1-1/2 hours

- 1/3 cup all-purpose flour
- 1/2 cup canola oil
- 1 large green pepper, chopped
- 1 large onion, chopped
- 1 cup chopped celery
- 1 can (15 ounces) tomato sauce
- 1 cup water
- 1 tablespoon Worcestershire sauce
- 1 teaspoon garlic powder
- 1 teaspoon paprika
- 1 teaspoon lemon juice
- 3/4 teaspoon Creole seasoning
- 2 pounds frozen cooked crawfish tails, thawed
- Hot cooked rice

■ In a Dutch oven, whisk flour and oil until smooth. Cook over medium-high heat for 5 minutes, whisking constantly. Reduce heat to medium; cook and stir 10 minutes longer or until mixture is reddish-brown.

■ Add the green pepper, onion and celery; cook and stir for 5 minutes. Add the tomato sauce, water, Worcestershire sauce, garlic powder, paprika, lemon juice and Creole seasoning. Bring to a boil. Reduce heat; cover and simmer for 45 minutes.

■ Stir in crawfish and heat through. Serve with rice.

Yield: 8 servings.

Editor's Note: The following spices may be substituted for 1 teaspoon Creole seasoning: 1/4 teaspoon each salt, garlic powder and paprika; and a pinch each of dried thyme, ground cumin and cayenne pepper.

Creole Tuna

Betty Bernat
LITTLETON, NEW HAMPSHIRE

Here's a speedy recipe that's been in my family for as long as I can remember. Because it relies on pantry staples, it's easy to make when you can't decide what to fix for dinner.

PREP/TOTAL TIME: 15 min.

- 1/4 cup chopped green pepper
- 2 tablespoons butter
- 2 tablespoons all-purpose flour
- 1/2 teaspoon sugar
- 1/2 teaspoon salt
- 1/8 teaspoon pepper
- 1/3 cup milk
- 1 can (14-1/2 ounces) stewed tomatoes
- 1 can (6 ounces) tuna, drained and flaked
- 1 teaspoon Creole seasoning
- Hot cooked rice, optional

■ In a large saucepan, saute green pepper in butter until tender. Stir in the flour, sugar, salt and pepper until blended. Gradually add milk, stirring constantly. Stir in tomatoes. Bring to a boil; cook and stir for 2 minutes. Add tuna and Creole seasoning; heat through. Serve with rice if desired.

Yield: 4 servings.

Shrimp and Olive Rigatoni

Elaine Sweet
DALLAS, TEXAS

This pasta dish is one of my family's favorite recipes. It's full of yummy ingredients. I hope your family enjoys the easy main course as much as we do.

Shrimp and Olive Rigatoni*

PREP: 20 min. ■ COOK: 20 min.

- 12 ounces uncooked rigatoni *or* large tube pasta
- 3 garlic cloves, minced
- 2 green onions, chopped
- 1 tablespoon olive oil
- 1 pound uncooked medium shrimp, peeled and deveined
- 3 tablespoons white wine *or* reduced-sodium chicken broth
- 1/4 cup minced fresh basil
- 2 tablespoons minced fresh parsley
- 1 teaspoon grated lemon peel
- 1/2 teaspoon salt
- 1/4 teaspoon coarsely ground pepper
- 1/4 teaspoon crushed red pepper flakes
- 1 can (2-1/4 ounces) sliced ripe olives, drained
- 1/2 cup sliced pimiento-stuffed olives
- 2 anchovy fillets, rinsed, drained and chopped
- 5 plum tomatoes, seeded and chopped
- 1 jar (2 ounces) sliced pimientos, drained
- 1/3 cup shredded Parmesan cheese
- Additional fresh basil, optional

■ Cook pasta according to package directions. Meanwhile, in a large nonstick skillet coated with cooking spray, saute garlic and onions in oil for 1 minute. Add shrimp and wine; cook for 3-5 minutes or until shrimp turn pink.

■ Remove from the heat; stir in the basil, parsley, lemon peel, salt, pepper and red pepper flakes. Gently add the olives and anchovies.

■ Drain the pasta; stir into skillet. Add tomatoes and pimientos; return to the heat and heat through. Sprinkle with cheese. Garnish with basil leaves if desired.

Yield: 6 servings.

***Nutrition Facts:** 1-2/3 cups equals 359 calories, 9 g fat (2 g saturated fat), 116 mg cholesterol, 793 mg sodium, 47 g carbohydrate, 3 g fiber, 23 g protein. **Diabetic Exchanges:** 3 starch, 2 lean meat, 1-1/2 fat.

Shrimp are available fresh or frozen (raw or cooked, peeled or in the shell.) Shrimp in the shell (fresh or frozen) are available in different varieties and sizes (medium, large, extra large, jumbo). Uncooked shrimp will have shells that range in color from gray or brown to pink or red. Fresh shrimp should have a firm texture with a mild odor.

Ruth Simon
BUFFALO, NEW YORK

Enjoy the comforting flavor of tuna noodle casserole in minutes with this version that starts with a convenient jar of Alfredo sauce. It's easy to make with other on-hand ingredients, such as frozen peas and canned tuna.

Tuna Noodle Skillet

PREP/TOTAL TIME: 30 min.

- 2 jars (16 ounces *each*) Alfredo sauce
- 1 can (14-1/2 ounces) chicken broth
- 1 package (16 ounces) wide egg noodles
- 1 package (10 ounces) frozen peas
- 1/4 teaspoon pepper
- 1 can (12 ounces) solid white water-packed tuna, drained and flaked

■ In a large skillet over medium heat, bring Alfredo sauce and broth to a boil. Add noodles; cover and cook for 7-8 minutes.

■ Reduce the heat; stir in peas and pepper. Cover and cook 4 minutes longer or until noodles are tender. Stir in tuna; heat through.

Yield: 6 servings.

Peppery Shrimp and Rice

Cynthia Schaible Boyll
LOVELAND, OHIO

This recipe satisfies my husband's yearning for shrimp over rice, which he enjoyed while growing up in Louisiana.

PREP: 10 min. ■ COOK: 30 min.

- 2 celery ribs, finely chopped
- 1 medium onion, chopped
- 1 tablespoon olive oil
- 1 garlic clove, minced
- 1 small green pepper, chopped
- 1 small sweet red pepper, chopped
- 1 can (15 ounces) tomato sauce
- 1/2 cup sherry *or* chicken broth
- 1 tablespoon chili sauce
- 2 teaspoons sugar
- 2 teaspoons dried basil
- 1 teaspoon dried oregano
- 1/2 teaspoon crushed red pepper flakes, optional
- 3/4 pound cooked medium shrimp, peeled and deveined
- 4 cups hot cooked rice

■ In a large nonstick skillet, saute celery and onion in oil for 3 minutes. Add garlic; cook 1 minute. Add peppers; cook 3 minutes longer.

■ Stir in the tomato sauce, sherry, chili sauce, sugar, basil, oregano and pepper flakes if desired. Bring to a boil. Reduce heat; simmer, uncovered, for 15-20 minutes or until vegetables are tender. Add shrimp; heat through. Serve with rice.

Yield: 4 servings.

Garlic Salmon Linguine

Theresa Hagan
GLENDALE, ARIZONA

A delightful garlic-seasoned main dish, my recipe calls for handy pantry ingredients, including pasta and canned salmon. I serve it with asparagus, rolls and fruit.

PREP/TOTAL TIME: 20 min.

- 1 package (16 ounces) linguine
- 3 garlic cloves, minced
- 1/3 cup olive oil
- 1 can (14-3/4 ounces) salmon, drained, bones and skin removed
- 3/4 cup chicken broth
- 1/4 cup minced fresh parsley
- 1/2 teaspoon salt
- 1/8 teaspoon cayenne pepper

■ Cook the linguine according to package directions. Meanwhile, in a large skillet, saute garlic in oil for 1 minute or until crisp-tender. Stir in the salmon, broth, parsley, salt and cayenne. Cook until heated through. Drain the linguine; add to salmon mixture and toss to coat.

Yield: 6 servings.

Robert Ulis
ALEXANDRIA, VIRGINIA
I love to cook and bake, and this is the first recipe I came up with on my own. It blends seafood, angel hair pasta, which I love, and an awesome cheesy white sauce.

Company Seafood Pasta

Company Seafood Pasta

PREP/TOTAL TIME: 30 min.

- 1 package (16 ounces) angel hair pasta
- 2 tablespoons all-purpose flour
- 2 cups (16 ounces) sour cream
- 3 cups (12 ounces) shredded Monterey Jack cheese
- 2 tablespoons butter
- 1 package (8 ounces) imitation flaked crabmeat
- 1/8 teaspoon pepper
- 1 pound fresh *or* frozen bay scallops, thawed and drained
- 1 pound cooked medium shrimp, peeled and deveined
- Minced fresh parsley, optional

■ Cook pasta according to package directions. Meanwhile, in a large saucepan, whisk flour and sour cream until smooth. Add cheese and butter; cook and stir over low heat until thickened. Remove from the heat; stir in crab and pepper. Set aside and keep warm.

■ Place the scallops in a large saucepan with 1/2 in. of water. Cover and cook over medium heat for 5-7 minutes or just until opaque.

■ Drain scallops; add to crab mixture. Add shrimp; cook and stir over low heat until shrimp turn pink. Drain pasta; toss with sauce. Sprinkle with parsley if desired.

Yield: 8 servings.

Sole Amandine

Marshall Simon
GRAND RAPIDS, MICHIGAN
It may have started off as an experiment, but the result was a great hit! The almonds add so much flavor to the fish in the following recipe.

PREP/TOTAL TIME: 20 min.

- 5 tablespoons butter, *divided*
- 1 tablespoon olive oil
- 1 pound sole *or* whitefish fillets
- All-purpose flour
- 1 egg, lightly beaten
- 1/4 cup slivered almonds, toasted
- 2 tablespoons lemon juice
- 1/4 cup dry white wine, optional
- Lemon wedges

■ In a large skillet, heat 4 tablespoons butter and oil over medium heat. Dip fillets in flour, then in egg. Place in skillet; cook until lightly browned and fish flakes easily with a fork, about 2 minutes on each side. Transfer to a platter and keep warm.

■ In the same skillet, melt remaining butter. Add the almonds, lemon juice, and wine if desired; heat through. Pour over fillets and garnish with lemon wedges.

Yield: 2-4 servings.

Salmon-Wrapped Asparagus*

Amy Clark

CHESAPEAKE, WASHINGTON

My inspiration for this deliciously different salmon dish came from a variety of Saturday morning cooking shows. Dinner guests always admire how pretty each fish bundle looks.

PREP/TOTAL TIME: 25 min.

- 2 pounds fresh asparagus, trimmed
- 1-1/2 pounds salmon fillets
- 1-1/2 cups water
- 1/2 cup dry white wine *or* chicken broth
- 1 tablespoon minced green onion
- 1 tablespoon minced chives
- 1 teaspoon salt
- 1/2 teaspoon whole black peppercorns

MUSHROOM SAUCE:

- 1/2 pound fresh mushrooms, sliced
- 1/2 cup sliced green onions
- 2 tablespoons butter
- 1 teaspoon olive oil
- 2 tablespoons all-purpose flour
- 1/2 teaspoon salt
- 1/8 teaspoon pepper
- 1 cup 2% milk
- 1 tablespoon minced chives

■ In a large skillet, bring 1/2 in. of water to a boil; add asparagus spears. Cover and cook for 2-4 minutes. Drain and immediately place asparagus in ice water; drain and pat dry.

■ Cut salmon widthwise into 1/4-in. thick slices. To form one bundle, place three to four slices cut side down, overlapping edges slightly; wrap around five to six asparagus spears. Secure with toothpicks. Repeat for remaining bundles.

■ In a large skillet, bring 1-1/2 cups water, wine, onion, chives, salt and peppercorns to a boil. Using a spatula, carefully add the bundles. Reduce heat; cover and simmer for 7-8 minutes or until fish flakes easily with a fork.

■ Meanwhile, for sauce, in a small skillet, saute mushrooms and green onions in butter and oil until tender. Stir in the flour, salt and pepper until blended. Gradually add milk. Bring to a boil; cook and stir for 2 minutes or until thickened. Add chives. Serve with bundles.

Yield: 6 servings.

***Nutrition Facts:** 1 bundle with 1/3 cup sauce equals 277 calories, 10 g fat (4 g saturated fat), 97 mg cholesterol, 710 mg sodium, 14 g carbohydrate, 4 g fiber, 29 g protein. **Diabetic Exchanges:** 3-1/2 lean meat, 2 vegetable, 1 fat.

Jambalaya

Gloria Kirchman

EDEN PRAIRIE, MINNESOTA

This Southern dish is my family's favorite. They love the hearty combination of sausage, shrimp and rice. I like that it cooks in one pot for a marvelous meal.

PREP: 20 min.
COOK: 30 min.

- 3/4 pound bulk hot *or* mild Italian sausage
- 1/2 cup chopped onion
- 1/2 cup chopped green pepper
- 1 garlic clove, minced
- 1 can (14-1/2 ounces) diced tomatoes, undrained
- 1 can (14-1/2 ounces) chicken broth
- 2 cups diced fully cooked ham
- 3/4 cup uncooked long grain rice
- 1 bay leaf
- 1/4 teaspoon dried thyme
- 1 pound fresh medium shrimp, peeled and deveined

■ In a large skillet, cook sausage until browned; drain. Stir in onion and green pepper until vegetables are tender. Add garlic; cook 1 minute longer. Add the tomatoes, broth, ham, rice, bay leaf and thyme; cover and simmer for 20-25 minutes or until tender.

■ Stir in the shrimp; cover and cook for 3-4 minutes or until the shrimp turn pink. Remove bay leaf.

Yield: 6-8 servings.

Angel Hair Pasta with Lobster*

Carole Resnick
CLEVELAND, OHIO

A light, lemon-garlic wine sauce enhances the flavor of tender lobster in this extra-special entree. Arugula adds a bit of color as well.

PREP: 25 min. ■ COOK: 15 min.

- 2 lobster tails (8 to 10 ounces *each*)
- 2 garlic cloves, minced
- 3 tablespoons olive oil
- 1/2 cup white wine *or* chicken broth
- 2 tablespoons tomato puree
- 1/2 teaspoon salt
- 1/4 teaspoon pepper
- 8 ounces uncooked angel hair pasta
- 1 cup fresh arugula *or* baby spinach, coarsely chopped
- 2 tablespoons lemon juice
- 1 tablespoon grated lemon peel
- Shredded Romano *or* Parmesan cheese, optional

■ Carefully remove the lobster meat from shells; cut into 1-in. pieces and set aside.

■ In a large skillet, saute garlic in oil for 1 minute. Add the wine, tomato puree, salt and pepper. Bring to a boil over medium heat. Reduce heat. Stir in lobster pieces; simmer, uncovered, for 5-6 minutes or until lobster is firm and opaque.

■ Meanwhile, cook pasta according to package directions. Drain pasta; add to lobster mixture and toss to coat. Stir in the arugula, lemon juice and peel; cook for 1-2 minutes or until arugula is wilted. Garnish with cheese if desired.

Yield: 4 servings.

***Nutrition Facts:** 1-1/2 cups (calculated without cheese) equals 290 calories, 8 g fat (1 g saturated fat), 72 mg cholesterol, 426 mg sodium, 31 g carbohydrate, 1 g fiber, 19 g protein. **Diabetic Exchanges:** 2 starch, 2 lean meat, 1-1/2 fat.

Keeping fresh lemon juice on hand is an easy way to add refreshing flavor to many recipes. Freeze extra lemon juice in ice cube trays. Then defrost the cubes when needed to use in poultry recipes, desserts, iced or hot teas and many other dishes.

Pesto Shrimp Pasta

PREP/TOTAL TIME: 30 min.

- 8 ounces uncooked spaghetti
- 3 tablespoons olive oil, *divided*
- 1 cup loosely packed fresh basil leaves
- 1/4 cup lemon juice
- 2 garlic cloves, peeled
- 1/2 teaspoon salt
- 1 pound fresh asparagus, trimmed and cut into 2-inch pieces
- 3/4 pound uncooked medium shrimp, peeled and deveined
- 1/8 teaspoon crushed red pepper flakes

■ Cook spaghetti according to package directions. Meanwhile, in a blender, combine 1 tablespoon oil, basil, lemon juice, garlic and salt; cover and process until smooth.

■ In a large skillet, saute the asparagus in remaining oil until crisp-tender. Add shrimp and pepper flakes. Cook and stir until shrimp turn pink.

■ Drain spaghetti; place in a large bowl. Add basil mixture; toss to coat. Add the shrimp mixture and mix well.

Yield: 4 servings.

Gloria Jones Grenga
NEWNAN, GEORGIA

There's no better way to celebrate the flavors of spring and summer than with a delicious pasta dish like this one. The asparagus tastes wonderful with the shrimp and basil, and a dash of red pepper puts zip into your dinner lineup.

page 210

OVEN ENTREES

Beef & Ground Beef

Robust beefy dishes are reliable, hearty and a mainstay in any busy cook's kitchen. You'll find plenty of tasty new twists on classics, such as meat loaf, beefy baked pastas, pot roast and shepherd's pie in this popular chapter.

Mexican Lasagna

Tina Newhauser
PETERBOROUGH, NEW HAMPSHIRE

Tortillas replace lasagna noodles in this beefy casserole that has a south-of-the-border twist. With salsa, enchilada sauce, chilies, cheese and refried beans, it's a fiesta of flavors!

Mexican Lasagna

PREP: 25 min. ■ BAKE: 40 min. + standing

- 1-1/4 pounds ground beef
- 1 medium onion, chopped
- 4 garlic cloves, minced
- 2 cups salsa
- 1 can (16 ounces) refried beans
- 1 can (15 ounces) black beans, rinsed and drained
- 1 can (10 ounces) enchilada sauce
- 1 can (4 ounces) chopped green chilies
- 1 envelope taco seasoning
- 1/4 teaspoon pepper
- 6 flour tortillas (10 inches)
- 3 cups (12 ounces) shredded Mexican cheese blend, *divided*
- 2 cups crushed tortilla chips
- Sliced ripe olives, guacamole, chopped tomatoes and sour cream, optional

■ In a large skillet, cook the beef and onion over medium heat until meat is no longer pink. Add garlic; cook 1 minute longer. Drain. Stir in the salsa, beans, enchilada sauce, chilies, taco seasoning and pepper; heat through.

■ Spread 1 cup of the meat mixture in a greased 13-in. x 9-in. baking dish. Layer with two tortillas, a third of the remaining meat mixture and 1 cup cheese. Repeat layers. Top with remaining tortillas and meat mixture.

■ Cover and bake at 375° for 30 minutes. Uncover; sprinkle with remaining cheese and top with tortilla chips.

■ Bake 10-15 minutes longer or until cheese is melted. Let stand for 10 minutes before serving. Garnish with olives, guacamole, tomatoes and sour cream if desired.

Yield: 12 servings.

Store garlic bulbs in a cool, dry and dark place in a container that is well-ventilated, like a mesh bag. Leaving the cloves on the bulb with the papery skin intact will help prevent them from drying out. Stored this way, the garlic should be good for up to 2 months.

Reuben Loaf

Darlene Loudon
CRESTON, IOWA

This meat loaf really captures the wonderful flavor of reuben sandwiches. When my family tires of regular meat loaf, I turn to this recipe that came from my niece.

Reuben Loaf

PREP: 20 min. ■ BAKE: 1 hour + standing

- 1 egg, lightly beaten
- 1 tablespoon ketchup
- 2 cups soft bread crumbs
- 1 teaspoon salt
- 2 pounds lean ground beef (90% lean)
- 1 can (8 ounces) sauerkraut, rinsed and well drained
- 4 ounces deli pastrami, chopped
- 1 cup (4 ounces) shredded Swiss cheese
- 1/4 cup sour cream
- 1 tablespoon prepared mustard

■ In a large bowl, combine the egg, ketchup, bread crumbs and salt. Crumble beef over mixture; mix well. Set aside. In another large bowl, combine sauerkraut, pastrami, cheese, sour cream and mustard.

■ Press a third of the beef mixture into a greased 9-in. x 5-in. loaf pan. Top with half of the pastrami mixture. Repeat layers. Top with remaining beef mixture.

■ Cover and bake at 350° for 1 hour or until no pink remains and a meat thermometer reads 160°; drain. Let stand for about 10 minutes before slicing.

Yield: 8 servings.

Tortilla Beef Bake*

Kim Osburn
LIGONIER, INDIANA

My family loves Mexican food, so I came up with this simple yet satisfying casserole that gets its spark from salsa. We like it so much that when I make it, there are rarely any leftovers.

PREP: 10 min.
BAKE: 30 min.

- 1-1/2 pounds ground beef
- 1 can (10-3/4 ounces) condensed cream of chicken soup, undiluted
- 2-1/2 cups crushed tortilla chips, *divided*
- 1 jar (16 ounces) salsa
- 1-1/2 cups (6 ounces) shredded cheddar cheese

■ In a large skillet, cook beef over medium heat until no longer pink; drain. Stir in soup. Sprinkle 1-1/2 cups tortilla chips in a greased shallow 2-1/2-qt. baking dish. Top with beef mixture, salsa and cheese.

■ Bake, uncovered, at 350° for 25-30 minutes or until bubbly. Sprinkle with remaining chips. Bake 3 minutes longer or until chips are lightly toasted.

Yield: 6 servings.

***Nutrition Facts:** 1 serving (1 each) equals 464 calories, 26 g fat (12 g saturated fat), 90 mg cholesterol, 1,083 mg sodium, 23 g carbohydrate, 4 g fiber, 29 g protein.

Lee Leuschner
CALGARY, ALBERTA

This old-fashioned pot roast with smooth pan gravy is one of my best beef recipes. It evokes memories of dinners at Mom's or Grandma's.

Savory Pot Roast

Savory Pot Roast

PREP: 15 min. ■ BAKE: 2-1/2 hours

- 1 rolled boneless beef chuck roast (6 pounds)
- 2 tablespoons canola oil

Salt and coarsely ground pepper

- 1 large onion, coarsely chopped
- 2 medium carrots, coarsely chopped
- 1 celery rib, coarsely chopped
- 2 cups water
- 1 can (14-1/2 ounces) beef broth
- 2 bay leaves

GRAVY:

- 1/4 cup butter, cubed
- 1/4 cup all-purpose flour
- 1 teaspoon lemon juice
- 4 to 5 drops hot pepper sauce

■ In a large skillet over medium-high heat, brown roast in oil on all sides. Transfer to a large roasting pan; season with salt and pepper. Add the onion, carrots and celery.

■ In a large saucepan, bring the water, broth and bay leaves to a boil. Pour over roast and vegetables. Cover and bake at 350° for 2-1/2 to 3 hours or until meat is tender, turning once.

■ Remove roast to a serving platter and keep warm. For gravy, strain pan juices, reserving 2 cups. Discard vegetables and bay leaves.

■ In a large saucepan over medium heat, melt butter; stir in flour until smooth. Gradually stir in pan juices. Bring to a boil; cook and stir for 2 minutes or until thickened. Stir in lemon juice and hot pepper sauce. Serve with roast.

Yield: 14-16 servings.

Editor's Note: Ask your butcher to tie two 3-pound chuck roasts together to form a rolled chuck roast.

Corned Beef 'n' Sauerkraut Bake

Susan Stahl
DULUTH, MINNESOTA

I love Reuben sandwiches, so this recipe was a dream come true! We especially like this casserole with my husband's homemade sauerkraut.

PREP: 10 min.
BAKE: 30 min.

- 1-3/4 cups sauerkraut, rinsed and well drained
- 1/2 pound thinly sliced deli corned beef, julienned
- 2 cups (8 ounces) shredded Swiss cheese
- 1/4 cup Thousand Island salad dressing
- 2 medium tomatoes, thinly sliced
- 6 tablespoons butter, *divided*
- 1 cup coarsely crushed seasoned rye crackers

■ In a greased 1-1/2 -qt. baking dish, layer half of the sauerkraut, corned beef and cheese. Repeat layers. Drop salad dressing by teaspoonfuls over the cheese. Arrange tomato slices over the top; dot with 2 tablespoons butter.

■ In a small saucepan, melt the remaining butter. Stir in the crumbs. Sprinkle over top of casserole. Bake, uncovered, at 400° for 30-35 minutes or until heated through.

Yield: 6 servings.

Debbie Brunssen
RANDOLPH, NEBRASKA

This hearty stromboli gets rave reviews from the whole gang. With a well-seasoned filling surrounded by tender Italian bread, what's not to love?

Hearty Sausage Stromboli

Hearty Sausage Stromboli*

PREP: 25 min. ■ BAKE: 15 min.

- 1/2 pound bulk Italian sausage
- 1/4 pound ground beef
- 1/2 cup chopped onion
- 1/2 cup sliced fresh mushrooms
- 1/4 cup chopped green pepper
- 1/2 cup water
- 1/3 cup tomato paste
- 2 tablespoons grated Parmesan cheese
- 1/2 teaspoon salt
- 1/4 teaspoon dried oregano
- 1/4 teaspoon minced garlic
- 1/8 teaspoon dried rosemary, crushed
- 1 loaf (1 pound) Italian bread
- 6 slices part-skim mozzarella cheese

■ In a large skillet, cook the sausage, beef, onion, mushrooms and green pepper over medium heat until meat is no longer pink; drain. Stir in the water, tomato paste, Parmesan cheese, salt, oregano, garlic and rosemary. Bring to a boil. Reduce heat; simmer, uncovered, for 5 minutes or until thickened.

■ Meanwhile, cut the top third off a loaf of bread; carefully hollow out bottom, leaving a 1/2-in. shell (discard removed bread or save for another use).

■ Line bottom half with three mozzarella cheese slices; top with the sausage mixture and remaining cheese. Replace bread top. Wrap sandwich loaf in foil.

■ Bake at 400° for 15-20 minutes or until cheese is melted. Let stand for 5 minutes before slicing.

Yield: 6 servings.

***Nutrition Facts:** 1 slice equals 411 calories, 16 g fat (7 g saturated fat), 41 mg cholesterol, 1,016 mg sodium, 44 g carbohydrate, 3 g fiber, 23 g protein.

Cranberry Beef Brisket*

Annette Bartle
LEES SUMMIT, MISSOURI

My mother-in-law gave me the recipe for this tender brisket. It yields a lot, so the leftover beef can be used in other recipes later in the week.

PREP: 15 min.
BAKE: 3-4 hours

- 1 beef brisket (4 to 5 pounds)
- 2 tablespoons canola oil
- 1 can (14 ounces) whole-berry cranberry sauce
- 1/2 cup beef broth
- 1/2 cup red wine *or* additional beef broth
- 1 envelope onion soup mix

■ In a large skillet, brown beef in oil on both sides. Transfer to a greased roasting pan. In a small bowl, combine the remaining ingredients; pour over beef.

■ Cover and bake at 350° for 3-4 hours or until meat is tender. Strain cooking juices if desired to serve with meat.

Yield: 10-12 servings.

Editor's Note: This is a fresh beef brisket, not corned beef.

***Nutrition Facts:** 8 ounces equals 273 calories, 9 g fat (3 g saturated fat), 64 mg cholesterol, 301 mg sodium, 14 g carbohydrate, 1 g fiber, 31 g protein. **Diabetic Exchanges:** 4 lean meat, 1 starch.

Spicy Bean and Beef Pie

Debra Dohy
MASSILLON, OHIO
My daughter helped me create this recipe one day when we wanted a one-dish meal that was something other than a casserole. It slices nicely and is a fun, satisfying dish.

Spicy Bean and Beef Pie

PREP: 20 min. ■ BAKE: 30 min.

- 1 pound ground beef
- 2 to 3 garlic cloves, minced
- 1 can (11-1/2 ounces) condensed bean with bacon soup, undiluted
- 1 jar (16 ounces) thick and chunky picante sauce, *divided*
- 1/4 cup cornstarch
- 1 tablespoon chopped fresh parsley
- 1 teaspoon paprika
- 1 teaspoon salt
- 1/4 teaspoon pepper
- 1 can (16 ounces) kidney beans, rinsed and drained
- 1 can (15 ounces) black beans, rinsed and drained
- 2 cups (8 ounces) shredded cheddar cheese, *divided*
- 3/4 cup sliced green onions, *divided*
- Pastry for double-crust pie (10 inches)
- 1 cup (8 ounces) sour cream
- 1 can (2-1/4 ounces) sliced ripe olives, drained

■ In a skillet, cook beef over medium heat until beef is no longer pink. Add garlic; cook 1 minute longer. Drain.

■ In a large bowl, combine soup, 1 cup picante sauce, cornstarch, parsley, paprika, salt and pepper. Fold in beans, 1-1/2 cups cheese, 1/2 cup onions and beef mixture.

■ Line pie plate with bottom pastry; fill with bean mixture. Top with remaining pastry; seal and flute edges. Cut slits in the top crust.

■ Bake at 425° for 30-35 minutes or until lightly browned. Let stand for 5 minutes before cutting. Top with sour cream, olives and remaining picante sauce, cheese and onions.

Yield: 8 servings.

To flute a pie crust, trim to 1 in. beyond the edge for a double-crust pie. Turn the overhang to form a built-up edge. Place index finger on edge, pointing out. Place thumb and index finger of other hand on outside edge; pinch dough around index finger to form a V shape. Continue around the edge.

Oven Swiss Steak

Jan Briggs
GREENFIELD, WISCONSIN

My whole family likes this version of Swiss steak because it is not very saucy, but is still chock full of veggies.

PREP: 20 min. ■ BAKE: 1-1/2 hours

- 1/4 cup all-purpose flour
- 1/2 teaspoon salt
- 1-1/2 pounds boneless beef round steak (3/4 inch thick), cut into 6 serving size pieces
- 1 tablespoon canola oil
- 1/3 cup white wine
- 1 can (14-1/2 ounces) diced tomatoes, undrained
- 1/2 cup finely chopped celery
- 1/2 cup sliced fresh mushrooms
- 1/2 cup finely chopped carrots
- 1 teaspoon beef bouillon granules
- 1/2 teaspoon Worcestershire sauce

■ Combine flour and salt. Sprinkle 1/2 teaspoon flour mixture over each piece of meat. Pound into the meat, turn over and repeat on other side. In a large skillet, brown meat on both sides in oil.

■ Transfer to an 11-in. x 7-in. baking dish, reserving pan drippings. Stir remaining flour mixture into skillet until smooth. Gradually add wine. Add the remaining ingredients.

■ Bring to a boil; cook and stir for 2 minutes or until thickened. Pour over the meat. Cover and bake at 350° for 1-1/2 hours or until the meat is tender.

Yield: 6 servings.

Round steak is a less-tender cut of beef and is best when tenderized or "Swissed" by pounding with a meat mallet before cooking.

Taco Casserole

PREP: 20 min.
BAKE: 20 min.

- 2-1/2 pounds ground beef
- 2 packages taco seasoning
- 2/3 cup water
- 1 can (16 ounces) kidney beans, rinsed and drained
- 1 cup (4 ounces) shredded Monterey Jack *or* pepper Jack cheese
- 2 eggs, lightly beaten
- 1 cup milk
- 1-1/2 cups biscuit/baking mix
- 1 cup (8 ounces) sour cream
- 1 cup (4 ounces) shredded cheddar cheese
- 2 cups shredded lettuce
- 1 medium tomato, diced
- 1 can (2-1/4 ounces) sliced ripe olives, drained

■ In a large skillet, cook beef over medium heat until meat is no longer pink; drain. Stir in taco seasoning and water. Bring to a boil. Reduce heat and simmer for 5 minutes. Stir in beans.

■ Spoon meat mixture into a greased 8-in. square baking dish. Sprinkle with Monterey Jack cheese. In a large bowl, combine the eggs, milk and biscuit mix until moistened. Pour over cheese.

■ Bake, uncovered, at 400° for 20-25 minutes or until lightly browned and a knife inserted near the center comes out clean. Spread with sour cream. Top with shredded cheddar cheese, lettuce, tomato and olives.

Yield: 6-8 servings.

Bonnie King
LANSING, MICHIGAN

When you're bored with traditional tacos, give this family-pleasing main dish a try. It puts the taste of the Southwest into a comforting casserole. To add even more flavor, you can also garnish with salsa, sour cream, chopped green onion or avocado. Yum!

Averleen Ressie
RICE LAKE, WISCONSIN

This meat loaf with a zesty chili sauce is sure to please any family. My son-in-law is in his glory when I serve the tasty entree. There are never any leftovers.

Chili Sauce Meat Loaf

Chili Sauce Meat Loaf*

PREP: 20 min. ■ BAKE: 55 min. + standing

- 1/3 cup plus 2 tablespoons chili sauce, *divided*
- 1 egg white
- 1 tablespoon Worcestershire sauce
- 3/4 cup quick-cooking oats
- 3/4 cup finely chopped onion
- 2 garlic cloves, minced
- 1 teaspoon dried thyme
- 1/2 teaspoon salt
- 1/2 teaspoon pepper
- 1-1/2 pounds lean ground beef (90% lean)

■ In a large bowl, combine 1/3 cup chili sauce, egg white, Worcestershire sauce, oats, onion, garlic, thyme, salt and pepper. Crumble beef over mixture and mix well.

■ Shape into a 9-in. x 4-in. loaf; place in an 11-in. x 7-in. baking dish coated with cooking spray.

■ Bake, uncovered, at 350° for 50 minutes. Brush with remaining chili sauce. Bake 5-10 minutes longer or until no pink remains and a meat thermometer reads 160°. Let stand for 10 minutes before slicing.

Yield: 6 servin

***Nutrition Fac** aturated fat), 69 mg cholesterol, 565 protein. **Diabetic Exchanges:** 3 l

Seasoned Rib Roast

Evelyn Gebhardt
KASILOF, ALASKA

Gravy made from the drippings of this boneless beef rib roast is exceptional. You can also use a ribeye roast with excellent results.

PREP: 10 min.
BAKE: 1-3/4 hours + standing

- 1-1/2 teaspoons lemon-pepper seasoning
- 1-1/2 teaspoons paprika
- 3/4 teaspoon garlic salt
- 1/2 teaspoon dried rosemary, crushed
- 1/4 teaspoon cayenne pepper
- 1 beef ribeye roast (3 to 4 pounds)

■ In a small bowl, combine the seasonings; rub over roast. Place roast fat side up on a rack in a shallow roasting pan.

■ Bake, uncovered, at 350° for 1-3/4 to 2-1/2 hours or until meat reaches desired doneness (for medium-rare, a meat thermometer should read 145°; medium, 160°; well-done, 170°). Remove to a warm serving platter. Let stand for 10-15 minutes before carving.

Yield: 6-8 servings.

Spaghetti Beef Casserole

Jane Radtke
GRIFFITH, INDIANA

We love spaghetti, and as the mother of three boys, this casserole has been a life saver! Fast and delicious, it was a favorite at pre-game meals and sports banquets.

Spaghetti Beef Casserole*

PREP: 25 min. ■ BAKE: 20 min.

- 1-1/2 pounds uncooked spaghetti
- 3 pounds ground beef
- 1 cup chopped onion
- 2/3 cup chopped green pepper
- 1 teaspoon minced garlic
- 2 cans (10-3/4 ounces *each*) condensed cream of mushroom soup, undiluted
- 2 cans (10-3/4 ounces *each*) condensed tomato soup, undiluted
- 1-1/3 cups water
- 1 can (8 ounces) mushroom stems and pieces, drained
- 3 cups (12 ounces) shredded cheddar cheese, *divided*

■ Cook spaghetti according to package directions. Meanwhile, in several large skillets, cook the beef, onion and green pepper over medium heat until meat is no longer pink. Add garlic; cook 1 minute longer. Drain. Stir in the soups, water and mushrooms.

■ Drain the spaghetti. Add spaghetti and 1 cup cheese to beef mixture. Transfer to two greased 13-in. x 9-in. baking dishes. Sprinkle with the remaining cheese. Cover and freeze one casserole for up to 3 months. Bake remaining casserole, uncovered, at 350° for 20-25 minutes or until cheese is melted.

■ TO USE FROZEN CASSEROLE: Thaw in the refrigerator overnight. Remove from the refrigerator 30 minutes before baking. Cover and bake at 350° for 1 to 1-1/4 hours or until heated through and cheese is melted.

Yield: 2 casseroles (8 servings each).

***Nutrition Facts:** 1 piece equals 434 calories, 17 g fat (8 g saturated fat), 66 mg cholesterol, 732 mg sodium, 43 g carbohydrate, 3 g fiber, 26 g protein.

To prevent spaghetti from sticking together when cooking, use a large pot and 3 quarts of water for every 8 ounces of pasta you plan to cook.

Southwestern Shepherd's Pie

Suzette Jury
KEENE, CALIFORNIA

This easy meal is robust and colorful with a zesty blend of South-of-the-border spices! It's great to cook once but have enough food for two meals.

Southwestern Shepherd's Pie

PREP: 35 min. ■ BAKE: 25 min.

- 3 pounds ground beef
- 1 cup chopped onion
- 2 cans (10 ounces *each*) enchilada sauce
- 2 tablespoons all-purpose flour
- 2 teaspoons chopped chipotle peppers in adobo sauce
- 1 teaspoon ground cumin
- 1 teaspoon dried oregano
- 2-1/2 cups water
- 2 cups milk
- 1/3 cup butter, cubed
- 1 teaspoon salt
- 4 cups mashed potato flakes
- 2 cans (4 ounces *each*) chopped green chilies, undrained
- 2 cups (8 ounces) shredded Mexican cheese blend, *divided*
- 2 cans (11 ounces *each*) Mexicorn, drained
- 2/3 cup chopped green onions
- Paprika

■ In a Dutch oven, cook beef and onion over medium heat until meat is no longer pink; drain. Add the enchilada sauce, flour, chipotle peppers, cumin and oregano; bring to a boil. Reduce heat; simmer, uncovered, for 5 minutes.

■ Meanwhile, in a large saucepan, combine the water, milk, butter and salt; bring to a boil. Remove from the heat. Stir in potato flakes until combined. Add chilies and 1/2 cup cheese.

■ Transfer meat mixture to two greased 11-in. x 7-in. baking dishes. Layer with corn, mashed potato mixture and remaining cheese. Sprinkle with green onions. Cover and freeze one casserole for up to 3 months.

■ Cover and bake the remaining casserole at 375° for 20 minutes. Uncover and bake 5-10 minutes longer or until bubbly. Sprinkle with paprika.

■ TO USE FROZEN CASSEROLE: Thaw in refrigerator overnight. Remove from refrigerator 30 minutes before baking.

■ Cover and bake at 375° for 20 minutes. Uncover and bake 15-20 minutes longer or until bubbly. Sprinkle with paprika.

Yield: 2 casseroles (7 servings each).

Joy Hagen
WEBSTER, SOUTH DAKOTA

This is a favorite recipe of ours. I recently served it at a potluck gathering and people loved it so much that they actually requested the recipe!

Reuben Casserole

Reuben Casserole

PREP: 20 min. ■ BAKE: 40 min.

- 5 cups uncooked egg noodles
- 2 cans (14 ounces *each*) sauerkraut, rinsed and well drained
- 2 cans (10-3/4 ounces *each*) condensed cream of chicken soup, undiluted
- 3/4 cup milk
- 1/2 cup chopped onion
- 3 tablespoons prepared mustard
- 3/4 pound sliced deli corned beef, chopped
- 2 cups (8 ounces) shredded Swiss cheese
- 2 slices day-old light rye bread
- 2 tablespoons butter, melted

■ Cook noodles according to package directions. Meanwhile, in a large bowl, combine the sauerkraut, soup, milk, onion and mustard.

■ Drain noodles; stir into sauerkraut mixture. Transfer to a greased 13-in. x 9-in. baking dish. Sprinkle with corned beef and cheese.

■ Place bread in a food processor; cover and process until mixture resembles coarse crumbs. Toss the crumbs with butter and sprinkle over the casserole.

■ Bake, uncovered, at 350° for 40-45 minutes or until bubbly.

Yield: 5 servings.

Zesty Beef Roast

Joan Enerson
WAUPACA, WISCONSIN

One day while making meatballs, I ran out of ketchup and used horseradish in the sauce. The dish was so tasty, I decided to try it on a roast. It, too, was a winner.

PREP: 20 min.
BAKE: 2 hours + standing

- 1 beef sirloin tip roast *or* boneless beef rump roast (3 pounds)
- 2 tablespoons canola oil
- 1 cup beef broth
- 1/4 to 1/3 cup prepared horseradish
- 1 cup chopped onion
- 1/4 teaspoon salt
- 1/4 teaspoon pepper
- 1/3 cup all-purpose flour
- 2/3 cup cold water

■ In a Dutch oven, brown roast on all sides in oil. Add broth. Spread horseradish over roast; sprinkle with onion, salt and pepper. Cover and bake at 350° for 2 hours or until tender, basting frequently. Remove roast from the pan; let stand for 10 minutes.

■ Meanwhile, pour pan juices into a large measuring cup; add enough water to equal 2 cups. Return to pan. Combine flour and cold water until smooth; gradually stir into pan juices. Bring to a boil; cook and stir for 2 minutes. Add additional water if a thinner gravy is desired. Slice roast and serve with gravy.

Yield: 6-8 servings.

Taste of Home Test Kitchen

We created this recipe for pasties as a way to use leftover pot roast. Just tuck cooked beef, carrots, potatoes and onion into pie pastry and your family will love the tender and oh-so flaky results!

Beef Pasties

Beef Pasties

PREP: 20 min. ■ BAKE: 20 min.

- 2 cups cubed cooked roast beef (1/4-inch pieces)
- 1-1/2 cup finely chopped cooked potatoes
- 1 cup beef gravy
- 1/2 cup finely chopped carrot
- 1/2 cup finely chopped cooked onion
- 1 tablespoon chopped fresh parsley
- 1/4 teaspoon dried thyme
- 1/2 teaspoon salt
- 1/8 to 1/4 teaspoon pepper
- Pastry for double-crust pie (9 inches)
- Half-and-half cream

■ In a large bowl, combine the first nine ingredients; set aside. On a lightly floured surface, roll out a fourth of the pastry into an 8-in. circle. Mound 1 cup filling on half of circle. Moisten edges with water; fold dough over filling and press the edges with a fork to seal.

■ Place on an ungreased baking sheet. Repeat with remaining pastry and filling. Cut slits in top of each; brush with cream. Bake at 450° for 20-25 minutes or until golden brown.

Yield: 4 servings.

Editor's Note: If using purchased pre-rolled pastry, cut each circle in half. Mound filling on half of the pastry; fold over, forming a wedge.

Simple Shepherd's Pie

Lera Joe Bayer
WIRTZ, VIRGINIA

Our son Charlie loves to help in the kitchen. When we have leftover mashed potatoes, he fixes this dish. It's a great meal alongside a crisp salad.

PREP: 20 min.
BAKE: 30 min.

- 1 pound ground beef
- 2 cans (10-3/4 ounces *each*) condensed cream of potato soup, undiluted
- 1-1/2 cups frozen peas, thawed
- 1-1/2 cups frozen sliced carrots, thawed
- 4 cups mashed potatoes (with added milk and butter)

■ In a large skillet, cook the beef over medium heat until no longer pink; drain. Add the soup, peas and carrots. Pour into a greased 11-in. x 7-in. baking dish. Top with the mashed potatoes.

■ Bake, uncovered, at 350° for 30-40 minutes or until heated through.

Yield: 4 servings.

Oven Stew and Biscuits

Bertha Brookmeier
EL CAJON, CALIFORNIA

Soy sauce and sesame seeds give this hearty casserole a slight Asian twist. The recipe came from my brother, who was a wonderful cook.

Oven Stew and Biscuits

PREP: 20 min. ■ BAKE: 45 min.

- 1/3 cup all-purpose flour
- 1 teaspoon salt
- 1/2 teaspoon pepper
- 2 pounds beef top sirloin, cut into 1-inch cubes
- 1/4 cup canola oil
- 1 can (14-1/2 ounces) stewed tomatoes
- 1 jar (4-1/2 ounces) sliced mushrooms, drained
- 1 large onion, thinly sliced
- 3 tablespoons soy sauce
- 3 tablespoons molasses
- 1 medium green pepper, cut into 1-inch pieces
- 1 tube (12 ounces) refrigerated buttermilk biscuits
- 1 teaspoon butter, melted
- Sesame seeds

■ In a large resealable plastic bag, combine the flour, salt and pepper. Add beef in batches; shake to coat. In a large skillet, brown beef in oil over medium heat. Stir in the tomatoes, mushrooms, onion, soy sauce and molasses.

■ Transfer to a greased 13-in. x 9-in. baking dish. Cover and bake at 375° for 20 minutes. Stir in the green pepper. Cover and bake 10 minutes longer.

■ Uncover and top with the biscuits. Brush biscuits with butter; sprinkle with sesame seeds. Bake 15-18 minutes more or until the biscuits are golden brown.

Yield: 6-8 servings.

Molasses is the by product of the process that refines sugarcane into table sugar. Blackstrap molasses is made from the third boiling of sugar syrup and is stronger, darker and more bitter than either light or dark molasses. Use blackstrap molasses with caution in cooking or baking because the intense flavor can be quite overwhelming.

Saucy Scalloped Pie

Jan Breitkreuz
ONOWAY, ALBERTA

This uncommon recipe features a ground beef shell and cheesy potato filling. I made this dish out of desperation one day and my family adored it.

Saucy Scalloped Pie

PREP: 25 min. ■ BAKE: 25 min.

- 1 package (5-1/4 ounces) cheesy scalloped potatoes
- 1 bottle (12 ounces) chili sauce
- 1 tablespoon Italian seasoning
- 1/2 cup dry bread crumbs
- 1/4 cup chopped onion
- 1 garlic clove, minced
- 1 pound ground beef
- 1 can (8 ounces) mushroom stems and pieces, drained
- 2 tablespoons grated Parmesan cheese

■ Prepare scalloped potatoes according to package directions. Meanwhile, combine chili sauce and Italian seasoning. In a large bowl, combine bread crumbs, onion, garlic and 1 cup chili sauce mixture. Crumble beef over mixture and mix well.

■ Press onto the bottom and up the sides of an ungreased 9-in. pie plate. Bake at 350° for 15 minutes or until no pink remains; drain. Add mushrooms and Parmesan cheese to scalloped potatoes. Spoon into meat shell.

■ Bake for 10 minutes or until potatoes are golden brown. Heat the remaining chili sauce mixture; serve with individual servings.

Yield: 4 servings.

Zucchini Supper

Mandy Anderson
EAST MOLINE, ILLINOIS

Nothing says "home sweet home" like the aroma of your favorite comfort food. My husband and I love this hearty casserole.

PREP: 25 min.
BAKE: 35 min.

- 1 pound ground beef
- 1 pound bulk pork sausage
- 4 cups chopped zucchini
- 1 pound process cheese (Velveeta), cubed
- 1 can (10-3/4 ounces) condensed cream of mushroom soup, undiluted
- 1 can (10-3/4 ounces) condensed cheddar cheese soup, undiluted
- 1 package (6 ounces) stuffing mix
- 3 eggs, lightly beaten
- 1 small onion, chopped
- 1/2 teaspoon salt
- 1/2 teaspoon garlic powder
- 1/4 teaspoon pepper

■ In a Dutch oven, cook beef and sausage over medium heat until no longer pink; drain. Stir in the remaining ingredients. Cook, stirring occasionally, until heated through.

■ Transfer to a greased 13-in. x 9-in. baking dish. Cover and bake at 350° for 30-35 minutes or until a thermometer reads 160°. Uncover and stir. Bake 4-6 minutes longer or until golden brown.

Yield: 8 servings.

Catherine Yoder
NEW PARIS, INDIANA

My children and husband aren't fond of veggies, so I snuck them into this lasagna and they hardly noticed! One pan feeds a crowd and the recipe is great for potlucks and even family reunions.

Sneaky Lasagna

Sneaky Lasagna

PREP: 25 min. ■ BAKE: 55 min. + standing

- 2 pounds ground beef
- 1 package (16 ounces) frozen California-blend vegetables
- 2 eggs
- 3 cups (24 ounces) 2% cottage cheese
- 2 jars (26 ounces *each*) spaghetti sauce
- 12 no-cook lasagna noodles
- 2 cups (8 ounces) shredded part-skim mozzarella cheese

■ In a Dutch oven, cook beef over medium heat until no longer pink. Meanwhile, cook vegetables according to package directions; drain. Finely chop the vegetables; place in a bowl. Stir in eggs and cottage cheese; set aside.

■ Drain beef; stir in spaghetti sauce. Spread 2 cups meat mixture into a greased 13-in. x 9-in. baking dish. Top with four noodles. Spread half of the vegetable mixture to edges of noodles. Layer with 2 cups meat mixture and 1 cup mozzarella cheese. Top with four noodles, remaining vegetable mixture and 2 cups meat mixture. Layer with remaining noodles, meat mixture and mozzarella cheese.

■ Cover and bake at 375° for 50 minutes or until a thermometer reads 160°. Uncover; bake 5-10 minutes longer or until bubbly and cheese is melted. Let stand for 15 minutes before cutting.

Yield: 10-12 servings.

Buttermilk Pot Roast

Anne Powers
MUNFORD, ALABAMA

Here is a melt-in-your-mouth roast with a very flavorful gravy that I've been making for years. It's always great for company.

PREP: 20 min.
BAKE: 2-1/4 hours

- 2 tablespoons Dijon mustard
- 1 boneless beef chuck roast (about 3-1/2 pounds)
- 4-1/2 teaspoons onion soup mix
- 1/4 teaspoon pepper
- 8 medium potatoes, peeled and halved
- 8 medium carrots, halved
- 8 small onions, cut into wedges
- 1 cup buttermilk

■ Spread mustard over roast; place in a Dutch oven. Sprinkle with soup mix and pepper. Arrange vegetables around roast; pour buttermilk over the top.

■ Cover and bake at 350° for 2-1/4 to 2-3/4 hours or until meat and vegetables are tender. Transfer meat and vegetables to a platter and keep warm.

■ Skim fat from drippings; bring to a boil. Cook until liquid is reduced to 1 cup; serve with beef and vegetables.

Yield: 8 servings.

Spoon Bread Tamale Bake*

Marjorie Mersereau
CORVALLIS, OREGON

This is a favorite comfort food for my family on winter nights—and all year round! Make it ahead for convenience, then pop in the oven to bake about an hour before dinner.

PREP: 25 min. ■ BAKE: 30 min.

- 1-1/2 pounds lean ground beef (90% lean)
- 1 large onion, chopped
- 1 small green pepper, chopped
- 1 garlic clove, minced
- 1 can (28 ounces) diced tomatoes, undrained
- 1-1/2 cups frozen corn
- 1 can (2-1/4 ounces) sliced ripe olives, drained
- 4-1/2 teaspoons chili powder
- 1/2 teaspoon salt
- 1/4 teaspoon pepper
- 1/2 cup cornmeal
- 1 cup water

TOPPING:

- 1-1/2 cups fat-free milk, *divided*
- 1/2 cup cornmeal
- 1/2 teaspoon salt
- 1/2 cup shredded reduced-fat cheddar cheese
- 2 tablespoons butter
- 1/2 cup egg substitute

■ In a Dutch oven coated with cooking spray, cook the beef, onion, green pepper and garlic over medium heat until meat is no longer pink; drain. Stir in the tomatoes, corn, olives, chili powder, salt and pepper. Bring to a boil. Reduce the heat and simmer, uncovered, for 5 minutes.

■ Combine cornmeal and water until smooth; gradually stir into the pan. Bring to a boil. Reduce heat; simmer, uncovered, for 10 minutes, stirring occasionally. Transfer to a 2-1/2-qt. baking dish coated with cooking spray.

■ In a small saucepan, bring 1 cup milk to a boil. Combine cornmeal, salt and remaining milk; slowly whisk into boiling milk. Cook and stir until mixture returns to a boil. Reduce heat; cook and stir for 3-4 minutes or until slightly thickened.

■ Remove from the heat; stir in cheese and butter until melted. Stir in egg substitute. Pour over meat mixture. Bake, uncovered, at 375° for 30-40 minutes or until topping is lightly browned.

Yield: 8 servings.

***Nutrition Facts:** 1 serving equals 331 calories, 12 g fat (6 g saturated fat), 55 mg cholesterol, 754 mg sodium, 30 g carbohydrate, 4 g fiber, 25 g protein. **Diabetic Exchanges:** 3 lean meat, 1-1/2 starch, 1 vegetable, 1/2 fat.

Farmhouse Dinner*

PREP: 20 min.
BAKE: 30 min.

- 1 pound ground beef
- 2 eggs
- 1/4 cup milk
- 1 can (14-3/4 ounces) cream-style corn
- 1 cup soft bread crumbs
- 1/4 cup finely chopped onion
- 2 teaspoons prepared mustard
- 1 teaspoon salt
- 1/2 cup dry bread crumbs
- 2 tablespoons butter, melted

Minced fresh parsley, optional

■ In a large skillet, cook the beef over medium heat until no longer pink; drain and set aside.

■ In a large bowl, combine eggs and milk. Add the corn, soft bread crumbs, onion, mustard, salt and beef.

■ Transfer to a greased 9-in. square baking dish. Toss dry bread crumbs with butter; sprinkle over meat mixture. Bake, uncovered, at 350° for 30 minutes or until golden brown. Sprinkle with parsley if desired.

Yield: 4-6 servings.

***Nutrition Facts:** 1 serving (1 each) equals 292 calories, 14 g fat (6 g saturated fat), 120 mg cholesterol, 843 mg sodium, 24 g carbohydrate, 1 g fiber, 19 g protein.

Deborah Binstock
SOUTH HEART, NORTH DAKOTA

After a hard day of working on our farm, we look forward to a down-home meal-in-one dinner like this. The buttered bread crumbs pair well with the mellow flavor of cream-style corn.

Poultry

Perfect for potlucks, casual get-togethers or weeknight meals, the hearty, satisfying oven-baked dinners and casseroles in this chapter use popular chicken or turkey as the main ingredient.

Pesto Chicken Lasagna

Michelle Larson
EVELETH, MINNESOTA

Pesto really perks up this scrumptious chicken lasagna. Plus, the marinara sauce adds a touch of sweetness. Serve it with warm, crusty bread to impress your friends.

Pesto Chicken Lasagna

PREP: 30 min. ■ BAKE: 55 min. + standing

- 1 large sweet red pepper, diced
- 1/4 cup finely chopped onion
- 1 tablespoon butter
- 4 garlic cloves, minced
- 1/4 cup all-purpose flour
- 2 cups milk
- 1/4 cup chicken broth
- 1-1/2 teaspoons dried basil
- 1 teaspoon dried oregano
- 2 cups cubed cooked chicken
- 1/2 cup prepared pesto
- 1 can (3.8 ounces) sliced ripe olives, drained
- 1 egg, lightly beaten
- 1 carton (15 ounces) ricotta cheese
- 1 package (4 ounces) crumbled feta cheese
- 2 cups marinara sauce
- 12 no-cook lasagna noodles
- 1 package (6 ounces) fresh baby spinach, chopped
- 2 cups (8 ounces) shredded part-skim mozzarella cheese

■ In a large saucepan, saute red pepper and onion in butter until tender. Add the garlic and cook 1 minute longer. Stir in the flour until blended; gradually stir in the milk, broth, basil and oregano. Bring to a boil over medium heat and cook and stir for 2 minutes or until thickened. Stir in the cooked chicken, pesto and olives. Remove from the heat.

■ In a large bowl, combine the lightly beaten egg, ricotta cheese and feta cheese.

■ Spread 1 cup marinara sauce in a greased 13-in. x 9-in. baking dish. Layer with four no-bake noodles, half of the ricotta mixture, half of the spinach, half of the pesto mixture and 2/3 cup of the mozzarella cheese. Repeat layers. Top with the remaining noodles, marinara sauce and mozzarella cheese.

■ Cover and bake at 375° for 45 minutes. Uncover and bake 10 minutes more or until a thermometer reads 160°. Let the lasagna stand 15 minutes before serving.

Yield: 12 servings.

Chipotle-Apple Chicken Breasts

Shannon Abdollmohammadi
WOODINVILLE, WASHINGTON

The sweetness of the apple, the smokiness of the bacon and the heat from the chipotle pepper blend so well in this delicious entree. It's my husband's favorite.

Chipotle-Apple Chicken Breasts*

PREP: 25 min. ■ BAKE: 15 min.

- 2 bacon strips, diced
- 1 small tart apple, peeled and coarsely chopped
- 2 tablespoons dried minced onion
- 2 tablespoons unsweetened applesauce
- 1/2 to 1 teaspoon chipotle peppers in adobo sauce, chopped
- 2 boneless skinless chicken breast halves (6 ounces *each*)
- 2 teaspoons olive oil
- 1 teaspoon all-purpose flour
- 1/2 cup unsweetened apple juice
- 1/4 teaspoon salt
- 1/8 teaspoon pepper

■ In a small skillet, cook the bacon over medium heat until crisp. Using a slotted spoon, remove to paper towels; drain, reserving 1 teaspoon of the drippings. Saute apple in drippings until tender. Add the onion, applesauce, chipotle peppers and bacon; saute 2 minutes longer.

■ Cut a pocket in each chicken breast half; stuff with apple mixture. In a small skillet, brown the chicken in oil on both sides.

■ Transfer to an ungreased 8-in. square baking dish. Bake, uncovered, at 425° for about 12-15 minutes or until a meat thermometer reads 170°.

■ Meanwhile, add the flour, apple juice, salt and pepper to the skillet; stir to loosen browned bits. Bring to a boil; cook and stir for 2 minutes or until thickened. Serve with the stuffed chicken.

Yield: 2 servings.

***Nutrition Facts:** 1 stuffed chicken breast half with 3 tablespoons sauce equals 335 calories, 12 g fat (3 g saturated fat), 99 mg cholesterol, 489 mg sodium, 19 g carbohydrate, 1 g fiber, 37 g protein. **Diabetic Exchanges:** 5 lean meat, 1-1/2 fat, 1 fruit.

Joann Jensen
LOWELL, INDIANA
The aroma of this moist, golden-brown chicken is almost as wonderful as its flavor, and Mom's oyster stuffing is to die for!

Roast Chicken with Oyster Stuffing

Roast Chicken With Oyster Stuffing

PREP: 35 min. ■ BAKE: 2 hours + standing

- 1 can (8 ounces) whole oysters
- 1 celery rib, chopped
- 1 small onion, chopped
- 1/4 cup butter, cubed
- 2 tablespoons minced fresh parsley
- 1/2 teaspoon Italian seasoning
- 3 cups cubed bread, lightly toasted
- 1 roasting chicken (6 pounds)
- 1/4 cup butter, melted
- 1 to 2 teaspoons paprika

■ Drain oysters, reserving liquid; coarsely chop oysters. Set aside. In a small skillet, saute celery and onion in butter until tender. Stir in parsley and Italian seasoning. Place bread cubes in a large bowl; add the butter mixture, oysters and 1/4 cup reserved oyster liquid.

■ Just before baking, loosely stuff chicken with stuffing. Place breast side up on a rack in a roasting pan; tie drumsticks together. Combine melted butter and paprika; brush over chicken.

■ Bake, uncovered, at 350° for about 2 to 2-1/2 hours or until a meat thermometer reads 180° for chicken and 165° for stuffing, basting occasionally with pan drippings. (Cover loosely with foil if chicken browns too quickly.)

■ Cover chicken and let stand for 10 minutes before removing stuffing and carving. Skim fat and thicken pan juices if desired.

Yield: 6 servings (4 cups stuffing).

Oven-Fried Chicken

Daucia Brooks
WESTMORELAND, TENNESSEE

Tarragon, ginger and cayenne pepper season the cornmeal coating that is used on my golden "fried" chicken. The moist meat and crunchy topping are sure to make this entree a mealtime mainstay at your house, too.

PREP: 10 min.
BAKE: 50 min.

- 1/2 cup cornmeal
- 1/2 cup dry bread crumbs
- 1 teaspoon dried tarragon
- 1 teaspoon ground ginger
- 1/2 teaspoon salt
- 1/4 teaspoon cayenne pepper
- 1/4 teaspoon pepper
- 3 egg whites
- 2 tablespoons fat-free milk
- 1/2 cup all-purpose flour
- 1 broiler/fryer chicken (3 to 4 pounds), cut up
- Refrigerated butter-flavored spray

■ In a shallow bowl, combine the first seven ingredients. In a second shallow bowl, combine egg whites and milk. Place flour in a third shallow bowl. Coat chicken with flour; dip in the egg white mixture, then roll in cornmeal mixture.

■ Place in a 15-in. x 10-in. x 1-in. baking pan coated with cooking spray. Bake, uncovered, at 350° for 40 minutes. Spritz with butter-flavored spray. Bake 10-15 minutes longer or until juices run clear.

Yield: 6 servings.

Fran Allen
ST. LOUIS, MISSOURI
Make everyone in your family happy with this easy, warm and truly comforting dish that tastes like a chicken potpie but with a Tater Tot crust.

Chicken Tater Bake

Chicken Tater Bake

PREP: 20 min. ■ BAKE: 40 min.

- 2 cans (10-3/4 ounces *each*) condensed cream of chicken soup, undiluted
- 1/2 cup 2% milk
- 1/4 cup butter, cubed
- 3 cups cubed cooked chicken
- 1 package (16 ounces) frozen peas and carrots, thawed
- 1-1/2 cups (6 ounces) shredded cheddar cheese, *divided*
- 1 package (32 ounces) frozen Tater Tots

■ In a large saucepan, combine the soup, milk and butter. Cook and stir over medium heat until heated through. Remove from the heat; stir in the chicken, peas and carrots, and 1 cup cheese.

■ Transfer to two greased 8-in. square baking dishes. Top with Tater Tots; sprinkle with remaining cheese.

■ Cover and freeze one casserole for up to 3 months. Cover and bake the remaining casserole at 350° for 35 minutes. Uncover; bake 5-10 minutes longer or until heated through.

■ TO USE FROZEN CASSEROLE: Remove from the freezer 30 minutes before baking (do not thaw). Cover and bake at 350° for 1-1/2 to 1-3/4 hours or until heated through.

Yield: 2 casseroles (6 servings each).

Turkey Pizza

PREP: 15 min.
BAKE: 25 min.

- 1 package (20 ounces) turkey Italian sausage links
- 1 teaspoon olive oil
- 2 tubes (13.8 ounces *each*) refrigerated pizza crust
- 1 can (15 ounces) pizza sauce
- 1 cup sliced red onion
- 1 can (14 ounces) water-packed artichoke hearts, rinsed, drained and chopped
- 2 large tomatoes, sliced
- 2 cups (8 ounces) shredded Italian cheese blend

■ In a large skillet, cook the sausage in oil over medium heat for 8-10 minutes or until no longer pink. Cut into 1/4-in. slices.

■ Press pizza dough into a greased 15-in. x 10-in. x 1-in. baking pan, building up edges slightly; seal seam. Prick dough thoroughly with a fork. Bake at 400° for 8 minutes or until lightly browned.

■ Spread with pizza sauce; top with sausage, onion, artichokes and tomatoes. Sprinkle with cheese. Bake for 15-20 minutes or until crust is golden brown.

Yield: 8 servings.

Taste of Home Test Kitchen

You'll never order a delivered pizza again after diving into this homemade version. Refrigerated pizza crust is topped with turkey sausage, artichoke hearts and cheese. The pizza is delicious and takes less time to make than waiting for the delivery man!

Ramona Fish
COLUMBUS, INDIANA

This creamy, comforting casserole is a terrific way to use up leftover turkey. I have diced and frozen cooked turkey in portions ready to use when someone requests this popular dish.

Spinach Turkey Noodle Bake

Spinach Turkey Noodle Bake*

PREP: 20 min. ■ BAKE: 45 min. + standing

- 2-1/2 cups uncooked yolk-free noodles
- 2 cups diced cooked turkey breast
- 1 can (10-3/4 ounces) reduced-fat reduced-sodium condensed cream of chicken soup, undiluted
- 1/4 teaspoon garlic salt
- 1/8 teaspoon dried rosemary, crushed
- Dash pepper
- 1 package (10 ounces) frozen chopped spinach, thawed and squeezed dry
- 1 cup (8 ounces) fat-free cottage cheese
- 3/4 cup shredded part-skim mozzarella cheese, *divided*
- 1/8 teaspoon paprika

■ Cook the noodles according to package directions; drain. Meanwhile, in a large bowl, combine the turkey, soup, garlic salt, rosemary and pepper. In another bowl, combine the spinach, cottage cheese and 1/2 cup mozzarella cheese.

■ In a 2-qt. baking dish coated with cooking spray, layer half of the noodles, turkey mixture and cottage cheese mixture. Repeat layers.

■ Cover and bake 350° for 35 minutes. Uncover and sprinkle with the remaining mozzarella cheese. Bake 10-15 minutes longer or until the edges are lightly browned; sprinkle with paprika. Let stand for about 5 minutes before serving.

Yield: 6 servings.

***Nutrition Facts:** 1 cup equals 242 calories, 4 g fat (2 g saturated fat), 53 mg cholesterol, 568 mg sodium, 21 g carbohydrate, 3 g fiber, 26 g protein. **Diabetic Exchanges:** 3 lean meat, 1-1/2 starch, 1/2 fat.

Golden Chicken With Rice

Sharon Juart
ROCHESTER MILLS, PENNSYLVANIA

Chicken and rice has never been so easy, or so delicious! This very tender chicken is served over creamy wild rice; finish the meal with steamed carrots or another favorite veggie.

PREP: 10 min.
BAKE: 2 hours

- 1 package (6 ounces) long grain and wild rice mix
- 1 can (10-3/4 ounces) condensed cream of mushroom soup, undiluted
- 1 can (10-3/4 ounces) condensed cream of celery soup, undiluted
- 1-1/2 cups water
- 4 chicken leg quarters
- 1 envelope onion soup mix

■ In a large bowl, combine the rice, contents of seasoning packet, cream soups and water. Spread into a greased 13-in. x 9-in. baking dish. Top with chicken; sprinkle with onion soup mix.

■ Cover and bake at 350° for 2 hours or until a meat thermometer reads 180° and the rice is tender.

Yield: 4 servings.

Chicken Penne Casserole

Carmen Vanosch
VERNON, BRITISH COLUMBIA

Here is my family's favorite casserole recipe. I make it every week or two and we never tire of it. I like that I can clean my kitchen and then relax while it bakes. It won't disappoint!

Chicken Penne Casserole

PREP: 35 min. ■ BAKE: 45 min.

- 1 pound boneless skinless chicken thighs, cut into 1-inch pieces
- 1/2 cup *each* chopped onion, green pepper and sweet red pepper
- 1 teaspoon *each* dried basil, oregano and parsley flakes
- 1/2 teaspoon salt
- 1/2 teaspoon crushed red pepper flakes
- 1 tablespoon canola oil
- 3 garlic cloves, minced
- 1-1/2 cups uncooked penne pasta
- 1 can (14-1/2 ounces) diced tomatoes, undrained
- 3 tablespoons tomato paste
- 3/4 cup chicken broth
- 2 cups (8 ounces) shredded part-skim mozzarella cheese
- 1/2 cup grated Romano cheese

■ In a large saucepan, saute the chicken, onion, peppers and seasonings in oil until chicken is no longer pink. Add garlic; cook 1 minute longer.

■ Cook pasta according to package directions. Meanwhile, process tomatoes and tomato paste in a blender; add to the chicken mixture. Stir in the broth. Bring to a boil. Reduce heat; cover and simmer for 10-15 minutes or until slightly thickened.

■ Drain pasta; toss with chicken mixture. Spoon half of the mixture into a greased 2-qt. baking dish. Sprinkle with half of the cheeses. Repeat layers.

■ Cover and bake at 350° for 30 minutes. Uncover; bake 15-20 minutes longer or until heated through.

Yield: 4 servings.

Diced green, sweet red and yellow peppers can be frozen without first boiling. Simply place the chopped peppers directly into freezer bags or containers, then label and date. The peppers will keep in your freezer for 3 to 6 months. Then, when a cooked dish calls for diced peppers, you can use them directly from your freezer.

Tomato-Cream Stuffed Chicken

Jaqui Humphrey
KIRKLAND, WASHINGTON

For a pretty presentation at your holiday gathering, reach for this impressive recipe. The sun-dried tomato sauce is great with the chicken as well as with grilled veggies.

Tomato-Cream Stuffed Chicken

PREP: 30 min. ■ BAKE: 20 min.

- 1/2 cup cream cheese, softened
- 1/2 cup shredded part-skim mozzarella cheese
- 1/2 cup chopped fresh spinach
- 1/2 cup oil-packed sun-dried tomatoes, chopped
- 2 garlic cloves, minced
- 4 bone-in chicken breast halves (8 ounces *each*)
- 1/4 teaspoon salt
- 1/4 teaspoon pepper
- 3 tablespoons butter
- 1 tablespoon olive oil

SAUCE:

- 3/4 cup white wine *or* chicken broth
- 1/4 cup oil-packed sun-dried tomatoes, chopped
- 3 teaspoons chopped shallot
- 3 garlic cloves, minced
- 6 fresh basil leaves, thinly sliced
- 3/4 cup heavy whipping cream
- 1/4 cup butter, cubed

■ In a small bowl, combine the first five ingredients. Carefully loosen the skin on one side of each chicken breast to form a pocket; spread cheese mixture under the skin. Sprinkle with salt and pepper. In a large skillet, brown chicken on both sides in butter and oil.

■ Transfer to an ungreased 13-in. x 9-in. baking dish. Bake, uncovered, at 400° for 20-25 minutes or until a meat thermometer reads 170°.

■ Meanwhile, in a small saucepan, combine wine, tomatoes, shallot, garlic and basil. Bring to a boil over medium-high heat; cook until reduced by half. Add cream and butter. Bring to a boil. Reduce heat; simmer, uncovered, until thickened, stirring occasionally. Serve with chicken.

Yield: 4 servings.

Shallots are a part of the onion family and have a mild onion-garlic flavor. In place of the chopped shallots in this recipe, use chopped onion plus a pinch of garlic powder or (if you like the taste of garlic) 1 minced small garlic clove.

Ann Herren
PULASKI, TENNESSEE
Everyone in my family loves this casserole, even my 80-year-old grandparents who aren't big fans of Mexican food. The combination of ingredients is delicious!

Spanish Rice Turkey Casserole

Spanish Rice Turkey Casserole

PREP: 30 min. ■ BAKE: 20 min.

- 2 packages (6.8 ounces *each*) Spanish rice and pasta mix
- 1/4 cup butter, cubed
- 4 cups water
- 1 can (14-1/2 ounces) diced tomatoes, undrained
- 1 can (10 ounces) diced tomatoes and green chilies, undrained
- 3 cups cubed cooked turkey *or* chicken
- 1 can (11 ounces) whole kernel corn, drained
- 1/2 cup sour cream
- 1 cup (4 ounces) shredded Mexican cheese blend, *divided*

■ In a large skillet, saute rice and vermicelli in butter until golden brown. Gradually stir in the water, tomatoes and contents of rice seasoning packets. Bring to a boil. Reduce heat; cover and simmer for 15-20 minutes or until rice is tender.

■ Meanwhile, in a large bowl, combine the turkey, corn, sour cream and 1/2 cup cheese. Stir in rice mixture.

■ Transfer to a greased 3-qt. baking dish. Sprinkle with remaining cheese (dish will be full). Bake, uncovered, at 375° for 20-25 minutes or until heated through.

Yield: 8 servings.

Tasty Mozzarella Chicken

Nancy Foust
STONEBORO, PENNSYLVANIA
This amazingly easy chicken dish is sure to be a family favorite after just one taste.

PREP: 15 min.
BAKE: 30 min.

- 1 egg
- 2 tablespoons water
- 2/3 cup dry bread crumbs
- 1 envelope onion soup mix
- 1/8 teaspoon pepper
- 6 boneless skinless chicken breast halves (5 ounces *each*)
- 1-1/2 cups spaghetti sauce
- 1 can (7 ounces) mushroom stems and pieces, drained
- 1 cup (4 ounces) shredded part-skim mozzarella cheese

■ In a shallow bowl, beat egg and water. In a second shallow bowl, combine the bread crumbs, soup mix and pepper. Dip chicken in egg mixture, then coat with crumb mixture.

■ Place in a greased 13-in. x 9-in. baking dish. Bake, uncovered, at 400° for 22-25 minutes or until a meat thermometer reads 170°.

■ Combine spaghetti sauce and mushrooms; spoon over chicken. Sprinkle with cheese. Bake 5-7 minutes longer or until sauce is bubbly and cheese is melted.

Yield: 6 servings.

Nancy Zimmerman
CAPE MAY COURT HOUSE, NEW JERSEY

The well-seasoned bread stuffing in this golden bird is sparked by a festive sweetness from the apples and raisins. It's a staple on our holiday menu!

Turkey with Apple Stuffing

PREP: 20 min. ■ BAKE: 3-3/4 hours + standing

- 1-1/2 cups chopped celery
- 3/4 cup chopped onion
- 3/4 cup butter, cubed
- 9 cups day-old cubed whole wheat bread
- 3 cups finely chopped apples
- 3/4 cup raisins
- 1-1/2 teaspoons salt
- 1-1/2 teaspoons dried thyme
- 1/2 teaspoon rubbed sage
- 1/4 teaspoon pepper
- 1 turkey (14 to 16 pounds)
- Additional butter, melted

■ In a Dutch oven, saute celery and onion in butter until tender. Remove from the heat; stir in the bread cubes, apples, raisins, salt, thyme, sage and pepper.

■ Just before baking, loosely stuff turkey with 4 cups stuffing. Place remaining stuffing in a greased 2-qt. baking dish; refrigerate until ready to bake. Skewer turkey openings; tie drumsticks together. Place breast side up on a rack in a roasting pan. Brush with melted butter.

■ Bake, uncovered, at 325° for 3-3/4 to 4 hours or until a meat thermometer reads 180° for the turkey and 165° for the stuffing, basting occasionally with pan drippings. (Cover loosely with foil if turkey browns too quickly.)

■ Bake additional stuffing, covered, for 20-30 minutes. Uncover; bake 10 minutes longer or until lightly browned. Cover turkey and let stand for 20 minutes before removing stuffing and carving. If desired, thicken pan drippings for gravy.

Yield: 10-12 servings.

Editor's Note: Stuffing may be prepared as directed and baked separately in a greased 3-qt. baking dish. Cover and bake at 325° for 30 minutes. Uncover and bake 10 minutes longer or until lightly browned.

Turkey and stuffing tips: To be sure the stuffing is done, a meat thermometer inserted at the center of the stuffing inside the bird should reach 165°. Always remove the stuffing before carving the bird, and never leave stuffing in a cooked turkey when storing in the refrigerator. And finally, don't let cooked turkey and stuffing stand at room temperature longer than 2 hours.

Chicken Tarragon

Ruth Peterson
JENISON, MICHIGAN

This easy-to-fix entree combines moist chicken breasts with zucchini, carrots and mushrooms. I love tarragon, so I make this dish often.

PREP: 15 min.
BAKE: 30 min.

- 4 boneless skinless chicken breast halves
- 1/2 teaspoon paprika
- 1/3 cup butter, *divided*
- 2 medium zucchini, julienned
- 4 small carrots, julienned
- 4 large mushrooms, sliced
- 2 tablespoons minced fresh tarragon *or* 2 teaspoons dried tarragon
- 1 tablespoon lemon juice
- 1/2 teaspoon salt
- 1/8 teaspoon pepper

■ Sprinkle the chicken with paprika. In a large skillet, brown chicken in 2 teaspoons butter. Place the vegetables in a greased 13-in. x 9-in. baking dish. Top with chicken.

■ Melt the remaining butter; stir in the tarragon, lemon juice, salt and pepper. Pour over chicken and vegetables. Cover and bake at 350° for 30-35 minutes or until chicken juices run clear and vegetables are tender.

Yield: 4 servings.

Anna Ginsberg
AUSTIN, TEXAS

Bacon, turkey and Swiss cheese are the base of these very unique yet always delightful enchiladas. You'll need about a cup of leftover turkey meat for this recipe.

Club-Style Turkey Enchiladas

Club-Style Turkey Enchiladas

PREP: 25 min. ■ BAKE: 30 min.

- 8 bacon strips, chopped
- 1/2 cup chopped sweet red pepper
- 1/3 cup chopped onion
- 10 ounces thinly sliced cooked turkey, shredded
- 1-1/2 cups (6 ounces) shredded Swiss cheese, *divided*
- 1/4 teaspoon salt
- 1/4 teaspoon pepper
- 8 yellow corn tortillas (6 inches), warmed
- 1 carton (10 ounces) refrigerated Alfredo sauce
- 1/4 cup milk
- 2 cups shredded lettuce
- 1 can (14-1/2 ounces) diced tomatoes, well drained

■ In a large skillet, saute the bacon, red pepper and onion until bacon is crisp and vegetables are tender; drain. Cool slightly.

■ In a large bowl, combine the turkey, bacon mixture, 1 cup cheese, salt and pepper. Place 1/2 cup turkey mixture down the center of each tortilla. Roll up and place seam side down in a greased 13-in. x 9-in. baking dish. Combine Alfredo sauce and milk; pour over top.

■ Cover and bake at 350° for 25 minutes. Uncover; sprinkle with the remaining cheese. Bake 5-10 minutes longer or until the cheese is melted. Garnish with lettuce and tomatoes.

Yield: 4 servings.

Chicken With Onions And Figs

Helen Conwell
PORTLAND, OREGON

Friends and family can't get enough tender chicken in this sweet onion and fig sauce. When prepared this way, the meat turns out moist every time.

PREP: 40 min.
BAKE: 35 min.

- 3 large red onions, halved and sliced
- 3 tablespoons butter
- 10 dried figs, coarsely chopped
- 1/4 cup honey
- 2 tablespoons lemon juice
- 1 garlic clove, minced
- 1 teaspoon salt
- 4 pounds boneless skinless chicken thighs
- 1 teaspoon paprika

■ In a large skillet, saute onions in butter until tender. Add the figs, honey, lemon juice, garlic and salt. Bring to a boil. Reduce heat; cover and simmer for 20 minutes or until mixture is thick, stirring occasionally.

■ Place chicken in two greased 13-in. x 9-in. baking dishes. Spoon onion mixture over chicken. Sprinkle with paprika. Bake at 350° for 35-40 minutes or until a meat thermometer reads 180°. Serve with pan juices.

Yield: 8 servings.

Coq au Vin

Linda Clark
STONEY CREEK, ONTARIO

Don't let the name fool you, because this upscale classic is deliciously home-style. The dish has potatoes, chicken, carrots and a ton of flavor in every bite.

Coq au Vin

PREP: 20 min. ■ BAKE: 50 min.

- 6 medium red potatoes, quartered
- 1/2 cup water
- 2 medium carrots, sliced
- 1 can (10-3/4 ounces) condensed cream of mushroom soup, undiluted
- 1/2 cup white wine *or* chicken broth
- 1-1/2 teaspoons chicken bouillon granules
- 1 teaspoon minced garlic
- 1/2 teaspoon dried parsley flakes
- 1/4 teaspoon dried thyme
- 1/4 teaspoon pepper
- 4 boneless skinless chicken breast halves (6 ounces *each*)
- 1/2 pound sliced fresh mushrooms
- 4 bacon strips, cooked and crumbled
- 1/3 cup chopped green onions

■ Place the potatoes and water in a microwave-safe dish; cover and microwave on high for 3 minutes. Add carrots; cook 4 minutes longer or until vegetables are tender. Drain.

■ In a large bowl, combine the soup, wine, bouillon, garlic, parsley, thyme and pepper. Cut each chicken breast half into three pieces. Add the chicken, potato mixture, mushrooms, bacon and onions to the soup mixture; stir to coat.

■ Carefully transfer to a greased 13-in. x 9-in. baking dish. Cover and bake at 350° for 50-55 minutes or until chicken is no longer pink.

Yield: 6 servings.

"Coq au Vin" is a traditional French dish that means "rooster in wine," although in most recipes, chicken or capon are used. Aside from wine and chicken, this old, rustic recipe also calls for lardons (or bacon), mushrooms, onions and garlic.

Turkey Tetrazzini

Irene Banegas
LAS CRUCES, NEW MEXICO

Your family will flip over this turkey and mushroom casserole. In fact, the creamy Parmesan-topped tetrazzini is so satisfying, no one will suspect that it's low in fat.

Turkey Tetrazzini*

PREP: 25 min. ■ BAKE: 25 min.

- 1/2 pound uncooked spaghetti
- 1/4 cup finely chopped onion
- 1 tablespoon butter
- 1 garlic clove, minced
- 3 tablespoons cornstarch
- 1 can (14-1/2 ounces) reduced-sodium chicken broth
- 1 can (12 ounces) fat-free evaporated milk
- 2-1/2 cups cubed cooked turkey breast
- 1 can (4 ounces) mushroom stems and pieces, drained
- 1/2 teaspoon seasoned salt
- Dash pepper
- 2 tablespoons grated Parmesan cheese
- 1/4 teaspoon paprika

■ Cook spaghetti according to package directions; drain.

■ In a large saucepan, saute onion in butter until tender. Add garlic; cook 1 minute longer. Combine cornstarch and broth until smooth; stir into the onion mixture. Bring to a boil; cook and stir for 2 minutes or until thickened.

■ Reduce heat to low. Add milk; cook and stir for 2-3 minutes. Stir in the spaghetti, turkey, mushrooms, seasoned salt and pepper.

■ Transfer to an 8-in. square baking dish coated with cooking spray. Cover and bake at 350° for 20 minutes. Uncover; sprinkle with cheese and paprika. Bake 5-10 minutes longer or until heated through.

Yield: 6 servings.

***Nutrition Facts:** 1-1/4 cups equals 331 calories, 5 g fat (2 g saturated fat), 51 mg cholesterol, 544 mg sodium, 41 g carbohydrate, 1 g fiber, 28 g protein. **Diabetic Exchanges:** 3 very lean meat, 2 starch, 1 vegetable, 1/2 fat-free milk.

Taste of Home Test Kitchen

Start the night off right with this mouthwatering dish from our Test Kitchen. Lemon pie filling is the secret ingredient to the moist chicken's full-flavored sauce.

Lemon Chicken with Rice

Lemon Chicken with Rice

PREP: 25 min. ■ BAKE: 40 min.

- 1/3 cup biscuit/baking mix
- 1 teaspoon seasoned salt
- 1/2 teaspoon pepper
- 4 bone-in chicken breast halves (12 ounces *each*), skin removed
- 1/4 cup olive oil
- 1-1/3 cups lemon pie filling
- 1/2 cup water
- 1/3 cup cider vinegar
- 1/4 cup soy sauce

TOMATO PARSLEY RICE:

- 2 cups water
- 1 teaspoon chicken bouillon granules
- 1/8 teaspoon pepper
- 2 cups uncooked instant rice
- 1 medium tomato, seeded and chopped
- 3 tablespoons minced fresh parsley

■ In a large resealable plastic bag, combine the biscuit mix, seasoned salt and pepper. Add chicken, one piece at a time, and shake to coat.

■ In a large skillet, brown chicken in oil on both sides; drain. Transfer to a 13-in. x 9-in. baking dish. In a small bowl, combine the pie filling, water, vinegar and soy sauce; pour over chicken.

■ Bake, uncovered, at 375° for 40-45 minutes or until a meat thermometer reads 170°.

■ In a large saucepan, bring the water, bouillon and pepper to a boil. Stir in the rice, tomato and parsley. Cover and remove from the heat; let stand for 5 minutes. Fluff with a fork. Serve with chicken.

Yield: 4 servings.

Garlic-Roasted Chicken and Potatoes

Beth Erbert
LIVERMORE, CALIFORNIA

This recipe has been in my "favorites" file for almost 20 years. My husband and I enjoyed it before we had kids, and now they love it, too. It's a real timesaver since it comes together so very easily.

PREP: 20 min.
BAKE: 1 hour

- 6 bone-in chicken thighs (about 2-1/4 pounds)
- 6 chicken drumsticks
- 6 medium red potatoes (about 2 pounds), cut into 1-inch cubes
- 24 garlic cloves, peeled
- 1/4 cup butter, melted
- 1 teaspoon salt, *divided*
- 1/4 cup maple syrup

■ Place the chicken, potatoes and garlic in a large roasting pan. Drizzle with butter; sprinkle with 3/4 teaspoon salt. Toss to coat. Bake, uncovered, at 400° for 40 minutes.

■ Combine the syrup and remaining salt; drizzle over chicken. Spoon pan juices over potatoes and garlic. Bake 20 minutes longer or until a meat thermometer reads 180° and potatoes are tender.

Yield: 6 servings.

Colorful Chicken Pizza

Kelli Stone
BOISE, IDAHO

I threw this pizza together on a hot summer night when I needed something quick to satisfy my fiance and me. Without a doubt, my experiment was a smashing success.

Colorful Chicken Pizza

PREP/TOTAL TIME: 25 min.

- 1 prebaked 12-inch pizza crust
- 2 tablespoons olive oil
- 1 package (6 ounces) ready-to-use grilled chicken breast strips
- 1/2 cup barbecue sauce
- 1/3 cup chopped onion
- 1-1/2 teaspoons minced garlic
- 1-1/2 cups (6 ounces) shredded pizza cheese blend
- 1/4 cup chopped sweet red pepper
- 1/4 cup chopped green pepper
- 2 ounces smoked Gouda cheese, shredded
- 2 tablespoons minced fresh basil

■ Place crust on an ungreased 12-in. pizza pan. Brush with oil. Combine the chicken, barbecue sauce, onion and garlic; spoon half over crust.

■ Sprinkle with pizza cheese. Top with remaining chicken mixture. Sprinkle with the peppers, Gouda cheese and basil.

■ Bake at 450° for 10-12 minutes or until cheese is melted.

Yield: 6 slices.

Chicken & Corn Bread Bake

PREP: 25 min.
BAKE: 25 min.

- 2-1/2 cups reduced-sodium chicken broth
- 1 small onion, chopped
- 1 celery rib, chopped
- 1/8 teaspoon pepper
- 4-1/2 cups corn bread stuffing mix, *divided*
- 4 cups cubed cooked chicken
- 1-1/2 cups (12 ounces) sour cream
- 1 can (10-3/4 ounces) condensed cream of chicken soup, undiluted
- 3 green onions, thinly sliced
- 1/4 cup butter, cubed

■ In a large saucepan, combine the broth, onion, celery and pepper. Bring to a boil. Reduce the heat; cover and simmer for 5-6 minutes or until vegetables are tender. Stir in 4 cups stuffing mix.

■ Transfer to a greased 13-in. x 9-in. baking dish. Top with chicken. In a small bowl, combine the sour cream, soup and green onions. Spread over chicken. Sprinkle with remaining stuffing mix; dot with butter.

■ Bake, uncovered, for 325° for 25-30 minutes or until heated through.

Yield: 8 servings.

Ann Hillmeyer
SANDIA PARK, NEW MEXICO

Here's Southern comfort food at its best! This filling casserole is delicious made with either chicken or turkey. It's often on the menu when I cook for my husband, our four children and their spouses and our 10 grandkids.

Pork

The irresistible flavor of pork, whether it comes in the form of finger-licking ribs, swift and savory tenderloin, smoky ham, convenient chops or juicy sausages, always makes a great meal. In this chapter, there are plenty of hearty oven entrees and robust casseroles to satisfy everyone.

Cheese-Stuffed Shells

Lori Mecca
GRANTS PASS, OREGON

When I was living in California, I tasted this rich cheesy pasta dish at a neighborhood Italian restaurant. I got the recipe and made a few changes to it in my own kitchen.

Cheese-Stuffed Shells

PREP: 35 min. ■ BAKE: 50 min.

- 1 pound bulk Italian sausage
- 1 large onion, chopped
- 1 package (10 ounces) frozen chopped spinach, thawed and squeezed dry
- 1 package (8 ounces) cream cheese, cubed
- 1 egg, lightly beaten
- 2 cups (8 ounces) shredded part-skim mozzarella cheese, *divided*
- 2 cups (8 ounces) shredded cheddar cheese
- 1 cup 4% cottage cheese
- 1 cup grated Parmesan cheese
- 1/4 teaspoon salt
- 1/4 teaspoon pepper
- 1/8 teaspoon ground cinnamon, optional
- 24 jumbo pasta shells, cooked and drained

SAUCE:

- 1 can (29 ounces) tomato sauce
- 1 tablespoon dried minced onion
- 1-1/2 teaspoons dried basil
- 1-1/2 teaspoons dried parsley flakes
- 2 garlic cloves, minced
- 1 teaspoon sugar
- 1 teaspoon dried oregano
- 1/2 teaspoon salt
- 1/4 teaspoon pepper

■ In a large skillet, cook the sausage and onion over medium heat until meat is no longer pink; drain. Transfer to a large bowl. Stir in the spinach, cream cheese and egg. Add 1 cup mozzarella cheese, cheddar cheese, cottage cheese, Parmesan cheese, salt, pepper and cinnamon if desired.

■ Stuff pasta shells with the sausage mixture. Arrange in two 11-in. x 7-in. baking dishes coated with cooking spray. Combine the sauce ingredients; spoon over shells.

■ Cover and bake at 350° for 45 minutes. Uncover; sprinkle with remaining mozzarella. Bake 5-10 minutes longer or until bubbly and cheese is melted. Let stand for 5 minutes before serving.

Yield: 12 servings.

Instead of draining jumbo pasta shells in a colander (which can cause them to tear), carefully remove them from the boiling water with a pair of tongs. Pour out any water inside the shells and drain on lightly greased waxed paper until you're ready to stuff them.

Corn Dog Casserole

Marcy Suzanne Olipane
BELLEVILLE, ILLINOIS

Reminiscent of traditional corn dogs, this fun entree really hits the spot on fall days. It's perfect for the football parties my husband and I often host.

Corn Dog Casserole

PREP: 25 min. ■ BAKE: 30 min.

- 2 cups thinly sliced celery
- 2 tablespoons butter
- 1-1/2 cups sliced green onions
- 1-1/2 pounds hot dogs
- 2 eggs
- 1-1/2 cups milk
- 2 teaspoons rubbed sage
- 1/4 teaspoon pepper
- 2 packages (8-1/2 ounces *each*) corn bread/muffin mix
- 2 cups (8 ounces) shredded sharp cheddar cheese, *divided*

■ In a small skillet, saute celery in butter for 5 minutes. Add onions; saute for 5 minutes longer or until vegetables are tender. Place in a large bowl; set aside.

■ Cut hot dogs lengthwise into quarters, then cut into thirds. In the same skillet, saute hot dogs for 5 minutes or until lightly browned; add to the vegetables. Set aside 1 cup.

■ In a large bowl, whisk the eggs, milk, sage and pepper. Add the remaining hot dog mixture. Stir in corn bread mixes. Add 1-1/2 cups of cheese. Spread into a shallow 3-qt. baking dish. Top with reserved hot dog mixture and remaining cheese.

■ Bake, uncovered, at 400° for 30 minutes or until golden brown.

Yield: 12 servings.

If you have washed, dried and chopped more green onions than you need in your recipe, store the leftovers in a covered glass jar in the refrigerator. They'll last a couple of weeks this way. Just shake them out as needed.

Doris Natvig
JESUP, IOWA

My mother's wonderful corn dressing recipe goes so well with pork chops, making them especially moist and tender. This main dish takes very little effort to prepare, and it's a winner every time.

Pork Chops with Corn Dressing

Pork Chops with Corn Dressing

PREP: 15 min. ■ BAKE: 1 hour

- 2 eggs, lightly beaten
- 2 cans (15 ounces *each*) cream-style corn *or* 1 can cream-style corn and 1 can (15-1/4 ounces) whole kernel corn, drained
- 1/4 cup butter, melted
- 1/3 cup chopped celery
- 2 tablespoons chopped pimiento
- 4 slices white bread, cubed (about 2 cups)
- 1/2 teaspoon paprika
- 1/2 teaspoon salt
- 1/2 teaspoon pepper
- 4 bone-in center-cut pork loin chops (about 1 inch thick and 7 ounces *each*)
- Additional paprika and salt

■ In a large bowl, combine the eggs, corn, butter, celery, pimiento, bread cubes, paprika, salt and pepper. Spoon into a greased 13-in. x 9-in. baking pan.

■ Arrange pork chops over dressing. Sprinkle with additional paprika and salt. Cover and bake at 350° for 30 minutes. Uncover and bake 30 minutes longer or until a meat thermometer reads 160°.

Yield: 4-6 servings.

Pork Chops And Sauerkraut

Delma Carretta
WALLINGFORD, CONNECTICUT

I make this hearty dish often for guests. I think the sauerkraut tastes very much like what we enjoyed in Munich restaurants when we visited Germany.

PREP: 20 min.
BAKE: 1 hour

- 3 cups sauerkraut, well drained
- 2 cups applesauce
- 1/2 cup chicken broth
- 1/2 pound sliced bacon, cooked and crumbled
- 1 tablespoon brown sugar
- 1 teaspoon dried thyme
- 1/2 teaspoon ground mustard
- 1/2 teaspoon dried oregano
- 1/2 teaspoon salt
- 1/2 teaspoon pepper
- 6 pork chops (1 inch thick and 7 ounces *each*)
- 2 tablespoons canola oil
- 1/4 teaspoon paprika

■ In a large bowl, combine the sauerkraut, applesauce, chicken broth, bacon, brown sugar and seasonings; spoon into an ungreased 13-in. x 9-in. baking dish.

■ In a large skillet, brown pork chops in oil; drain. Place chops over the sauerkraut mixture. Sprinkle with paprika. Cover and bake at 350° for 1 to 1-1/4 hours or until a meat thermometer reads 160°.

Yield: 6 servings.

Dianne Esposite
NEW MIDDLETOWN, OHIO

I'm always on the lookout for good, quick dishes to fix for my family, and get a lot of recipes from friends. This zippy casserole was brought to a get-together at my house, and people raved over it!

Pork and Green Chili Casserole

Pork and Green Chili Casserole

PREP: 20 min. ■ BAKE: 30 min.

- 1-1/2 pounds boneless pork, cut into 1/2-inch cubes
- 1 tablespoon canola oil
- 1 can (15 ounces) black beans, rinsed and drained
- 1 can (10-3/4 ounces) condensed cream of chicken soup, undiluted
- 1 can (14-1/2 ounces) diced tomatoes, undrained
- 2 cans (4 ounces *each*) chopped green chilies
- 1 cup quick-cooking brown rice
- 1/4 cup water
- 2 to 3 tablespoons salsa
- 1 teaspoon ground cumin
- 1/2 cup shredded cheddar cheese

■ In a large skillet, saute pork in oil until no pink remains; drain. Add the beans, soup, tomatoes, chilies, rice, water, salsa and cumin; cook and stir until bubbly.

■ Pour into an ungreased 2-qt. baking dish. Bake, uncovered, at 350° for 30 minutes or until bubbly. Sprinkle with cheese; let stand a few minutes before serving.

Yield: 6 servings.

Spinach Ravioli Bake

Susan Kehl
PEMBROKE PINES, FLORIDA

This entree is unbelievably simple to prepare yet tastes delicious. The fact that you use frozen ravioli—straight from the bag without boiling or thawing—saves so much time.

PREP: 5 min.
BAKE: 40 min.

- 2 cups spaghetti sauce
- 1 package (25 ounces) frozen sausage ravioli *or* ravioli of your choice
- 2 cups (8 ounces) shredded part-skim mozzarella cheese
- 1 package (10 ounces) frozen chopped spinach, thawed and squeezed dry
- 1/4 cup grated Parmesan cheese

■ Place 1 cup of the spaghetti sauce in a greased shallow 2-qt. baking dish. Top with half of the ravioli, mozzarella, spinach and Parmesan cheese. Repeat layers.

■ Bake, uncovered, at 350° for 40-45 minutes or until heated through and cheese is melted.

Yield: 4-6 servings.

Pork Hot Dish

Marie Leadens
MAPLE GROVE, MINNESOTA

This recipe is a winner...I know, because I once entered it in a contest and it took first prize! This hot dish works well for our family of 10 and is a favorite at parties.

Pork Hot Dish

PREP: 20 min. ■ BAKE: 45 min.

- 1 pound boneless pork, cut into bite-size pieces
- 1/2 cup chopped celery
- 1/4 cup chopped sweet red *or* green pepper
- 1/4 cup chopped onion
- 1 tablespoon canola oil
- 1 package (10 ounces) medium egg noodles, cooked and drained
- 1 can (10-3/4 ounces) condensed cream of mushroom soup, undiluted
- 1 can (10-3/4 ounces) condensed cream of chicken soup, undiluted
- 1 can (16-1/2 ounces) cream-style corn
- 1/2 cup milk
- 1 teaspoon salt
- 1/4 teaspoon pepper
- 1 cup crushed saltines
- 3 tablespoons butter, melted

■ In a large skillet, over medium heat, cook the pork, celery, red pepper and onion in oil until the meat is browned and vegetables are tender. In a large bowl, combine the pork mixture, noodles, soups, corn, milk, salt and pepper.

■ Transfer to an ungreased 13-in. x 9-in. baking dish. Combine the cracker crumbs and butter; sprinkle over the top. Bake, uncovered, at 350° for 45-50 minutes or until the meat is tender.

Yield: 8-10 servings.

Give limp celery a second chance to season entrees, soups and stews. Cut the ends from any limp stalks. Place in a jar or glass of cold water. Refrigerate for several hours or overnight.

Corny Pork Chops

Ralph Petterson
SALT LAKE CITY, UTAH

My grandmother began making this recipe in the 1950s, and it remains a family favorite today. As simple as it seems, the corn dressing complements the pork beautifully.

Corny Pork Chops

PREP: 15 min. ■ BAKE: 45 min.

- 4 bone-in pork loin chops (3/4 to 1 inch thick and 7 ounces *each*)
- 1 teaspoon salt, *divided*
- 1/4 teaspoon pepper, *divided*
- 1 tablespoon canola oil
- 1 can (15-1/4 ounces) whole kernel corn, drained
- 2 celery ribs, diced
- 1 cup soft bread crumbs
- 1/3 cup ketchup
- 1 tablespoon chopped green onion

■ Season pork chops with 1/2 teaspoon salt and 1/8 teaspoon pepper. In a large skillet, brown pork in oil on both sides.

■ Combine the corn, celery, bread crumbs, ketchup, onion, and remaining salt and pepper; place in a greased 11-in. x 7-in. baking dish. Top with chops.

■ Cover and bake at 350° for 45-55 minutes or until a meat thermometer reads 160°.

Yield: 4 servings.

Oven-Barbecued Spareribs

PREP: 30 min.
BAKE: 1-1/2 hours

- 6 pounds pork spareribs
- 3 cups ketchup
- 1-1/2 cups packed brown sugar
- 3/4 cup chopped onion
- 1 teaspoon garlic powder
- 4 to 5 teaspoons Liquid Smoke, optional

■ Cut ribs into serving-size pieces; place on a rack in a shallow roasting pan. Bake, uncovered, at 350° for 30 minutes.

■ Meanwhile, in a large saucepan, combine the remaining ingredients. Simmer, uncovered, for 20 minutes, stirring occasionally. Drain ribs; pour sauce over all.

■ Cover and bake for 30-40 minutes or until tender. Uncover; bake 30 minutes longer, basting several times with sauce.

Yield: 6-8 servings.

LaVerna Mjones
MOORHEAD, MINNESOTA

This dish, which is one of my family's favorites, is often at the heart of our special meals. All our married children live nearby, so we often have family gatherings. Whenever I prepare these spareribs, I need a large quantity—everyone asks for seconds.

Phyllis Sheeley
ALTONA, ILLINOIS

This hearty casserole has become one of my family's most requested. It's easy to make and a delicious way to use sausage. I even make it for brunch. Try it with cream of chicken soup, too.

Sausage Potato Casserole

Sausage Potato Casserole

PREP: 15 min. ■ BAKE: 1 hour 35 min.

- 1 pound bulk pork sausage
- 1 can (10-3/4 ounces) condensed cream of mushroom soup, undiluted
- 3/4 cup milk
- 1/4 cup chopped onion
- 1/2 teaspoon salt
- 1/4 teaspoon pepper
- 3 cups thinly sliced peeled potatoes (about 1-1/4 pounds)
- 1 cup (4 ounces) shredded cheddar cheese

■ In a large skillet, cook sausage over medium heat until no longer pink; drain. In a large bowl, combine the soup, milk, onion, salt and pepper.

■ In an ungreased 11-in. x 7-in. baking dish, layer half the potatoes, soup mixture and sausage; repeat layers.

■ Cover and bake at 350° for 1-1/2 hours or until potatoes are tender. Uncover and sprinkle with cheese. Bake 5 minutes longer or until cheese is melted.

Yield: 4-6 servings.

Mostaccioli

Nancy Mundhenke
KINSLEY, KANSAS

Even though we're not Italian, this rich, cheesy pasta dish is a tradition for holidays and special occasions. It has all the flavor of lasagna without the work of layering the ingredients.

PREP: 15 min.
BAKE: 45 min.

- 1 pound uncooked mostaccioli
- 1-1/2 pounds bulk Italian sausage
- 1 jar (28 ounces) meatless spaghetti sauce
- 1 egg, lightly beaten
- 1 carton (15 ounces) ricotta cheese
- 2 cups (8 ounces *each*) shredded part-skim mozzarella cheese
- 1/2 cup grated Romano cheese

■ Cook pasta according to package directions; drain. Crumble sausage into a Dutch oven. Cook over medium heat until no longer pink; drain. Stir in spaghetti sauce and pasta. In a large bowl, combine the egg, ricotta cheese and mozzarella cheese.

■ Spoon half of the pasta mixture into a greased shallow 3-qt. baking dish; layer with cheese mixture and remaining pasta mixture.

■ Cover and bake at 375° for 40 minutes or until a meat thermometer reads 160°. Uncover and top with Romano cheese. Bake 5 minutes longer or until heated through.

Yield: 10-12 servings.

Potluck Casserole

Janet Wielhouwer
GRAND RAPIDS, MICHIGAN

Whenever I take this dish to family picnics and potlucks—which is quite often—people compare it to tuna casserole. It reminds folks of my mother's cooking.

Potluck Casserole*

PREP: 1-1/4 hours ■ BAKE: 20 min.

- 1/2 pound boneless pork, cut into 3/4-inch cubes
- 1 cup sliced celery
- 1/4 cup chopped onion
- 2 tablespoons water
- 2 cups cooked noodles
- 1 can (10-3/4 ounces) condensed cream of mushroom soup, undiluted
- 1 cup frozen peas
- 1/4 teaspoon salt, optional
- 1/8 teaspoon pepper
- 3 tablespoons seasoned *or* plain dry bread crumbs

■ In a large skillet coated with cooking spray, brown pork over medium heat until no longer pink. Add the celery, onion and water; cover and simmer for 1 hour or until pork is tender.

■ Remove from the heat; add the noodles, soup, peas, salt if desired and pepper.

■ Transfer to an ungreased 11-in. x 7-in. baking dish; sprinkle with bread crumbs. Bake, uncovered, at 350° for 20 minutes or until bubbly.

Yield: 4 servings.

***Nutrition Facts:** 1/4 recipe (prepared with yolk-free noodles, reduced-fat soup and plain bread crumbs; calculated w/o added salt) equals 244 calories, 5 g fat (0 saturated fat), 51 mg cholesterol, 440 mg sodium, 26 g carbohydrate, 0 fiber, 22 g protein. **Diabetic Exchanges:** 2 lean meat, 1-1/2 starch, 1 vegetable.

It's a snap to make seasoned bread crumbs. Simply break slices of dried bread into pieces and process in a blender or food processor until fine. Then season with dried basil and oregano, garlic and onion powder, grated Parmesan cheese, salt and paprika according to your family's tastes.

Italian Shepherd's Pie

Cindy Gage
BLAIR, NEBRASKA

For a stick-to-your-ribs main dish that's deliciously different, give this pie a try! The Italian sausage goes well with mashed potatoes, and both get a new twist served in a crust.

Italian Shepherd's Pie

PREP: 20 min. ■ BAKE: 50 min.

- 1 unbaked pastry shell (9 inches)
- 1 pound bulk Italian sausage
- 1 cup (8 ounces) cream-style cottage cheese
- 1 egg
- 1-1/2 cups warm mashed potatoes (without added milk and butter)
- 1/4 cup sour cream
- 1/2 teaspoon dried oregano
- 1/2 to 3/4 teaspoon salt
- 1/8 teaspoon pepper
- 2 teaspoons butter, melted
- 1 cup (4 ounces) shredded cheddar cheese
- Cherry tomatoes, quartered
- Minced fresh parsley, optional

■ Line unpricked pastry shell with a double thickness of heavy-duty foil. Bake at 450° for 7 minutes. Remove from the oven and remove foil; set aside. Reduce heat to 350°.

■ In a skillet, cook sausage until no longer pink; drain well on paper towels. Place cottage cheese and egg in a blender; cover and process until smooth. Transfer to a large bowl; stir in potatoes, sour cream, oregano, salt and pepper.

■ Place sausage in pastry shell; top with potato mixture. Drizzle with butter. Bake for 50-60 minutes or until set. Sprinkle with cheese; let stand for a few minutes until cheese is melted. Garnish with the tomatoes tossed with minced parsley if desired.

Yield: 6-8 servings.

For the fluffiest mashed potatoes, use only russets and be careful not to overbeat. Cook just until tender; immediately drain and let them stand uncovered for 1-2 minutes.

Renee Schwebach
DUMONT, MINNESOTA

Frozen green peas add lovely color to this comforting meal-in-one. The easy, cheesy entree is a terrific way to use baked ham from a holiday feast or dinner party.

Ham 'n' Noodle Hot Dish

Ham 'n' Noodle Hot Dish

PREP: 15 min. ■ BAKE: 30 min.

- 3 tablespoons butter, *divided*
- 2 tablespoons all-purpose flour
- 1 cup milk
- 1 cup (4 ounces) shredded process cheese (Velveeta)
- 1/2 teaspoon salt
- 2 cups diced fully cooked ham
- 1-1/2 cups elbow macaroni *or* medium noodles, cooked and drained
- 1 cup frozen peas, thawed
- 1/4 cup dry bread crumbs
- 1/2 teaspoon dried parsley flakes

■ In a saucepan, melt 2 tablespoons butter; stir in flour until smooth. Gradually add milk. Bring to a boil over medium heat; cook and stir for 2 minutes. Remove from the heat; stir in cheese and salt until cheese is melted.

■ Add the ham, noodles and peas. Pour into a greased 1-qt. baking dish. Melt remaining butter; add bread crumbs and parsley. Sprinkle over casserole.

■ Bake, uncovered, at 350° for 30 minutes or until heated through.

Yield: 4 servings.

Ham and Cheese Souffle

Airy Murray
WILLIAMSPORT, MARYLAND

I like to serve this tasty dish for brunch along with fresh fruit. Not only is it easy, but everyone enjoys it. Make it the night before, then the next day all you need to do is bake it.

PREP: 15 min. + chilling
BAKE: 40 min. + standing

- 16 slices white bread (crusts removed), cubed
- 16 slices (about 1 pound) ham, cut into bite-size pieces
- 2 cups (8 ounces) shredded cheddar cheese
- 2 cups (8 ounces) shredded Swiss cheese
- 5 eggs, lightly beaten
- 3 cups milk
- 1 teaspoon ground mustard
- 1/2 teaspoon onion salt
- 2-1/2 cups crushed cornflakes
- 1/3 cup butter, melted

■ In a greased 13-in. x 9-in. baking dish, layer half of the bread, ham, cheddar cheese and Swiss cheese. Repeat layers. In a small bowl, whisk the eggs, milk, mustard and onion salt; pour over layered mixture.

■ Cover and refrigerate overnight. Combine cornflakes and butter; sprinkle on top. Bake at 375° for 40 minutes or until a knife inserted near the middle comes out clean. Let stand 10 minutes before serving.

Yield: 8-10 servings.

Denise Dowd
ST. LOUIS, MISSOURI

This recipe is great for a busy week because it makes enough pork for two meals. Serve one tenderloin with the potatoes for a family dinner, then use the leftover in another recipe later in the week.

Herbed Pork and Potatoes

Herbed Pork and Potatoes

PREP: 10 min. ■ BAKE: 40 min.

- 1/2 cup olive oil
- 3 teaspoons minced fresh thyme *or* 1 teaspoon dried thyme
- 2 teaspoons minced garlic
- 2 teaspoons dried minced onion
- 2 teaspoons minced fresh rosemary *or* 1/2 teaspoon dried rosemary, crushed
- 1 teaspoon seasoned salt
- 1 teaspoon coarsely ground pepper
- 1 teaspoon ground mustard
- 2 pork tenderloins (1 pound *each*)
- 1 pound small red potatoes, quartered

■ In a small bowl, combine the first eight ingredients. Place the pork in a large shallow baking pan. Drizzle with three-fourths of the herb mixture. Toss potatoes with remaining herb mixture; place around pork.

■ Bake, uncovered, at 375° for 40-45 minutes or until a meat thermometer reads 160° and potatoes are tender. Let pork stand for 5 minutes before slicing.

Yield: 3-4 servings with potatoes plus 1 pound leftover pork.

Pork Chops And Chilies Casserole

Mickey O'Neal
CHULA VISTA, CALIFORNIA

A real estate agent who wanted to list my house dropped off this recipe at my door. I didn't sell the house, but the recipe has saved my life many times!

PREP: 15 min.
BAKE: 30 min.

- 4 pork rib chops (3/4 to 1 inch thick)
- 1 tablespoon canola oil
- 1 medium onion, chopped
- 1 can (4 ounces) chopped green chilies
- 1/2 cup chopped celery
- 1-1/2 cups uncooked instant rice
- 1 can (10-3/4 ounces) condensed cream of mushroom soup, undiluted
- 1-1/3 cups water
- 3 tablespoons soy sauce

■ In a large skillet, over medium-high heat, brown pork chops on both sides in oil. Remove and set aside. In the same skillet, saute the onion, chilies and celery until onion is tender. Stir in rice; saute until lightly browned. Add all remaining ingredients.

■ Place in a greased 2-qt. casserole. Top with pork chops. Bake at 350° for about 30 minutes or until a meat thermometer reads 160° and the rice is tender.

Yield: 4 servings.

Hearty Ribs & Beans

Marlene Muckenhirn
DELANO, MINNESOTA

This is one of my favorite ways to prepare spareribs. The celery and red pepper add color to the meaty meal, which always gets rave reviews from family and friends.

Hearty Ribs & Beans

PREP: 25 min. ■ BAKE: 2-1/4 hours

- 3 to 3-1/2 pounds country-style pork spareribs
- 1/4 cup water
- 1 can (14-1/2 ounces) tomato sauce
- 1 envelope onion soup mix
- 1/3 cup packed brown sugar
- 2 tablespoons prepared mustard
- 1/8 teaspoon hot pepper sauce
- 2 cans (15-1/2 ounces *each*) great northern beans, rinsed and drained
- 2 cans (15-1/2 ounces *each*) kidney beans, rinsed and drained
- 1-1/2 cups thinly sliced celery
- 1 sweet red pepper, thinly sliced

■ Place ribs in an ungreased 13-in. x 9-in. baking dish; add water. Cover and bake at 350° for 1-1/2 hours. Drain, reserving liquid; skim fat. Set ribs aside.

■ Add enough water to liquid to equal 1 cup; place in a saucepan. Add tomato sauce, soup mix, brown sugar, mustard and hot sauce. Simmer for 10 minutes; reserve 1/2 cup.

■ To the remaining sauce, add the beans, celery and red pepper. Pour into the baking dish; add ribs. Pour reserved sauce over ribs. Cover and bake for 45 minutes.

Yield: 6-8 servings.

Country-style

pork ribs are the meaty ribs from the rib end of the pork loin. They are sold (with and without bones) both in slabs and individually.

Sally Holbrook
PASADENA, CALIFORNIA

When I was growing up, Mom often made this tasty casserole in the summer for family and guests. It's a great use of garden vegetables, and the sausage adds that comforting flavor everyone craves. I'm sure you'll enjoy it as much as we do.

Sausage Pie

PREP: 20 min. ■ BAKE: 30 min.

- 16 fresh pork sausage links (about 1 pound)
- 1/2 medium green pepper, chopped
- 1/2 medium sweet red pepper, chopped
- 1 tablespoon canola oil
- 3 cups cooked long grain rice
- 4 to 5 medium tomatoes, peeled and chopped
- 1 package (10 ounces) frozen corn, thawed
- 1 cup (4 ounces) shredded cheddar cheese
- 2 tablespoons minced fresh parsley
- 1 tablespoon Worcestershire sauce
- 1 teaspoon salt
- 1 teaspoon dried basil
- 1 cup soft bread crumbs
- 2 tablespoons butter, melted

■ Place sausages on a rack in a baking pan. Bake at 350° for 15 minutes or until lightly browned and no longer pink. Cut into 1-in. pieces; set aside.

■ In a large skillet, saute peppers in oil for 3 minutes or until crisp-tender. Transfer to a 3-qt. baking dish. Add the sausages and the next eight ingredients.

■ Combine bread crumbs and butter; sprinkle over top. Bake, uncovered, at 350° for 30-40 minutes or until heated through.

Yield: 6-8 servings.

In 1835, English Lord Sandys commissioned two chemists from Worcestershire, John Lea and William Perrins, to duplicate a sauce he had acquired during his travels in India. The pungent batch proved disappointing and wound up in the cellar. When the pair stumbled upon the aged concoction 2 years later, they tasted it and were pleasantly surprised by its unique flavor.

Ham 'n' Cheese Pasta

Karen Kopp
INDIANAPOLIS, INDIANA

My mother would prepare this yummy comfort food whenever we had leftover ham. And now my kids love it, too! The addition of horseradish makes the sauce tangy. To speed things up, I often use process cheese instead of making a cheese sauce from scratch. Luckily, the recipe can be doubled easily.

PREP: 15 min.
BAKE: 30 min.

- 8 ounces uncooked medium pasta shells
- 1 pound process cheese (Velveeta), cubed
- 1/2 cup milk
- 2 tablespoons ketchup
- 1 tablespoon prepared horseradish
- 2 cups cubed fully cooked ham
- 1 package (8 ounces) frozen peas, thawed

■ Cook pasta according to package directions. Meanwhile, in a microwave-safe bowl, combine cheese and milk. Cover and microwave on high for 2 minutes; stir. Heat 1-2 minutes longer or until smooth, stirring twice. Stir in ketchup and horseradish until blended.

■ Drain pasta and place in a large bowl. Stir in the ham, peas and cheese sauce.

■ Transfer to a greased 2-qt. baking dish. Cover and bake at 350° for 30-35 minutes or until bubbly.

Yield: 4 servings.

Cherry-Stuffed Pork Loin

James Korzenowski
FENNVILLE, MICHIGAN

This simple pork roast is moist and has a delightful stuffing. Perfect for guests, it looks and tastes impressive, and the gravy is a great addition.

Cherry-Stuffed Pork Loin

PREP: 55 min. ■ **BAKE:** 1-1/2 hours + standing

- 1 cup dried cherries
- 1/2 cup water
- 2/3 cup chopped onion
- 1/2 cup chopped celery
- 1/2 cup minced fresh parsley
- 1/4 cup shredded carrot
- 1 tablespoon rubbed sage
- 1 teaspoon minced fresh rosemary
- 3 tablespoons butter
- 1/2 teaspoon minced garlic
- 2-1/2 cups salad croutons
- 1 cup chicken broth
- 1/2 teaspoon pepper, *divided*
- 1/4 teaspoon ground nutmeg
- 1/4 teaspoon almond extract
- 1 boneless whole pork loin roast (about 3 pounds)

GRAVY:

- 1-3/4 cups chicken broth
- 1/2 cup water
- 1/2 cup heavy whipping cream
- 1/2 teaspoon minced fresh rosemary

■ In a small saucepan, bring cherries and water to a boil, Remove from the heat; set aside (do not drain).

■ In a large skillet, saute the onion, celery, parsley, carrot, sage and rosemary in butter until tender. Add garlic; cook 1 minute longer. Remove from the heat. Stir in the croutons, broth, 1/4 teaspoon pepper, nutmeg, extract and cherries. Let stand until liquid is absorbed.

■ Cut a lengthwise slit down the center of the roast to within 1/2 in. of bottom. Open roast so it lies flat; cover with plastic wrap. Flatten to 3/4-in. thickness. Remove plastic; spread stuffing over meat to within 1 in. of edges. Close roast; tie several times with kitchen string and secure ends with toothpicks. Place fat side up on a rack in a shallow roasting pan. Sprinkle with remaining pepper.

■ Bake, uncovered, at 350° for 1-1/2 to 2 hours or until a meat thermometer reads 160°. Let stand for 10-15 minutes before slicing. Meanwhile, add broth and water to roasting pan; stir to loosen browned bits. Pour into a small saucepan. Bring to a boil over medium-high heat; cook until reduced by half. Stir in cream and rosemary. Bring to a boil. Reduce heat; simmer, uncovered, until thickened. Serve with roast.

Yield: 10-12 servings.

Joyce Leigh
GRAND JUNCTION, COLORADO

This hearty sausage dish has been a family favorite for more than 20 years. My four children were raised on it. It's easy to throw together, and it tastes wonderful.

Country Pizza Pie

Country Pizza Pie

PREP: 25 min. ■ BAKE: 35 min. + standing

- 1 unbaked pastry shell (9 inches)
- 1 pound bulk Italian sausage
- 1 small onion, chopped
- 4 eggs, lightly beaten
- 1 cup (4 ounces) shredded cheddar cheese
- 1/2 cup 2% milk
- 1/2 teaspoon dried oregano
- 1/8 teaspoon pepper
- 1 can (8 ounces) pizza sauce
- 6 slices part-skim mozzarella cheese

■ Line unpricked pastry shell with a double thickness of heavy-duty foil. Bake at 450° for 8 minutes. Remove foil; bake 5 minutes longer. Cool on a wire rack. Reduce heat to 350°.

■ In a large skillet, cook sausage and onion over medium heat until meat is no longer pink; drain. Transfer to a large bowl. Stir in the eggs, cheddar cheese, milk, oregano and pepper. Pour into crust.

■ Bake for 30-35 minutes or until a knife inserted near the center comes out clean. Spread pizza sauce over sausage mixture; top with cheese. Bake 5-8 minutes longer or until cheese is melted. Let stand for 10 minutes before cutting.

Yield: 6 servings.

Roasted Pork Tenderloin and Vegetables

Diane Martin
BROWN DEER, WISCONSIN

There are no complicated steps to follow when preparing this roasted medley of tender pork and veggies. Just season it with herbs, then pop it in the oven for less than an hour.

PREP: 10 min.
BAKE: 30 min.

- 2 pork tenderloins (3/4 pound *each*)
- 2 pounds red potatoes, quartered
- 1 pound carrots, halved and cut into 2-inch pieces
- 1 medium onion, cut into wedges
- 1 tablespoon olive oil
- 2 teaspoons dried rosemary, crushed
- 1 teaspoon rubbed sage
- 1/2 teaspoon salt
- 1/4 teaspoon pepper

■ Place the pork in a shallow roasting pan coated with cooking spray; arrange the potatoes, carrots and onion around pork. Drizzle with oil. Combine the seasonings; sprinkle over the meat and vegetables.

■ Bake, uncovered, at 450° for 30-40 minutes or until a meat thermometer reads 160°, stirring vegetables occasionally.

Yield: 6 servings.

Fish & Seafood

A great way to take a break from meat and potatoes is with these delicious oven entrees that showcase fish or seafood. You'll find classic meals such as tuna and seafood casseroles, lasagna and baked fish. It's always a well-received change of scenery at the family dinner table!

Seafood 'n' Shells Casserole

Taste of Home Test Kitchen
Poaching the cod before baking prevents it from watering out this comforting casserole. With pasta and vegetables, the satisfying dish will warm you up on chilly nights.

Seafood 'n' Shells Casserole*

PREP: 25 min. ■ BAKE: 25 min.

- 6 cups water
- 1 teaspoon lemon-pepper seasoning
- 1 bay leaf
- 2 pounds cod fillets, cut into 1-inch pieces
- 1 cup uncooked small pasta shells
- 1 medium sweet red pepper, chopped
- 1 medium green pepper, chopped
- 1 medium onion, chopped
- 1 tablespoon butter
- 3 tablespoons all-purpose flour
- 2-1/2 cups fat-free evaporated milk
- 3/4 teaspoon salt
- 1/2 teaspoon dried thyme
- 1/4 teaspoon pepper
- 1 cup (4 ounces) shredded Mexican cheese blend

■ In a large skillet, bring the water, lemon-pepper and bay leaf to a boil. Reduce heat; carefully add cod. Cover and simmer for 5-8 minutes or until fish flakes easily with a fork; drain and set aside. Discard bay leaf.

■ Cook pasta according to the package directions. Meanwhile, in a large saucepan, saute the peppers and onion in butter over medium heat until tender. Stir in flour until blended. Gradually stir in milk. Bring to a boil; cook and stir for 2 minutes or until thickened. Stir in salt, thyme and pepper. Remove from heat; stir in cheese until melted.

■ Drain pasta. Stir fish and pasta into sauce. Transfer to a 2-qt. baking dish coated with cooking spray. Cover and bake at 350° for 25-30 minutes or until heated through.

Yield: 6 servings.

***Nutrition Facts:** 1 cup equals 389 calories, 9 g fat (6 g saturated fat), 83 mg cholesterol, 732 mg sodium, 35 g carbohydrate, 2 g fiber, 39 g protein. **Diabetic Exchanges:** 4 lean meat, 1-1/2 fat, 1 starch, 1 vegetable, 1 fat-free milk.

To cut a bell pepper, hold it by the stem and, using a chef's knife, slice from the top of the pepper down. Use this easy technique to slice around the seeds when a recipe calls for julienned or chopped peppers.

Tuna 'n' Pea Casserole

Jackie Smulski
LYONS, ILLINOIS

Turn to this recipe when you want a tuna casserole that tastes a little different—the horseradish adds an unexpected flavor. It's a tried-and-true favorite that never fails.

Tuna 'n' Pea Casserole

PREP: 20 min. ■ BAKE: 40 min.

- 8 ounces uncooked egg noodles
- 2 cans (10-3/4 ounces *each*) condensed cream of mushroom soup, undiluted
- 1/2 cup mayonnaise
- 1/2 cup 2% milk
- 2 to 3 teaspoons prepared horseradish
- 1/2 teaspoon dill weed
- 1/8 teaspoon pepper
- 1 cup frozen peas, thawed
- 1 can (4 ounces) mushroom stems and pieces, drained
- 1 small onion, chopped
- 1 jar (2 ounces) diced pimientos, drained
- 2 cans (6 ounces *each*) tuna, drained and flaked
- 1/4 cup dry bread crumbs
- 1 tablespoon butter, melted

■ Cook noodles according to package directions. Meanwhile, in a large bowl, combine the soup, mayonnaise, milk, horseradish, dill and pepper. Stir in the peas, mushrooms, onion, pimientos and tuna.

■ Drain noodles; stir into soup mixture. Transfer to a greased 2-qt. baking dish. Toss bread crumbs and butter; sprinkle over the top.

■ Bake, uncovered, at 375° for 40-45 minutes or until bubbly.

Yield: 6 servings.

Company Swordfish

Callie Berger
DIAMOND SPRINGS, CALIFORNIA

This fantastic entree is so easy to prepare! We're not big fish eaters in my family, but the plates are always scraped clean when this is on the table.

PREP: 10 min.
BAKE: 25 min.

- 4 swordfish *or* halibut steaks (7 ounces each)
- 2 jars (7-1/2 ounces *each*) marinated artichoke hearts, drained and chopped
- 1/2 cup oil-packed sun-dried tomatoes, drained and chopped
- 4 shallots, chopped
- 2 tablespoons butter, melted
- 1 teaspoon lemon juice

■ Place fish in a greased 13-in. x 9-in. baking dish. In a small bowl, combine the artichokes, tomatoes and shallots; spread over fish. Drizzle with butter and lemon juice.

■ Cover and bake at 425° for 15 minutes. Uncover; bake 6-8 minutes longer or until fish just turns opaque.

Yield: 4 servings.

Sundra Hauck
BOGALUSA, LOUISIANA

Pasta is popular in our home, so my favorite menu must have it in the main course. In this sensational dish, pasta complements the shrimp our local fishermen bring in—a true standby that never fails.

Sunday Shrimp Pasta Bake

Sunday Shrimp Pasta Bake

PREP: 30 min. ■ BAKE: 25 min.

- 12 ounces uncooked vermicelli
- 1 medium green pepper, chopped
- 5 green onions, chopped
- 6 tablespoons butter, cubed
- 6 garlic cloves, minced
- 2 tablespoons all-purpose flour
- 2 pounds cooked medium shrimp, peeled and deveined
- 1 teaspoon celery salt
- 1/8 teaspoon pepper
- 1 pound process cheese (Velveeta), cubed
- 1 can (10 ounces) diced tomatoes and green chilies, drained
- 1 can (4 ounces) mushroom stems and pieces, drained
- 1 tablespoon grated Parmesan cheese

■ Cook vermicelli according to package directions. Meanwhile, in a large skillet, saute green pepper and onions in butter until tender. Add garlic; cook 1 minute longer. Gradually stir in flour until blended. Stir in shrimp, celery salt and pepper; cook, uncovered, over medium heat for 5-6 minutes or until heated through.

■ In a microwave-safe bowl, combine the process cheese, tomatoes and mushrooms. Microwave, uncovered, on high for 3-4 minutes or until cheese is melted, stirring occasionally. Add to shrimp mixture. Drain vermicelli; stir into skillet.

■ Pour into a greased 13-in. x 9-in. baking dish. Sprinkle with Parmesan cheese. Bake, uncovered, at 350° for 25-30 minutes or until heated through.

Yield: 8 servings.

Roasted Sea Scallops

Marguerite Shaeffer
SEWELL, NEW JERSEY

We like scallops because of their availability here year-round, and they're affordable compared to some seafood. These scallops are delicately seasoned with roasted tomatoes and can be served over rice or even toasted garlic bread.

PREP: 10 min.
BAKE: 25 min.

- 1 large tomato, chopped
- 1 medium onion, chopped
- 1 tablespoon minced fresh parsley
- 1 tablespoon olive oil
- 1-1/2 teaspoons paprika
- 1/2 teaspoon salt
- 1/4 teaspoon pepper
- 12 sea scallops (2 ounces *each*)
- Hot cooked rice, optional

■ In an ungreased 3-qt. baking dish, combine the first seven ingredients. Bake, uncovered, at 400° for 10 minutes or until bubbly.

■ Stir in the scallops. Bake 15 minutes longer or until the scallops are firm and opaque. Serve with rice if desired.

Yield: 4 servings.

Jennifer Maslowski
NEW YORK, NEW YORK

Olives, onion, dill and feta cheese combine in this tangy, Greek-inspired topping to boost the flavor of tilapia or your favorite whitefish.

Broiled Greek Fish Fillets

Broiled Greek Fish Fillets*

PREP/TOTAL TIME: 25 min.

- 8 tilapia fillets (4 ounces *each*)
- 1/4 teaspoon salt
- 1/4 teaspoon pepper
- 1/4 cup plain yogurt
- 2 tablespoons butter, softened
- 1 tablespoon lime juice
- 1 small red onion, finely chopped
- 1/2 cup pitted Greek olives
- 1 teaspoon dill weed
- 1/2 teaspoon paprika
- 1/4 teaspoon garlic powder
- 1/2 cup crumbled feta cheese

■ Sprinkle tilapia with salt and pepper. Place on a broiler pan coated with cooking spray.

■ In a small bowl, combine the yogurt, butter and lime juice. Stir in the onion, olives and seasonings. Spread down the middle of each fillet; sprinkle with feta cheese.

■ Broil 3-4 in. from the heat for 6-9 minutes or until fish flakes easily with a fork.

Yield: 8 servings.

***Nutrition Facts:** 1 fillet equals 169 calories, 7 g fat (3 g saturated fat), 68 mg cholesterol, 353 mg sodium, 3 g carbohydrate, 1 g fiber, 23 g protein. **Diabetic Exchanges:** 3 lean meat, 1-1/2 fat.

Crab & Penne Casserole

PREP: 20 min.
BAKE: 40 min.

- 1-1/2 cups uncooked penne pasta
- 1 jar (15 ounces) Alfredo sauce
- 1-1/2 cups imitation crabmeat, chopped
- 1 medium yellow summer squash, sliced
- 1 medium zucchini, sliced
- 1 tablespoon dried parsley flakes
- 1/8 to 1/4 teaspoon crushed red pepper flakes
- 1-1/2 cups (6 ounces) shredded part-skim mozzarella cheese
- 2 tablespoons dry bread crumbs
- 2 teaspoons butter, melted

■ Cook pasta according to package directions. Meanwhile, in a large bowl, combine the Alfredo sauce, crab, yellow squash, zucchini, parsley and pepper flakes. Drain pasta; add to the sauce mixture and toss to coat.

■ Transfer to a greased 13-in. x 9-in. baking dish. Sprinkle with cheese. Cover and bake at 325° for 35 minutes or until heated through.

■ Toss the bread crumbs and butter; sprinkle over the casserole. Bake, uncovered, 5-6 minutes longer or until browned.

Yield: 6 servings.

Crab & Penne Casserole

Bernadette Bennett
WACO, TEXAS

Purchased Alfredo sauce lends creaminess to this crab casserole while red pepper flakes kick up the heat. Summer squash and zucchini bring garden-fresh goodness to the comforting main dish. It's light and satisfying at the same time.

Baked Whole Salmon

Dixie Harmon
BAINVILLE, MONTANA

We don't get much fresh seafood around here. So when I see some whole salmon in the grocery store, I snap it up and make this elegant entree.

Baked Whole Salmon

PREP: 1 hour ■ BAKE: 1 hour

- 3/4 cup white wine *or* chicken broth
- 3/4 cup chopped celery leaves
- 1 small onion, finely chopped
- 2 lemon slices
- 8 fresh basil leaves
- 2 teaspoons dried tarragon
- 1 teaspoon dried rosemary, crushed
- 1/4 teaspoon dried thyme
- 1 whole salmon (about 10 pounds)
- 1-1/2 teaspoons salt

WINE SAUCE:

- 2 green onions, chopped
- 1/2 cup butter
- 6 tablespoons all-purpose flour
- 2-1/3 cups water
- 2-1/3 cups white wine *or* chicken broth
- 2 egg yolks, lightly beaten
- 1/2 cup heavy whipping cream

Salt and pepper to taste

■ In a saucepan over medium heat, combine the first eight ingredients. Bring to a boil. Reduce heat; simmer, uncovered, for 30 minutes.

■ Remove head and tail from salmon if desired. Place a double thickness of heavy-duty foil on a baking sheet (longer than the length of the fish). Grease foil. Place salmon on foil; sprinkle the cavity with salt. Pour herb sauce over fish. Fold foil over fish and seal tightly.

■ Bake at 375° for 60-75 minutes or until fish flakes easily with a fork.

■ Place salmon on a serving platter and keep warm. Strain cooking juices, reserving 1/3 cup. In a large saucepan, saute green onions in butter until tender. Stir in flour until blended. Gradually stir in the water, wine and reserved cooking juices. Bring to a boil; cook and stir for 2 minutes or until thickened.

■ Reduce heat. Stir a small amount of hot liquid into egg yolks; return all to the pan, stirring constantly. Add the cream, salt and pepper. Cook and stir until mixture reaches 160°. Serve with the salmon.

Yield: 12-14 servings.

Cheesy Tuna Lasagna

Virginia Ferris

LYONS, MICHIGAN

This wonderful casserole was added to my recipe collection many years ago. The tuna and three-cheese blend wins over doubters who say they aren't fond of seafood.

PREP: 15 min. ■ BAKE: 25 min. + standing

- 1 medium onion, chopped
- 2 tablespoons butter
- 1 can (12 ounces) tuna, drained and flaked
- 1 can (10-3/4 ounces) condensed cream of mushroom soup, undiluted
- 1/2 cup 2% milk
- 1/2 teaspoon garlic salt
- 1/2 teaspoon dried oregano
- 1/4 teaspoon pepper
- 9 lasagna noodles, cooked and drained
- 1-1/2 cups (12 ounces) 4% cottage cheese
- 8 ounces sliced part-skim mozzarella cheese
- 1/4 cup grated Parmesan cheese

■ In a large saucepan, saute onion in butter until tender. Stir in the tuna, soup, milk, garlic salt, oregano and pepper until combined. Spread 3/4 cupful into a greased 11-in. x 7-in. baking dish.

■ Layer with three noodles (trimming if necessary), 3/4 cup of the tuna mixture, half of the cottage cheese and a third of the mozzarella cheese. Repeat layers. Top with the remaining noodles, tuna mixture and mozzarella cheese. Sprinkle with Parmesan cheese.

■ Bake, uncovered, at 350° for 25-30 minutes or until bubbly. Let stand for 10-15 minutes before serving.

Yield: 6-8 servings.

If you have leftover noodles from your lasagna, cut the leftovers into 1/4- or 1/2-inch strips and put them in a heavy-duty resealable plastic bag. They freeze well and make quick hearty additions to soup later in the week.

Italian-Style Walleye

Cathy Lueschen

COLUMBUS, NEBRASKA

Herbs and melted cheese dress up fillets in this recipe. When I want a quick fish dinner, this is the recipe I turn to.

PREP/TOTAL TIME: 25 min.

- 4 to 6 walleye fillets (about 1-1/2 pounds)
- 1 can (15 ounces) tomato sauce
- 2 tablespoons chopped fresh parsley
- 1 teaspoon Italian seasoning
- 1/2 teaspoon dried basil
- 1/4 teaspoons salt
- 1/8 teaspoon pepper
- 1 cup (4 ounces) shredded part-skim mozzarella cheese

■ Place walleye in a greased shallow 3-qt. or 13-in. x 9-in. baking dish. In a small bowl, combine the tomato sauce, parsley, Italian seasoning, basil, salt and pepper; pour over the fish.

■ Bake, uncovered, at 350° for 15 minutes. Sprinkle with mozzarella cheese. Bake 5-10 minutes longer or until fish flakes easily with a fork.

Yield: 4-6 servings.

Jaelynne Smigel
VANCOUVER, BRITISH COLUMBIA

My husband can't get enough of these mini casseroles and is disappointed when there aren't any leftovers. Although the hearty hot dishes are great for any day of the week, they are a mainstay on my holiday menus.

Individual Seafood Casseroles

PREP: 25 min. ■ BAKE: 20 min.

- 1/3 cup chopped onion
- 1/3 cup butter, cubed
- 1/3 cup all-purpose flour
- 1/2 teaspoon salt
- 1/2 teaspoon white pepper
- 1 cup 2% milk
- 1 cup heavy whipping cream
- 3 tablespoons *each* finely chopped sweet red and green pepper
- 2 teaspoons curry powder
- 1 teaspoon ground mustard
- 1/4 teaspoon *each* ground ginger, ground turmeric and dried thyme
- 1/2 teaspoon lemon juice
- 3 to 5 drops hot pepper sauce
- 3 cans (6 ounces *each*) crabmeat, drained, flaked and cartilage removed
- 1 can (6 ounces) tuna, drained and flaked
- 1/4 pound cooked medium shrimp, peeled and deveined
- 2 hard-cooked eggs, chopped

TOPPING:

- 1/2 cup shredded cheddar cheese
- 1/4 cup dry bread crumbs
- 1/4 teaspoon garlic powder
- 1 tablespoon *each* chopped sweet red and green pepper

■ In a large saucepan, saute onion in butter until tender. Stir in flour, salt and pepper until blended. Gradually whisk in milk and cream. Bring to a boil; cook and stir for 2 minutes or until thickened and bubbly. Stir in the peppers, seasonings, lemon juice and pepper sauce until blended.

■ Remove from the heat; add the crab, tuna, shrimp and eggs. Transfer to six greased ovenproof 10-oz. dishes.

■ For topping, combine the cheese, bread crumbs and garlic powder. Sprinkle over seafood mixture.

■ Bake, uncovered, at 350° for 15 minutes. Sprinkle with peppers. Bake 5-8 minutes longer or until heated through and edges are bubbly.

Yield: 6 servings.

Cajun-Style Catfish

Irene Cliett
CEDAR BLUFF, MISSISSIPPI

This dish features the green pepper, onion and celery combination common to Cajun cooking, but it's not too spicy. It's a colorful and flavorful way to serve our locally raised catfish.

PREP: 30 min.
BAKE: 15 min.

- 1/2 cup chopped onion
- 1/2 cup chopped celery
- 1/2 cup chopped green pepper
- 1 tablespoon olive oil
- 1 can (14-1/2 ounces) diced tomatoes and green chilies, undrained
- 1/2 cup sliced fresh mushrooms
- 1 can (2-1/4 ounces) sliced ripe olives, drained
- 1/2 teaspoon garlic powder
- 4 catfish fillets (6 ounces *each*)
- 1/4 cup grated Parmesan cheese

■ In a large skillet, saute the onion, celery and green pepper in oil until tender. Add the tomatoes, mushrooms, olives and garlic powder. Bring to a boil. Reduce heat; simmer, uncovered, for 10 minutes or until heated through.

■ Place the catfish in an ungreased 13-in. x 9-in. baking dish. Top with vegetable mixture; sprinkle with cheese. Bake, uncovered, at 400° for 15-20 minutes or until fish flakes easily with a fork.

Yield: 4 servings.

Seafood Tortilla Lasagna

Sharon Sawicki
CAROL STREAM, ILLINOIS

My husband and I enjoy lasagna, seafood and Mexican fare. I combined all three into this deliciously different entree. It's a tempting change of pace from Italian-style lasagna.

Seafood Tortilla Lasagna

PREP: 40 min. ■ BAKE: 30 min. + standing

- 1 jar (20 ounces) picante sauce
- 1-1/2 pounds uncooked medium shrimp, peeled and deveined
- 1/8 teaspoon cayenne pepper
- 1 tablespoon olive oil
- 4 to 6 garlic cloves, minced
- 1/3 cup butter
- 1/3 cup all-purpose flour
- 1 can (14-1/2 ounces) chicken broth
- 1/2 cup heavy whipping cream
- 15 corn tortillas (6 inches), warmed
- 1 package (16 ounces) imitation crabmeat, flaked
- 3 cups (12 ounces) shredded Colby-Monterey Jack cheese

Sour cream and minced fresh cilantro, optional

■ Place picante sauce in a blender; cover and process until smooth. Set aside. In a large skillet cook shrimp and cayenne in oil for about 3 minutes or until shrimp turn pink. Add the garlic; cook 1 minute longer. Remove and set aside.

■ In the same skillet, melt the butter. Stir in flour until smooth. Gradually add broth. Bring to a boil; cook and stir for 2 minutes or until thickened. Reduce heat. Stir in cream and picante sauce; heat through.

■ Spread 1/2 cup of sauce in a greased 13-in. x 9-in. baking dish. Layer with six tortillas, half of the shrimp, crab and sauce and 1-1/4 cups cheese. Repeat layers. Tear or cut the remaining tortillas; arrange over cheese. Sprinkle with remaining cheese.

■ Bake, uncovered, at 375° for 30-35 minutes or until bubbly. Let stand 15 minutes before cutting. Garnish with sour cream and minced cilantro if desired.

Yield: 12 servings.

Michele Field
BURTONSVILLE, MARYLAND

Crabmeat is very plentiful here in Maryland, and this entree is one of my favorite ways to eat it. My sister-in-law Darlene gave me this recipe, and that simple gesture truly helped me feel like part of the family.

Crab Quiche

Crab Quiche

PREP: 10 min. ■ BAKE: 1 hour

- 1/2 cup mayonnaise
- 2 tablespoons all-purpose flour
- 2 eggs, beaten
- 1/2 cup milk
- 2 cans (6 ounces *each*) flaked crabmeat, drained
- 1/3 cup chopped green onions
- 1 tablespoon minced fresh parsley
- 2 cups (8 ounces) shredded Swiss cheese
- 1 unbaked pastry shell (9 inches)

■ In a large bowl, combine the mayonnaise, flour, eggs and milk. Stir in the crab, onion, parsley and cheese. Spoon into the pastry shell.

■ Bake at 350° for 1 hour or until a knife inserted near the center comes out clean.

Yield: 6-8 servings.

To avoid water on the bottom of the pie when making a quiche, use an oven thermometer to check your oven temperature. To avoid overbaking, do the "knife test" when the quiche has set around the edges but seems a little soft in the very center. The quiche is done if the knife inserted near the center comes out clean.

Creole Baked Tilapia*

Carolyn Collins
FREEPORT, TEXAS

Since I'm originally from Louisiana, I love Creole cooking. My tilapia is quick and easy as well as healthy. It's great served with your favorite rice dish. Enjoy!

PREP/TOTAL TIME: 25 min.

- 4 tilapia fillets (6 ounces *each*)
- 1 can (8 ounces) tomato sauce
- 1 small green pepper, thinly sliced
- 1/2 cup chopped red onion
- 1 teaspoon Creole seasoning

■ Place tilapia in an ungreased 13-in. x 9-in. baking dish. In a small bowl, combine the tomato sauce, green pepper, onion and Creole seasoning; pour over the fillets.

■ Bake, uncovered, at 350° for 20-25 minutes or until fish flakes easily with a fork.

Yield: 4 servings.

Editor's Note: The following spices may be substituted for 1 teaspoon of Creole seasoning: 1/4 teaspoon *each* salt, garlic powder and paprika; and a pinch *each* of dried thyme, ground cumin and cayenne pepper.

***Nutrition Facts:** 1 fish fillet with 1/3 cup topping equals 166 calories, 2 g fat (1 g saturated fat), 83 mg cholesterol, 488 mg sodium, 6 g carbohydrate, 1 g fiber, 33 g protein. **Diabetic Exchanges:** 5 lean meat, 1 vegetable.

Lucille Pennington
ORMOND BEACH, FLORIDA

We have friends from up North who come to Florida each winter. They enjoy eating fresh seafood with a green salad and strawberry pie. This casserole is one of their favorites!

Florida Seafood Casserole

Florida Seafood Casserole

PREP: 15 min. ■ BAKE: 25 min.

- 1/3 cup finely chopped onion
- 1/4 cup butter, cubed
- 1/4 cup all-purpose flour
- 1/2 teaspoon salt
- 1/2 teaspoon pepper
- 1 cup milk
- 1 cup half-and-half cream
- 2 cups cooked long grain rice
- 1 cup chopped cooked peeled shrimp
- 1 cup crabmeat, drained, flaked and cartilage removed
- 1 can (8 ounces) sliced water chestnuts, drained
- 2 tablespoons lemon juice
- 1 tablespoon chopped pimientos
- 1 tablespoon minced fresh parsley
- 1 cup (4 ounces) shredded cheddar cheese, *divided*

■ In a small saucepan, saute onion in butter. Stir in the flour, salt and pepper until blended. Gradually whisk in milk and cream. Bring to a boil. Cook and stir for 2 minutes or until thickened. Remove from the heat; stir in the rice, shrimp, crab, water chestnuts, lemon juice, pimientos, parsley and 1/2 cup cheese.

■ Transfer to a greased 2-1/2-qt. baking dish. Bake at 350° for 25-30 minutes or until heated through. Sprinkle with remaining cheese.

Yield: 6 servings.

Tasty Tuna Casserole*

PREP: 20 min.
BAKE: 25 min.

- 2 cups uncooked elbow macaroni
- 1 can (12 ounces) white water-packed solid tuna
- 1 can (8 ounces) tomato sauce
- 4 ounces reduced-fat cream cheese, cubed
- 1 small onion, finely chopped
- 1/4 teaspoon salt
- 1/2 teaspoon dried oregano

■ Cook the macaroni according to the package directions. Meanwhile, in a large bowl, combine the remaining ingredients. Drain macaroni and stir into tuna mixture.

■ Transfer to a 2-qt. baking dish coated with cooking spray. Cover and bake at 350° for 20-25 minutes or until heated through.

Yield: 4 servings.

***Nutrition Facts:** 1-1/2 cups equals 334 calories, 9 g fat (5 g saturated fat), 56 mg cholesterol, 851 mg sodium, 33 g carbohydrate, 2 g fiber, 29 g protein. **Diabetic Exchanges:** 3 lean meat, 2 starch, 1 fat.

Elsie Epp
NEWTON, KANSAS

Reduced-fat cream cheese adds a delightful creaminess to this easy, tomato-y and lighter twist on classic tuna casserole. You won't have to disguise it so that your kids will eat it because it's delicious enough as it is! I like to serve it with crusty bread.

Breads & Salads

Creating a full meal is a cinch with this brand new, beautiful bonus chapter that is chock-full of delicious accompaniments to the main entrees featured in the previous pages of the book. From tasty biscuits to easy-to-fix cole slaws, there are plenty of main-dish pairings to choose from.

Cheddar Skillet Corn Bread

Terri Adrian
LAKE CITY, FLORIDA

Here's a tasty spin on traditional corn bread that uses yogurt, cream-style corn and cheddar cheese. It's so delicious that it may become your new favorite!

Cheddar Skillet Corn Bread

PREP/TOTAL TIME: 30 min.

- 2 tablespoons butter
- 2 packages (8-1/2 ounces *each*) corn bread/muffin mix
- 2 eggs, lightly beaten
- 1/2 cup milk
- 1/2 cup plain yogurt
- 1 can (14-3/4 ounces) cream-style corn
- 1/2 cup shredded cheddar cheese

HONEY BUTTER:

- 1/2 cup butter, softened
- 2 tablespoons honey

■ Place butter into a deep 10-in. ovenproof skillet. Place in a 400° oven for 4-6 minutes or until melted.

■ Meanwhile, in a large bowl, combine the corn bread mix, eggs, milk and yogurt until blended. Stir in corn and cheese. Pour into hot skillet. Bake at 400° for 20-25 minutes or until a toothpick inserted near the center comes out clean. Cut into wedges.

■ In a small bowl, cream the butter and honey. Serve with warm corn bread.

Yield: 1 loaf (12 wedges).

Freezing honey helps to keep it from crystallizing. It will never freeze solid since the moisture content of honey is low. It will, however, become thick and sludgy. When thawed to room temperature, the honey should return to its original consistency.

Coffee Lover's Coffee Cake

Gale Lalmond
DEERING, NEW HAMPSHIRE

I had this cake at a friend's brunch and she graciously shared the recipe. Now people always request it from me because it's so tasty and always a hit.

Coffee Lover's Coffee Cake*

PREP: 25 min. ■ BAKE: 25 min.

- 1/3 cup sugar
- 4-1/2 teaspoons instant coffee granules
- 1-1/2 teaspoons ground cinnamon

BATTER:

- 3 tablespoons butter, softened
- 1/2 cup sugar
- 1 egg
- 1 teaspoon vanilla extract
- 1-1/2 cups all-purpose flour
- 1 teaspoon baking powder
- 1/2 teaspoon baking soda
- 1/8 teaspoon salt
- 1 cup (8 ounces) plain yogurt
- 2 tablespoons chopped walnuts *or* pecans

■ In a small bowl, combine the sugar, coffee granules and cinnamon; set aside. In a large bowl, beat butter and sugar until crumbly, about 2 minutes. Beat in egg and vanilla. Combine the flour, baking powder, baking soda and salt; add to the butter mixture alternately with the yogurt, beating just until combined.

■ Spread half of the batter evenly into a 9-in. square baking pan coated with cooking spray; sprinkle with half of the reserved sugar mixture. Repeat layers; cut through batter with a knife to swirl. Sprinkle with nuts.

■ Bake at 350° for 25-30 minutes or until a toothpick inserted near the center comes out clean. Cool for 5 minutes on a wire rack. Serve warm.

Yield: 9 servings.

***Nutrition Facts:** 1 piece equals 219 calories, 6 g fat (3 g saturated fat), 37 mg cholesterol, 206 mg sodium, 36 g carbohydrate, 1 g fiber, 4 g protein. **Diabetic Exchanges:** 2 starch, 1 fat.

Dana Herbert
GOSHEN, UTAH
This fresh and hearty salad is a smart change-of-pace. It's crunchy, creamy and simply delicious. You'd never guess it's on the light side!

Fresh Broccoli Salad

Fresh Broccoli Salad*

PREP/TOTAL TIME: 20 min.

- 6 cups fresh broccoli florets
- 1 can (8 ounces) sliced water chestnuts, drained
- 1/2 cup dried cranberries
- 1/4 cup chopped red onion
- 3/4 cup reduced-fat mayonnaise
- 3/4 cup fat-free plain yogurt
- 1-1/2 teaspoons sugar
- 1-1/2 teaspoons cider vinegar
- 1-1/2 teaspoons Dijon mustard
- 1/4 teaspoon salt
- 1/8 teaspoon pepper
- 1/4 cup slivered almonds, toasted

■ In a large bowl, combine the broccoli, water chestnuts, cranberries and onion.

■ In a small bowl, whisk together mayonnaise, yogurt, sugar, vinegar, mustard, salt and pepper. Pour over salad; toss to coat. Just before serving, sprinkle with almonds.

Yield: 9 servings.

***Nutrition Facts:** 3/4 cup equals 144 calories, 8 g fat (1 g saturated fat), 7 mg cholesterol, 272 mg sodium, 16 g carbohydrate, 3 g fiber, 3 g protein. **Diabetic Exchanges:** 1-1/2 fat, 1 vegetable, 1/2 starch.

Sour Cream & Chive Biscuits*

Priscilla Gilbert
INDIAN HARBOUR BEACH, FLORIDA

Chives add a nice, mild onion flavor to just about any dish, be it soup, dip, baked potato or buttery spread. They truly make a great addition to these biscuits.

PREP/TOTAL TIME: 20 min.

- 3 cups biscuit/baking mix
- 3 tablespoons minced chives
- 2/3 cup water
- 2/3 cup sour cream

■ In a large bowl, combine biscuit mix and chives. Stir in water and sour cream just until moistened.

■ Drop by heaping tablespoonfuls onto a baking sheet coated with cooking spray. Bake at 450° for 8-10 minutes or until lightly browned. Serve warm.

Yield: 16 biscuits.

***Nutrition Facts:** 1 biscuit equals 112 calories, 5 g fat (2 g saturated fat), 7 mg cholesterol, 287 mg sodium, 14 g carbohydrate, trace fiber, 2 g protein. **Diabetic Exchanges:** 1 starch, 1 fat.

Parmesan Knots

Jane Paschke
DULUTH, MINNESOTA

These novel knots are handy because they can be made ahead of time and re-heated when needed. They're easy to make, too, because they start with refrigerated biscuits.

Parmesan Knots*

PREP/TOTAL TIME: 15 min.

- 1 tube (12 ounces) refrigerated buttermilk biscuits
- 1/4 cup canola oil
- 3 tablespoons grated Parmesan cheese
- 1 teaspoon garlic powder
- 1 teaspoon dried oregano
- 1 teaspoon dried parsley flakes

- Cut each biscuit into thirds. Roll each piece into a 3-in. rope and tie into a knot; tuck ends under. Place 2 in. apart on a greased baking sheet. Bake at 400° for 8-10 minutes or until golden brown.
- In a large bowl, combine the remaining ingredients; add the warm knots and gently toss to coat.

Yield: 2-1/2 dozen.

***Nutrition Facts:** 1 knot equals 46 calories, 2 g fat (trace saturated fat), trace cholesterol, 105 mg sodium, 6 g carbohydrate, trace fiber, 1 g protein. **Diabetic Exchanges:** 1/2 starch, 1/2 fat.

Freezer Coleslaw*

PREP: 25 min. + freezing

- 1 medium head cabbage (about 2 pounds), shredded
- 1 teaspoon salt
- 2 cups sugar
- 1 cup cider vinegar
- 1/4 cup water
- 1 teaspoon celery seed
- 1 teaspoon mustard seed
- 1 large carrot, shredded
- 1/2 cup finely chopped green pepper

- In a large bowl, combine the cabbage and salt; let stand for 1 hour.
- In a large saucepan, combine the sugar, vinegar, water, celery seed and mustard seed. Bring to a boil; boil for 1 minute. Remove from the heat; cool.
- Add the carrot, green pepper and vinegar mixture to the cabbage mixture; stir to combine. Transfer to large freezer bags; seal and freeze for up to 2 months.
- Remove from the freezer 2 hours before serving. Serve with a slotted spoon.

Yield: 10 servings.

***Nutrition Facts:** 1 serving (3/4 cup) equals 185 calories, trace fat (trace saturated fat), 0 cholesterol, 256 mg sodium, 46 g carbohydrate, 3 g fiber, 2 g protein.

Donna Sasser Hinds
MILWAUKIE, OREGON

Loaded with crunch, my sweet-tart slaw can be made ahead for a family gathering. There's no mayonnaise in the dressing, so it's perfect to take to a picnic. You can also double the recipe so you have extra to serve later.

Pretty Pepper Salad

Colette Gerow
RAYTOWN, MISSOURI

This terrific salad goes great with grilled chicken or ribs. Peppers come in all different colors and varieties—try using your favorite.

Pretty Pepper Salad

PREP/TOTAL TIME: 20 min.

- 2 medium green peppers, cut into rings
- 1 medium sweet yellow pepper, cut into rings
- 1 medium sweet red pepper, cut into rings
- 1 medium red onion, cut into rings
- 1 jar (6-1/2 ounces) marinated quartered artichoke hearts, drained
- 1 can (2-1/4 ounces) sliced ripe olives, drained
- 1/4 cup canola oil
- 3 tablespoons lemon juice
- 1/2 to 1 teaspoon minced fresh oregano
- 1/2 teaspoon sugar
- 1/2 teaspoon salt
- 1/4 to 1/2 teaspoon paprika

■ In a large bowl, combine the peppers, onion, artichokes and olives. In a small bowl, whisk the remaining ingredients. Pour over pepper mixture and toss to coat. Chill until serving. Serve with a slotted spoon.

Yield: 9 servings.

Chili-Cheese Corn Muffins*

Taste of Home Test Kitchen

Add chilies and cheese to a boxed mix and what do you get? Easy muffins with zip. Our Test Kitchen shares the recipe.

PREP/TOTAL TIME: 30 min.

- 1 package (8-1/2 ounces) corn bread/muffin mix
- 1 egg, lightly beaten
- 1/3 cup 2% milk
- 1/2 cup shredded Mexican cheese blend
- 1 can (4 ounces) chopped green chilies, drained

■ In a large bowl, combine the corn bread mix, egg and milk just until blended. Stir in the cheese and chilies. Coat the muffin cups with cooking spray or use paper liners; fill three-fourths full with batter.

■ Bake at 400° for 20-22 minutes or until a toothpick inserted near the center comes out clean. Cool for 5 minutes before removing from pan to a wire rack. Serve warm.

Yield: 8 muffins.

***Nutrition Facts:** 1 muffin equals 167 calories, 6 g fat (3 g saturated fat), 40 mg cholesterol, 369 mg sodium, 23 g carbohydrate, 1 g fiber, 5 g protein. **Diabetic Exchanges:** 1-1/2 starch, 1 fat.

Collette Reynolds
RALEIGH, NORTH CAROLINA

My young nephew refuses to eat any potato salad but mine! Italian salad dressing, sour cream and bacon give it a one-of-a-kind flavor.

Potato Salad with Bacon

Potato Salad with Bacon

PREP: 45 min. + chilling

- 3 pounds red potatoes (about 12 medium)
- 4 hard-cooked eggs
- 3/4 cup sour cream
- 2/3 cup mayonnaise
- 1 teaspoon salt
- 1 teaspoon prepared mustard
- 1/2 teaspoon garlic powder
- 1/4 teaspoon pepper
- 11 bacon strips, cooked and crumbled
- 1/2 cup chopped celery
- 1/4 cup chopped green onions
- 1/4 cup Italian salad dressing

■ Cut potatoes into 1/2-in. cubes; place in a large Dutch oven and cover with water. Bring to a boil. Reduce heat; cover and simmer for 10-15 minutes or until tender. Drain and cool to room temperature.

■ Cut eggs in half; chop egg whites and set aside. In a small bowl, mash egg yolks. Stir in the sour cream, mayonnaise, salt, mustard, garlic powder and pepper; set aside.

■ In a large bowl, combine the potatoes, bacon, egg whites, celery, onions and Italian dressing. Fold in mayonnaise mixture. Cover and refrigerate for at least 2 hours before serving.

Yield: 16 servings.

Cashew-Pear Tossed Salad

Arlene Muller
KINGWOOD, TEXAS

A friend who does a lot of catering fixed this salad for our staff Christmas party several years ago, and we all asked for the recipe. The unexpected sweet-salty mix and lovely dressing make it a hit with everyone.

PREP/TOTAL TIME: 15 min.

- 1 bunch romaine, torn
- 1 cup (4 ounces) shredded Swiss cheese
- 1 cup salted cashews
- 1 medium pear, thinly sliced
- 1/2 cup dried cranberries

POPPY SEED VINAIGRETTE:

- 2/3 cup olive oil
- 1/2 cup sugar
- 1/3 cup lemon juice
- 2 to 3 teaspoons poppy seeds
- 2 teaspoons finely chopped red onion
- 1 teaspoon prepared mustard
- 1/2 teaspoon salt

■ In a large salad bowl, combine the romaine, cheese, cashews, pear and cranberries. In a small bowl, whisk the vinaigrette ingredients. Drizzle over salad and toss to coat.

Yield: 15 servings.

Freezer Crescent Rolls*

Kristine Buck
PAYSON, UTAH

Bake up sweet convenience with this freezer-friendly dough. The recipe was handed down to me from my aunt, who is an awesome cook! I love having homemade rolls available any time.

PREP: 30 min. + freezing ■ BAKE: 15 min.

- 3 teaspoons active dry yeast
- 2 cups warm water (110° to 115°)
- 1/2 cup butter, softened
- 2/3 cup nonfat dry milk powder
- 1/2 cup sugar
- 1/2 cup mashed potato flakes
- 2 eggs
- 1-1/2 teaspoons salt
- 6 to 6-1/2 cups all-purpose flour

■ In a large bowl, dissolve yeast in warm water. Add the butter, milk powder, sugar, potato flakes, eggs, salt and 3 cups flour. Beat until smooth. Stir in enough of the remaining flour to form a firm dough.

■ Turn onto a heavily floured surface; knead 8-10 times. Divide dough in half. Roll each portion into a 12-in. circle; cut each circle into 16 wedges. Roll up wedges from the wide ends and place point side down 2 in. apart on waxed paper-lined baking sheets. Curve ends to form crescents.

■ Cover and freeze. When firm, transfer to a large resealable plastic freezer bag. Freeze for up to 4 weeks.

■ TO USE FROZEN ROLLS: Arrange frozen rolls 2 in. apart on baking sheets coated with cooking spray. Cover and thaw in the refrigerator overnight.

■ Let rise in a warm place for 1 hour or until doubled. Bake at 350° for 15-17 minutes or until golden brown. Serve warm.

Yield: 32 rolls.

***Nutrition Facts:** 1 roll equals 141 calories, 3 g fat (2 g saturated fat), 21 mg cholesterol, 160 mg sodium, 23 g carbohydrate, 1 g fiber, 4 g protein. **Diabetic Exchanges:** 1-1/2 starch, 1/2 fat.

Parmesan-Ranch Pan Rolls

PREP: 30 min. + rising
BAKE: 20 min.

- 2 loaves (1 pound *each*) frozen bread dough, thawed
- 1 cup grated Parmesan cheese
- 1/2 cup butter, melted
- 1 envelope buttermilk ranch salad dressing mix
- 1 small onion, finely chopped

■ On a lightly floured surface, divide the dough into 18 portions; shape each into a ball. In a small bowl, combine the cheese, butter and ranch dressing mix.

■ Roll balls in cheese mixture; arrange in two greased 9-in. square baking pans. Sprinkle with onion. Cover and let rise in a warm place until doubled, about 45 minutes.

■ Bake at 350° for 20-25 minutes or until golden brown. Remove rolls from the pans to wire racks.

Yield: 1-1/2 dozen.

Trisha Kruse

EAGLE, IDAHO

My mom taught me this easy recipe, which is great for feeding a crowd. There is never a crumb left over. Mom made her own bread dough, but using frozen dough is my shortcut. The combination of the Parmesan cheese, dressing mix and onion is a real winner.

Denise Baumert
DALHART, TEXAS

This traditional salad is one of my mother-in-law's favorites. It's fun to eat because of its crunchy texture, and the raisins give it a slightly sweet flavor. Plus, it's easy to prepare. It's a good way to get kids to eat their vegetables, too.

Carrot Raisin Salad*

PREP/TOTAL TIME: 10 min.

- 4 cups shredded carrots (about 4 large)
- 3/4 to 1-1/2 cups raisins
- 1/4 cup mayonnaise
- 2 tablespoons sugar
- 2 to 3 tablespoons milk

■ Place carrots and raisins in a large bowl. In a small bowl, combine the mayonnaise, sugar and enough milk to achieve dressing consistency. Pour over carrot mixture; toss to coat.

Yield: 8 servings.

***Nutrition Facts:** 1 cup equals 110 calories, 2 g fat (0 saturated fat), 2 mg cholesterol, 80 mg sodium, 24 g carbohydrate, 0 fiber, 1 g protein. **Diabetic Exchanges:** 1 vegetable, 1 fruit, 1/2 fat.

Creamy Coleslaw*

Dianne Esposite
NEW MIDDLETOWN, OHIO

Cabbage, carrots and green pepper are blended with a tasty dressing that gets its zest from a hint of mustard in this special recipe from my mom. When we set this slaw on the table, it disappears fast.

PREP: 10 min. + chilling

- 3 to 4 cups shredded cabbage
- 1 cup shredded carrots
- 1 cup thinly sliced green pepper
- 1/2 cup mayonnaise
- 1/4 cup lemon juice
- 1 to 2 tablespoons sugar
- 1 tablespoon prepared mustard
- 1 teaspoon celery seed
- 1 teaspoon salt

■ In a large salad bowl, toss the cabbage, carrots and green pepper. In a small bowl, whisk the remaining ingredients. Pour over the cabbage mixture and toss to coat. Chill for at least 2-3 hours.

Yield: 6-8 servings.

***Nutrition Facts:** 1 serving (3/4 cup) equals 125 calories, 11 g fat (2 g saturated fat), 5 mg cholesterol, 401 mg sodium, 6 g carbohydrate, 1 g fiber, 1 g protein.

Cucumber Salad

Mary Lou Boyce
WILMINGTON, DELAWARE

Add a fresh-tasting touch to your menu with this favorite salad. The crunchy cucumbers are tossed with onion, green pepper and a sweet-tart dressing seasoned with celery seed.

PREP: 15 min. + chilling

- 7 cups thinly sliced peeled cucumbers
- 2 cups sugar
- 1 large onion, chopped
- 1 medium green pepper, chopped
- 1 cup cider vinegar
- 1 tablespoon salt
- 1 tablespoon celery seed

■ In a large serving bowl, combine all ingredients. Cover and refrigerate for at least 1 hour, stirring occasionally. Serve with a slotted spoon.

Yield: 8-10 servings.

A good way to keep shredded carrots on hand is to shred a lot of carrots at once and freeze them in plastic bags in 1-cup portions.

Muggs Nash
BLOOMINGTON, MINNESOTA

This is a perfect salad for potlucks and other occasions year-round because the ingredients are available during the winter and summer.

Marinated Italian Salad

Marinated Italian Salad

PREP: 30 min. + marinating

- 4 cups fresh broccoli florets
- 3 cups fresh caulifloweret s
- 1/2 pound sliced fresh mushrooms
- 2 celery ribs, chopped
- 4 green onions, thinly sliced
- 1 can (8 ounces) sliced water chestnuts, drained
- 1 bottle (16 ounces) Italian salad dressing
- 1 envelope Italian salad dressing mix
- 1 pint cherry tomatoes, halved
- 1 can (2-1/4 ounces) sliced ripe olives, drained

■ In a large serving bowl, combine broccoli, cauliflower, mushrooms, celery, onions and water chestnuts. In a small bowl, whisk salad dressing and dressing mix; drizzle over vegetables and toss to coat.

■ Cover and refrigerate overnight. Just before serving, add tomatoes and olives; toss to coat.

Yield: 12 servings.

Spiral Pasta Salad

Darlene Kileel
RIVERVIEW, NEW BRUNSWICK

I have two kids and am always on the go, so I appreciate recipes that I can prepare ahead of time. This super salad, topped with a homemade dressing, is easy to fix.

PREP/TOTAL TIME: 30 min.

- 3 cups cooked drained spiral pasta
- 1/2 cup chopped green pepper
- 1/2 cup sliced celery
- 1/2 cup chopped tomato
- 1/2 cup shredded carrot

DRESSING:

- 1/4 cup *each* canola oil, cider vinegar and chopped onion
- 2 tablespoons ketchup
- 4 teaspoons sugar
- 1/2 teaspoon salt, optional
- 1/4 teaspoon *each* garlic powder, dried oregano, ground mustard and paprika

■ In a large bowl, combine the pasta, green pepper, celery, tomato and carrot. In a small bowl, whisk the dressing ingredients. Pour over salad and toss to coat. Refrigerate until serving.

Yield: 6 servings.

Sweet Milk Dinner Rolls

Merle Dyck
ELKFORD, BRITISH COLUMBIA

A hint of sweetness in these tender buns brings many compliments. Served warm with butter or jam, they're a big hit at any meal. They also taste good reheated!

Sweet Milk Dinner Rolls

PREP: 20 min. + rising ■ BAKE: 35 min.

- 1 package (1/4 ounce) active dry yeast
- 2 cups warm milk (110° to 115°)
- 1/2 cup sugar
- 2 tablespoons butter, melted
- 1 teaspoon salt
- 4 to 5 cups all-purpose flour

■ In a large bowl, dissolve yeast in warm milk. Add the sugar, butter, salt and 3 cups flour. Beat until smooth. Add enough remaining flour to form a soft dough.

■ Turn onto a floured surface; knead until smooth and elastic, about 6-8 minutes. Place in a greased bowl, turning once to grease top. Cover and let rise in a warm place until doubled, about 1 hour.

■ Punch dough down. Turn onto a floured surface; divide into 16 pieces. Shape each into a ball. Place 2 in. apart on greased baking sheets. Cover and let rise until doubled, about 30 minutes.

■ Bake at 350° for 35-40 minutes or until golden brown. Remove from pans to wire racks. Serve warm.

Yield: 16 rolls.

It's important to preheat the oven before baking because baked items need the correct oven temperature to help them rise and cook properly. Preheating the oven takes 15 to 20 minutes and can be done while preparing the recipe.

Brittany Tyrrell
MANCHESTER, IOWA

A light dressing made of cream cheese and yogurt are combined to coat this tasty fruit medley. Miniature marshmallows add just the right touch of sweetness.

Creamy Fruit Salad

Creamy Fruit Salad

PREP/TOTAL TIME: 30 min.

- 1 can (11 ounces) mandarin oranges, drained
- 1 can (8-1/4 ounces) sliced peaches, drained
- 1 can (8 ounces) pineapple chunks, drained
- 1 cup miniature marshmallows
- 4 ounces cream cheese, softened
- 1/2 cup plain yogurt
- 1/4 cup sugar

■ In a large bowl, combine the oranges, peaches, pineapple and marshmallows. In a small bowl, beat the cream cheese, yogurt and sugar until smooth; pour over fruit and toss to coat. Refrigerate for about 15 minutes.

Yield: 4 servings.

To keep marshmallows from turning hard, store them in the freezer. When thawed, they're like fresh. To separate sticky marshmallows, place a spoonful of powdered sugar in the bag and shake it well. A few marshmallows may need to be separated by hand.

Round Cheese Bread

PREP: 10 min
BAKE: 20 min. + cooling

- 1-1/2 cups biscuit/baking mix
- 1 cup (4 ounces) shredded part-skim mozzarella cheese
- 1/4 cup grated Parmesan cheese
- 1/2 teaspoon dried oregano
- 1/2 cup milk
- 1 egg, lightly beaten
- 2 tablespoons butter, melted
- Additional Parmesan cheese

■ In a large bowl, combine the biscuit mix, mozzarella cheese, Parmesan cheese, oregano, milk and egg (batter will be thick).

■ Spoon into a greased 9-in. round baking pan. Drizzle with butter; sprinkle with additional Parmesan cheese.

■ Bake at 400° for 20-25 minutes or until a toothpick inserted near the center comes out clean. Cool for 10 minutes. Cut into wedges. Serve warm.

Yield: 6-8 servings.

Deborah Bitz
MEDICINE HAT, ALBERTA

This savory loaf has an Italian flair. Warm buttery wedges are tasty with a pasta dinner or tossed salad. The recipe is convenient to throw together because it starts with a baking mix and relies on kitchen staples and other easy-to-find ingredients.

Caraway Beer Bread

Janet Newmyer
WILBER, NEBRASKA

This moist and tender loaf boasts a mild beer and caraway flavor that can hold its own with hearty soups and chili. It's also yummy with ham salad, cream cheese and jam.

Caraway Beer Bread

PREP: 10 min. ■ **BAKE:** 40 min. + cooling

- 2-1/2 cups biscuit/baking mix
- 2 tablespoons sugar
- 1 teaspoon caraway seeds
- 2 eggs
- 1 cup beer *or* nonalcoholic beer
- 3 tablespoons butter, melted

■ In a large bowl, combine the biscuit mix, sugar and caraway seeds. In a small bowl, whisk the eggs, beer and butter until smooth. Stir into dry ingredients just until moistened.

■ Pour into a 9-in. x 5-in. loaf pan coated with cooking spray. Bake at 350° for 40-45 minutes or until a toothpick inserted near the center comes out clean. Cool for 10 minutes before removing to a wire rack.

Yield: 1 loaf (12 slices).

Bacon-Apple Cider Biscuits

Taste of Home Test Kitchen

The sweet and salty flavors of apple and bacon make these special biscuits stand out. Be prepared to make more—they're gonna go fast!

PREP: 20 min.
BAKE: 15 min.

- 2 cups all-purpose flour
- 2 teaspoons baking powder
- 2 teaspoons brown sugar
- 1/2 teaspoon salt
- 1/4 teaspoon baking soda
- 1/4 teaspoon apple pie spice
- 8 tablespoons cold butter, cubed, *divided*
- 5 bacon strips, cooked and crumbled
- 3/4 cup apple cider *or* juice
- 1/8 teaspoon ground cinnamon

■ In a large bowl, combine the first six ingredients. Cut in 7 tablespoons butter until mixture resembles coarse crumbs. Add bacon. Stir in cider just until combined.

■ Turn dough onto a lightly floured surface; knead 8-10 times. Roll into a 10-in. x 6-in. rectangle. Melt the remaining butter; brush over dough. Sprinkle with cinnamon.

■ Cut into eight rectangles. Place 1 in. apart on an ungreased baking sheet. Bake at 450° for 12-15 minutes or until golden brown. Serve warm.

Yield: 8 biscuits.

Taste of Home Test Kitchen
Basic biscuit mix gets a makeover with cheese, green onions and garlic powder. Brushing the breadsticks with melted butter when they come out of the oven adds to the eye appeal.

Cheesy Onion Breadsticks

Cheesy Onion Breadsticks

PREP/TOTAL TIME: 25 min.

- 1 cup biscuit/baking mix
- 1/4 cup milk
- 1/2 cup shredded cheddar cheese
- 2 green onions, finely chopped
- 1/4 teaspoon garlic powder
- 1 tablespoon butter, melted

■ In a large bowl, combine the biscuit mix, milk, cheese, onions and garlic powder. Turn onto a lightly floured surface; knead 8-10 times.

■ Roll into an 8-in. x 6-in. rectangle. Cut lengthwise into eight strips. Place on a greased baking sheet. Bake at 375° for 12-15 minutes or until golden brown. Brush with the butter.

Yield: 8 breadsticks.

Garlic and onion powders tend to absorb moisture from the air, especially during warm weather months. Store them in airtight spice jars to keep them as free from moisture and humidity as possible.

Vegetable Macaroni Salad

Mary Kay Dillingham
OVERLAND PARK, KANSAS

This salad is super easy and versatile. Even the leftovers taste great the next day!

PREP/TOTAL TIME: 20 min.

- 1 cup uncooked elbow macaroni
- 1/2 cup mayonnaise
- 1/4 cup sliced celery
- 1/4 cup chopped pitted green olives
- 1/4 cup sliced green onions
- 1/4 cup shredded cheddar cheese
- 2 tablespoons sliced radishes
- 1 tablespoon minced fresh parsley
- 1 tablespoon white vinegar
- 1 teaspoon prepared mustard
- 1/4 to 1/2 teaspoon salt
- 1/4 teaspoon celery seed
- Dash pepper

■ Cook macaroni according to the package directions. Meanwhile, in a large bowl, combine remaining ingredients.

■ Drain macaroni and rinse in cold water. Add macaroni to mayonnaise mixture; toss to coat. Chill until serving.

Yield: 4 servings.

Mixed Bean Salad

Merle Dyck
ELKFORD, BRITISH COLUMBIA

Making this colorful salad a day ahead gives it time to marinate. We love its flavorful tangy-sweet dressing.

PREP: 15 min. + chilling

- 1/2 cup sugar
- 1/3 cup cider vinegar
- 1/3 cup canola oil
- 1/2 teaspoon salt
- 1/8 teaspoon pepper
- 1 can (16 ounces) kidney beans, rinsed and drained
- 1 can (14-1/2 ounces) cut wax beans, drained
- 1 can (14-1/2 ounces) cut green beans, drained
- 3 celery ribs, sliced
- 1/2 medium green pepper, chopped
- 1/4 cup chopped onion

■ In a small saucepan, combine the sugar, vinegar, oil, salt and pepper. Cook and stir over medium heat until sugar is dissolved. Remove from the heat; cool slightly.

■ In a large salad bowl, combine the remaining ingredients. Drizzle with dressing; toss to coat. Cover and refrigerate overnight. Serve with a slotted spoon.

Yield: 8 servings.

Tangy Caesar Salad

Paula Stewart
CRAWFORDVILLE, GEORGIA

When time is tight, I like to toss together this zippy salad. It's a breeze to make with bottled Caesar dressing and Caesar salad croutons.

PREP/TOTAL TIME: 15 min.

- 8 cups torn romaine
- 1/4 cup creamy Caesar salad dressing
- 1 tablespoon lemon juice
- 1/2 teaspoon pepper
- 1 cup Caesar salad croutons
- 1/3 cup grated Parmesan cheese

■ Place romaine in a large salad bowl. In a small bowl, whisk the salad dressing, lemon juice and pepper; drizzle over romaine and toss to coat. Top with croutons and cheese.

Yield: 6-8 servings.

Garlic Cheese Bread

Janet Rodakowski
WENTZVILLE, MISSOURI

Crunchy slices of this buttery and perfectly seasoned Garlic Cheese Bread make a finger-lickin' feast of any Italian dinner!

PREP/TOTAL TIME: 15 min.

- 1 cup butter, softened
- 1 cup (4 ounces) shredded Parmesan cheese
- 1/2 cup finely chopped onion
- 1 tablespoon garlic powder
- 2 teaspoons minced chives
- 2 teaspoons minced fresh parsley
- 1 loaf (1 pound) French bread, halved lengthwise
- 1 cup (4 ounces) shredded part-skim mozzarella cheese
- 1/2 cup shredded cheddar cheese

■ In a small bowl, combine the first six ingredients; spread over cut sides of bread. Sprinkle with mozzarella and cheddar cheeses.

■ Place on an ungreased baking sheet. Broil 4-6 in. from the heat for 2-3 minutes or until lightly browned. Cut into slices.

Yield: 8 servings.

Herbed Onion Focaccia

Krista Frank
RHODODENDRON, OREGON

This full-flavored bread doesn't require butter. I always hear oohs and aahs when guests take their first bite. It's best served warm, but the next day it makes great-tasting toast!

Herbed Onion Focaccia

PREP: 30 min. + rising ■ BAKE: 20 min.

- 1 cup water (70° to 80°)
- 1/3 cup finely chopped onion
- 1 tablespoon sugar
- 1-1/2 teaspoons salt
- 1 teaspoon grated Parmesan cheese
- 1/2 teaspoon garlic powder
- 1/2 teaspoon dried basil
- 1/2 teaspoon dill weed
- 1/2 teaspoon pepper
- 3 cups all-purpose flour
- 2 teaspoons active dry yeast

TOPPING:

- 1 tablespoon olive oil
- 1/2 teaspoon grated Parmesan cheese
- 1/2 teaspoon dried parsley flakes
- 1/4 teaspoon salt
- 1/8 teaspoon pepper

■ In bread machine pan, place the first 11 ingredients in order suggested by manufacturer. Select dough setting (check dough after 5 minutes of mixing; add 1 to 2 tablespoons of water or flour if needed).

■ When cycle is completed, turn dough onto a greased baking sheet and punch down (dough will be sticky). With lightly oiled hands, pat dough into a 9-in. circle. Brush with oil; sprinkle with the cheese, parsley, salt and pepper. Cover and let rise in a warm place until doubled, about 45 minutes.

■ Bake at 400° for 18-20 minutes or until golden brown. Cut into wedges; serve warm.

Yield: 1 loaf (16 slices).

Always follow the directions in your instruction manual when adding ingredients to a bread machine. Many manuals also help adapt standard recipes for use in your bread machine.

General Recipe Index

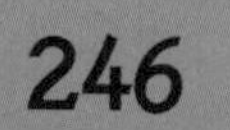

DRIED FRUIT

FISH & SEAFOOD

Oven

Stovetop

FRUIT *(also see specific kinds)*

GROUND BEEF

(also see Beef)

Oven

Slow Cooker

Stovetop

HAM & PROSCIUTTO

Oven

Slow Cooker

PEACHES

PEARS

PEPPERONI

PEPPERS

PINEAPPLE

PORK

(also see Bacon & Turkey Bacon; Ham & Prosciutto; Sausage)

Oven

Slow Cooker

Stovetop

POTATOES & SWEET POTATOES

RICE

SALADS

SANDWICHES

SAUCES

SAUSAGE

Oven

Slow Cooker

Stovetop

SIDE DISHES

SOUPS & CHOWDERS

(also see Chili; Stews)

Alphabetical Recipe Index

R

S

T

V

W

Z